IMAGES
of America

ISLETON

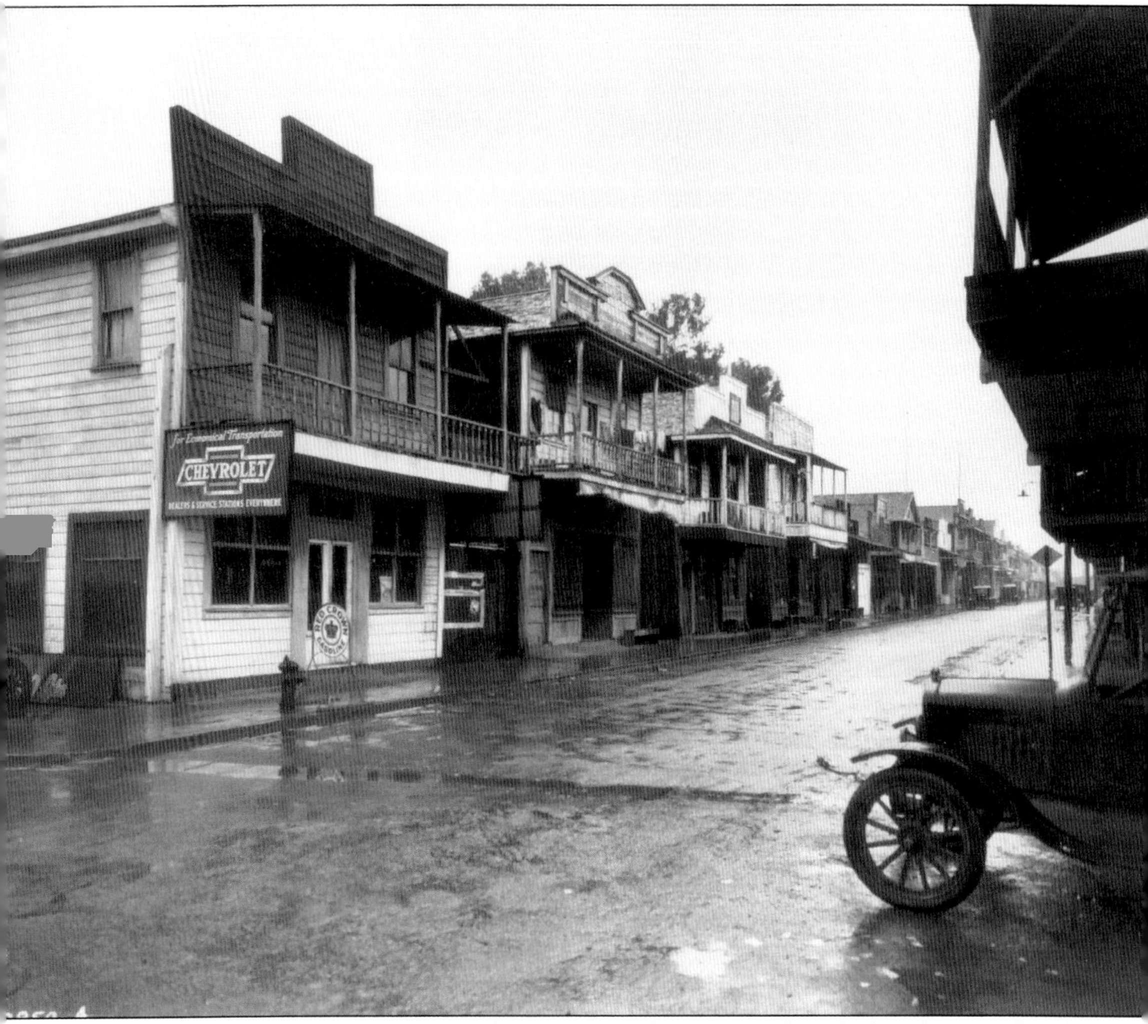

Chevy Sign. The old Main Street Chinatown in Isleton is seen here before the 1926 fire that completely destroyed the entire two blocks. The wood buildings were very close together and the fire was raging by the time the volunteer firemen arrived. The Chinese and Japanese communities quickly organized and rebuilt their homes and stores; however, this time they covered the exterior with metal siding to slow the spread of future fires.

IMAGES
of America

ISLETON

Bruce Crawford

ARCADIA
PUBLISHING

ISBN 978-0-7385-2863-2

Published by Arcadia Publishing
Charleston, South Carolina

Printed in the United States of America

Library of Congress Catalog Card Number: 2003113270

For all general information contact Arcadia Publishing at:
Telephone 843-853-2070
Fax 843-853-0044
E-Mail sales@arcadiapublishing.com
For customer service and orders:
Toll-Free 1-888-313-2665

Visit us on the Internet at www.arcadiapublishing.com

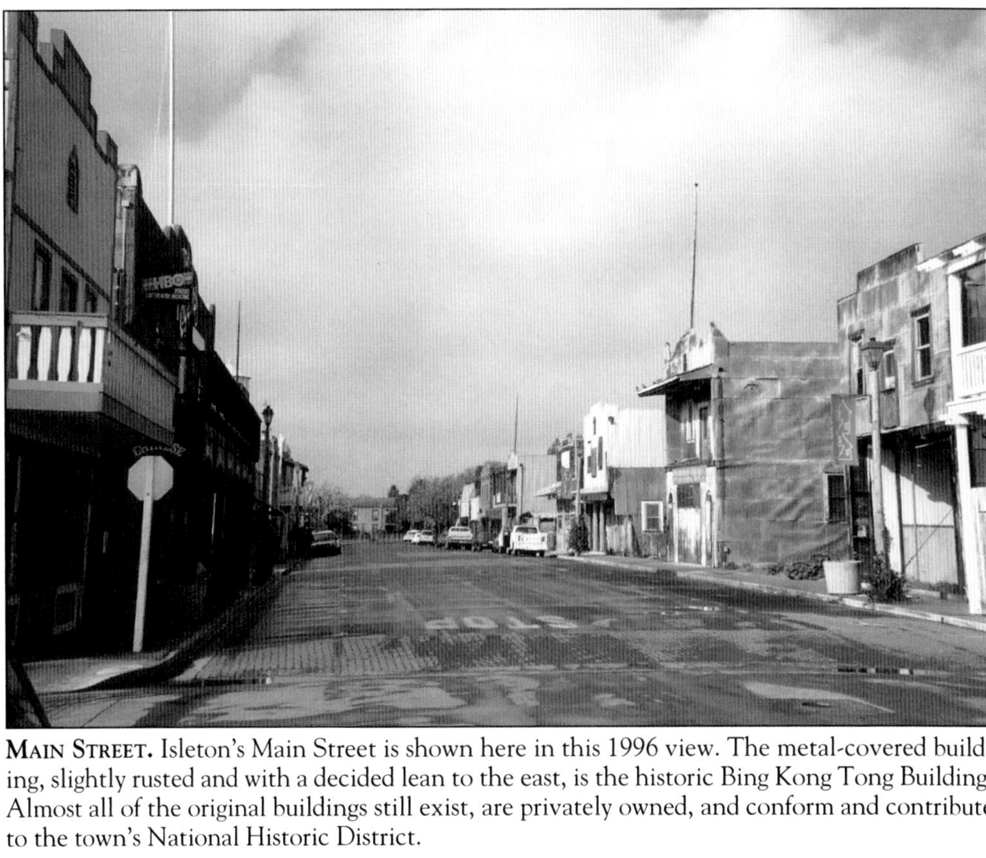

MAIN STREET. Isleton's Main Street is shown here in this 1996 view. The metal-covered building, slightly rusted and with a decided lean to the east, is the historic Bing Kong Tong Building. Almost all of the original buildings still exist, are privately owned, and conform and contribute to the town's National Historic District.

Contents

ACKNOWLEDGMENTS

A large amount of crucial help came together to make this book possible. The Isleton Historical Society loaned many pictures, and archivist Ed Conception contributed hours of work by collecting, reproducing photographs, and giving needed advice. Joanne McLoud, Sumi Lee, and Ben Levy all helped me with formatting, and John Poultney helped with editing and moral support. Several people from Isleton submitted old photographs, among them were Denis Van de Meale (tractors), the Gardiners (family photographs), and Bob Dunn (old city pictures). Others that contributed stories and photographs were Evelyn Silva, Armand Fonseca, Cheryl Apple, and Bert Blackwelder.

A special thanks to Linda Gonzales, Isleton's city clerk, who helped to locate and make available selections from the city's archive, and to the mayor who suggested that we make extra scans. Thanks also go out to the Lions Club, Olivia Glavin, Bill and Alda Lee, Marion Wong, and John Perez for their support.

This collection of Isleton's picturesque past is the work of a dedicated community that appreciates its vivid and dynamic history.

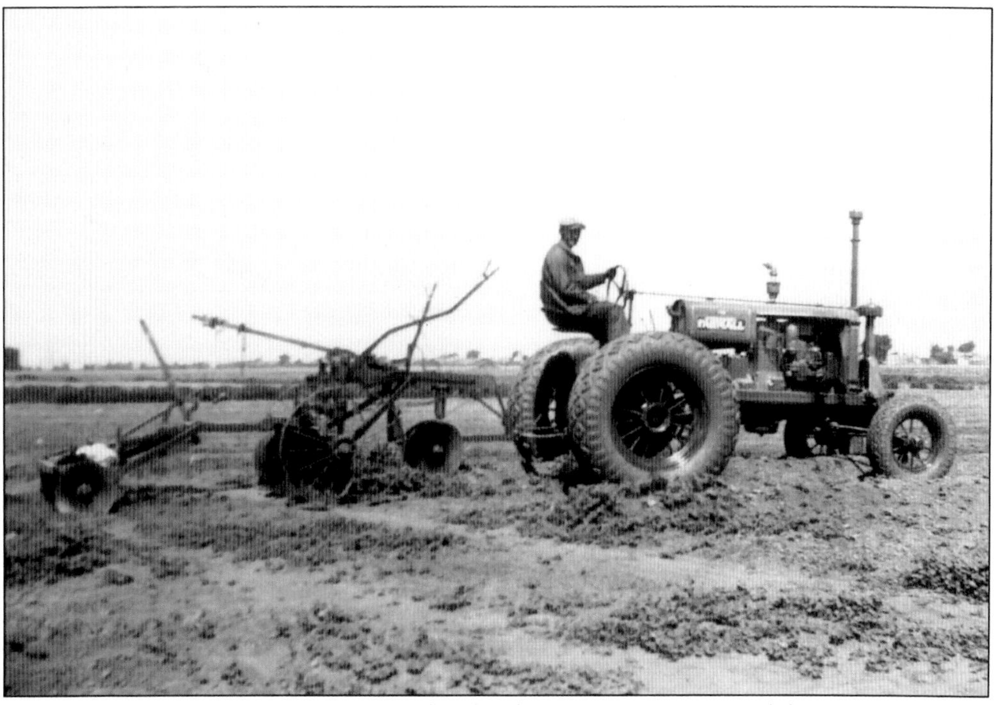

ASPARAGUS RIDGING. Hubert Van de Maele ridges his asparagus in 1938 with his Farmall F-30.

INTRODUCTION

Every year, during the Father's Day weekend, nearly 300,000 people join the throng that comes to the Crawdad Festival in Isleton, California. Throughout the year, many others make the short drive from San Francisco and Sacramento to enjoy the scenic wonders and dynamic history of this Delta city. The California Delta is not only one of California's best recreational attractions, but it is an invaluable resource of water, agriculture, and a complex mix of ecosystems. Isleton sits in the heart of the Delta, situated equally between San Francisco, Stockton, Sacramento, and San Jose, and is perfectly located for a short drive to a scenic, quiet place. But it wasn't always so quiet here.

This small town—less than 1,000 people—sits below river level between the Sacramento and San Joaquin Rivers, a few miles before they flow into San Francisco Bay. Isleton is much more than a festival to freshwater crustaceans. Behind the extensive levee system is an extremely valuable part of California history, one of the best farming areas in the world, and a recreational system that is natural, healthy, educational, and fun.

Long occupied by a large number of Native Americans, or "Indians" as they were known for many years, the Delta was settled during the American Civil War in the 1860s and quickly became a community of farmers and workers. The vast majority of workers first came from China. Driven by civil strife at home—and reports of wealth in America—these men helped to tame the rivers and to transform the marshy land into working farms.

The marsh land, shifting waterways, and countless islands presented an extensive and unruly landscape that needed planning, organization and manpower. Using the recently unemployed Chinese workers (many of whom had toiled to build railroads across the state), the reclamation project began. Levees were built and channels created by those who had learned the techniques in their homeland on the Yangtze River. Once these giant rivers were somewhat tamed, the marshlands needed to be pumped, plowed, planted, and harvested. Beneath the fine river silt were layers of thick peat soil. This rich deposit, when combined with California's Mediterranean climate, grows almost anything, and in record amounts.

As farmers moved into the Delta, the need for back-breaking labor increased. Hence, the Chinese built more than levees. Working on the farms, they built their own community in Isleton. This vibrant town was replete with the customs, values, and family life with which these migrants were familiar. The two-block Main Street, hub of the Chinese community in Isleton, still stands and is registered today as a national historic district. In the center of this community was the Tong Building, a large two-story building in the middle of Main Street. It was not only the "government" of the Chinese town, it was the focus of culture, news, gambling, and the place to settle disagreements.

Farming soon boomed in the Delta. The first crops were potatoes, followed by sweet potatoes, asparagus, pears, tomatoes, corn, and wheat. With laws that prohibited more Chinese immigrants, these citizens were replaced by the Japanese. Settling in Isleton, the Japanese built their businesses, churches and homes next to the Chinese, and these buildings are also on the National Historic Register. The Japanese made significant contributions to this ethnic mix of hard work and community, but this labor pool was depleted with the outbreak of World War II, and they were replaced with Filipino, Portuguese, and Middle Eastern workers. With pears and asparagus in worldwide demand, canneries began to spring up around Isleton. Before long over 3,000 people lived in Isleton and worked in seven canneries in the area. Hard-working immigrants scrubbed their children, sent them to segregated schools, and worked from dawn to dusk to improve their lives.

Isleton is in Sacramento County, and a long way down-river from the administrative capital of California. This river town has a mixed history—gambling, drinking, and sordid night activities were common in the early years. The county government didn't seem to mind that this small levee community had a culture all its own. However, with the Japanese moved to internment camps, the Chinese slowly moving to better jobs in bigger cities, and the asparagus crops diminishing, Isleton fell into a long downturn. Big farms began to replace the smaller ones, and the need for labor was replaced with machinery. The canneries closed down and the population of Isleton decreased dramatically.

Isleton became almost a ghost town located in one of the nicest spots in the world. But the memories of the good life remained. On the weekends, and during summer vacations, city folks came to "Crawdad Town" to relax and enjoy the pleasures of the river. Both the Chinese and Japanese hold yearly reunions to explain to their children and grandchildren their roots. Today the vibrant tourism and recreation are beginning to revive the "Heart of the Delta."

The Isleton Historical Society was started in the early 1990s when the Bing Kong Tong Association of San Francisco deeded their aged Tong Building to the society. Since then, the society has been raising the funds necessary to restore this precious artifact, and collecting and preserving our historic past. The community supports our efforts and has donated hundreds of photographs and documents to help me with this book. To help with the project, citizens have offered to do everything from conducting garage sales to editing.

The Delta's great recreational opportunities attract thousands to the area every year. Besides fishing contests for stripers and sturgeon, boat races, water skiing, sailing, wind surfing, and house boating, the Delta attracts bird watchers and naturalists who love to just watch the river flow by. Artists, movie producers, and writers have all found their spots in the Delta. Egrets, beavers, hawks, cranes, and countless fish make the Delta their home. Large sturgeon and huge flocks of geese remind us of the balance of this precious ecosystem.

When the Crawdad Festival comes around, and Isleton's quiet slow pace is interrupted by thousands of curious tourists, the disruption is welcomed. The town is happy to share some of the natural and human history with our kin from suburbia and the "big city." Isleton is a friendly city with small-town values, lost in a time when people knew almost everybody in town. Meeting at the post office, bakery, or "watering hole" on a daily basis, we are working together to discover the past, put on a giant festival, and share our heritage with California.

One

The Water and the Land

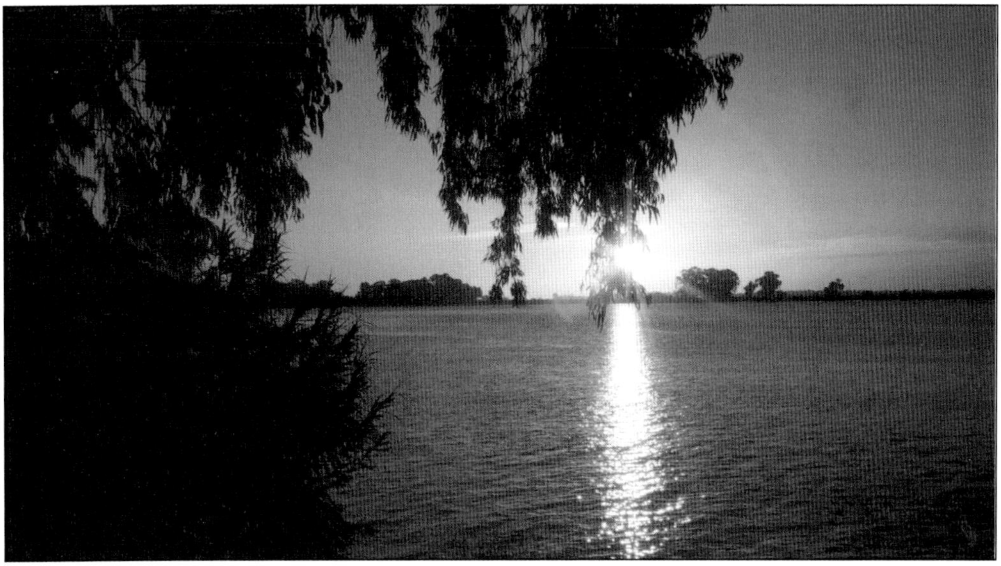

Sacramento River. The Sacramento River flows from north to south and can flood from November to May. Intense rainstorms and snowmelt combine to create giant floods, the largest of which was in 1861–1862, when Sacramento and Rio Vista were all under water. The Sacramento River is fed by the McCloud, Pitt, Feather, Yuba, American, Mokelumne, and Consumes rivers once it reaches the Delta. Water flow is regulated to maintain control for the Delta and for the California Aqueduct; the latter provides water for farms in Kern County and for the large population in Los Angeles. The Sacramento River's flow is regulated by several dams, but the two major ones are in Oroville and Shasta.

Managing the massive Sierra snow melt in early May has been a Delta problem as long as anyone can remember. Generally, the rivers from Mount Whitney to Mount Shasta flow into the Central Valley basin and join as they flow into San Francisco Bay. However, the snowmelt usually takes place in only a few short weeks and the rivers, streams, canyons, sloughs, and inlets become roaring torrents of water and debris. As the Delta drain clogs up, water fills the land. Delta floods are renowned for their degree and extent.

To tame the fertile Delta, it took Chinese workers building levees, farmers with dreams, large dredges, pumps, and pioneer families who would not be washed away.

Infinite marshland, deep river channels, drifting islands, mud flats, tule groves, oak-studded highlands, sandbars, and balsa groves were the way of life for Native Californians in the Delta. Waterfowl, shellfish, salmon, and abundant game nurtured one of the largest native populations in northern California. The vast labyrinth of water routes kept the early explorers from venturing very far into this maze. They wrote off the Delta as unsuitable for habitation.

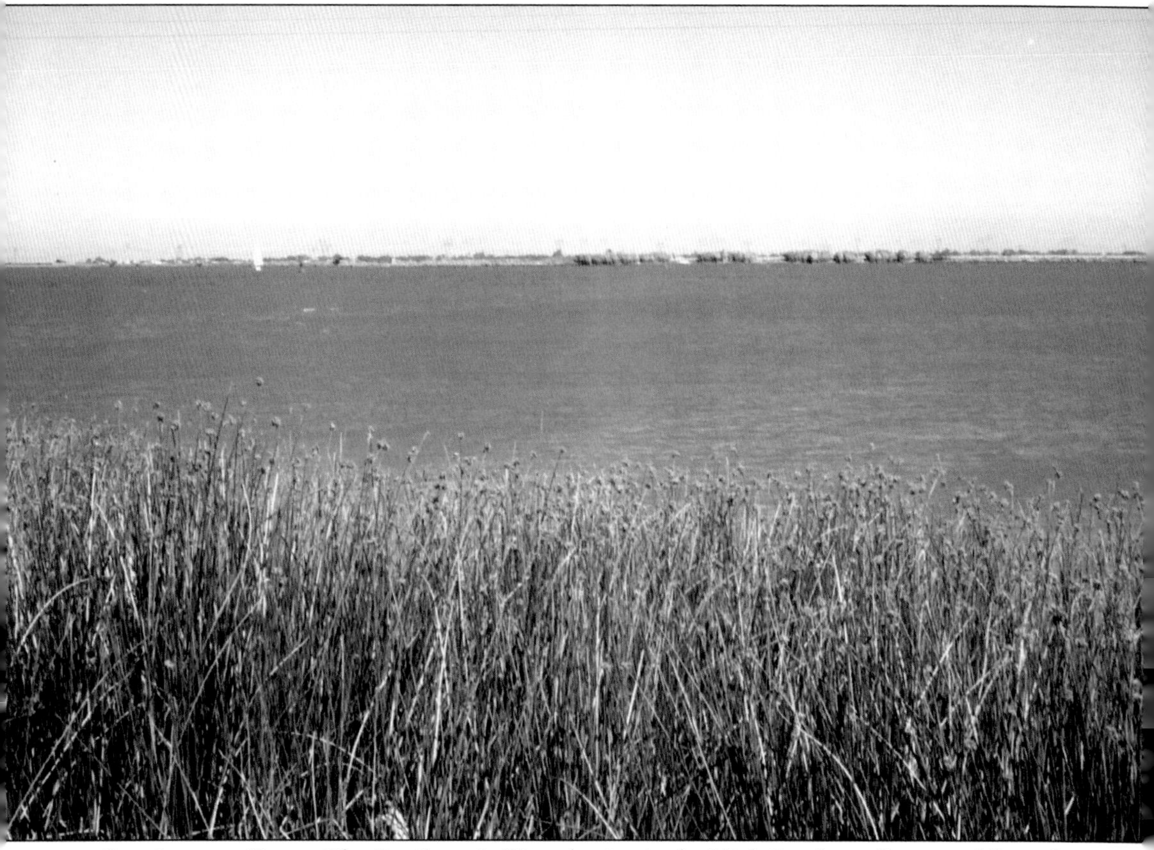

SAN JOAQUIN RIVER. The San Joaquin River begins in the High Southern Sierra and flows from south to north. It has less flow than the Sacramento River, but floods just as often. The limited bottomland and the variety of sources contribute to its flood capacity. The San Joaquin is fed by the Kings, Merced, Stanislaus, Touloumne, and Calavares Rivers. It joins the Sacramento River near Antioch. This view is from the Antioch Bridge looking upriver. Large ocean vessels use this channel to transport to docks in Stockton. This working river serves farms from Kings County to Contra Costa County.

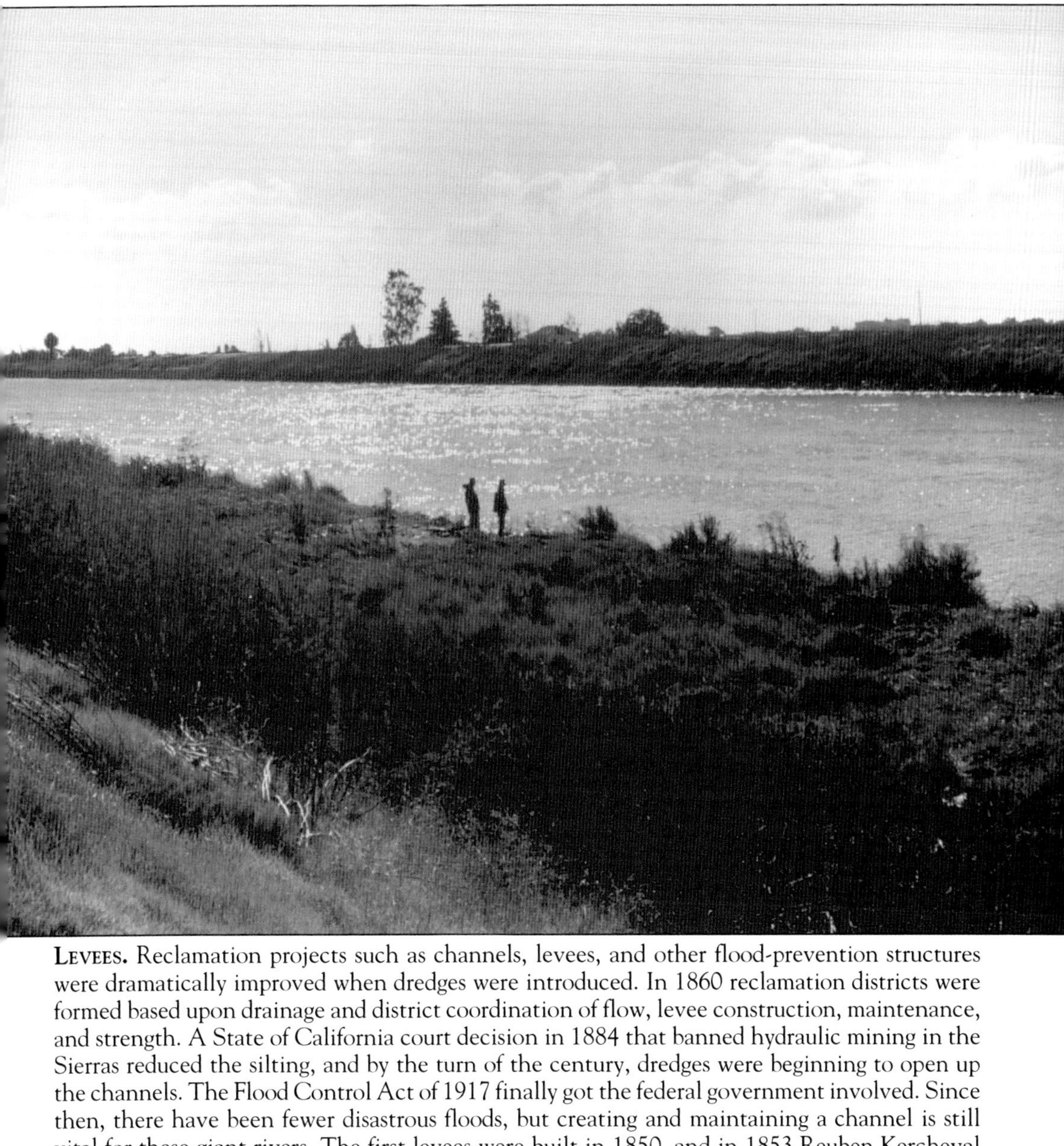

Levees. Reclamation projects such as channels, levees, and other flood-prevention structures were dramatically improved when dredges were introduced. In 1860 reclamation districts were formed based upon drainage and district coordination of flow, levee construction, maintenance, and strength. A State of California court decision in 1884 that banned hydraulic mining in the Sierras reduced the silting, and by the turn of the century, dredges were beginning to open up the channels. The Flood Control Act of 1917 finally got the federal government involved. Since then, there have been fewer disastrous floods, but creating and maintaining a channel is still vital for these giant rivers. The first levees were built in 1850, and in 1853 Reuben Kercheval hired Chinese laborers to build a levee 3 feet high, 3 feet across, and 13 feet wide at the base. It was about ten miles long, and the workers were paid about $1 per acre. These early levees soon failed, and by the turn of the century the levees were increased to eight feet in height. This view is looking across the Sacramento River just below Isleton. Sherman Island is on the other side. This is where Reuben Kercheval built the first levees and started farming. His wife developed the levees on Andrus Island.

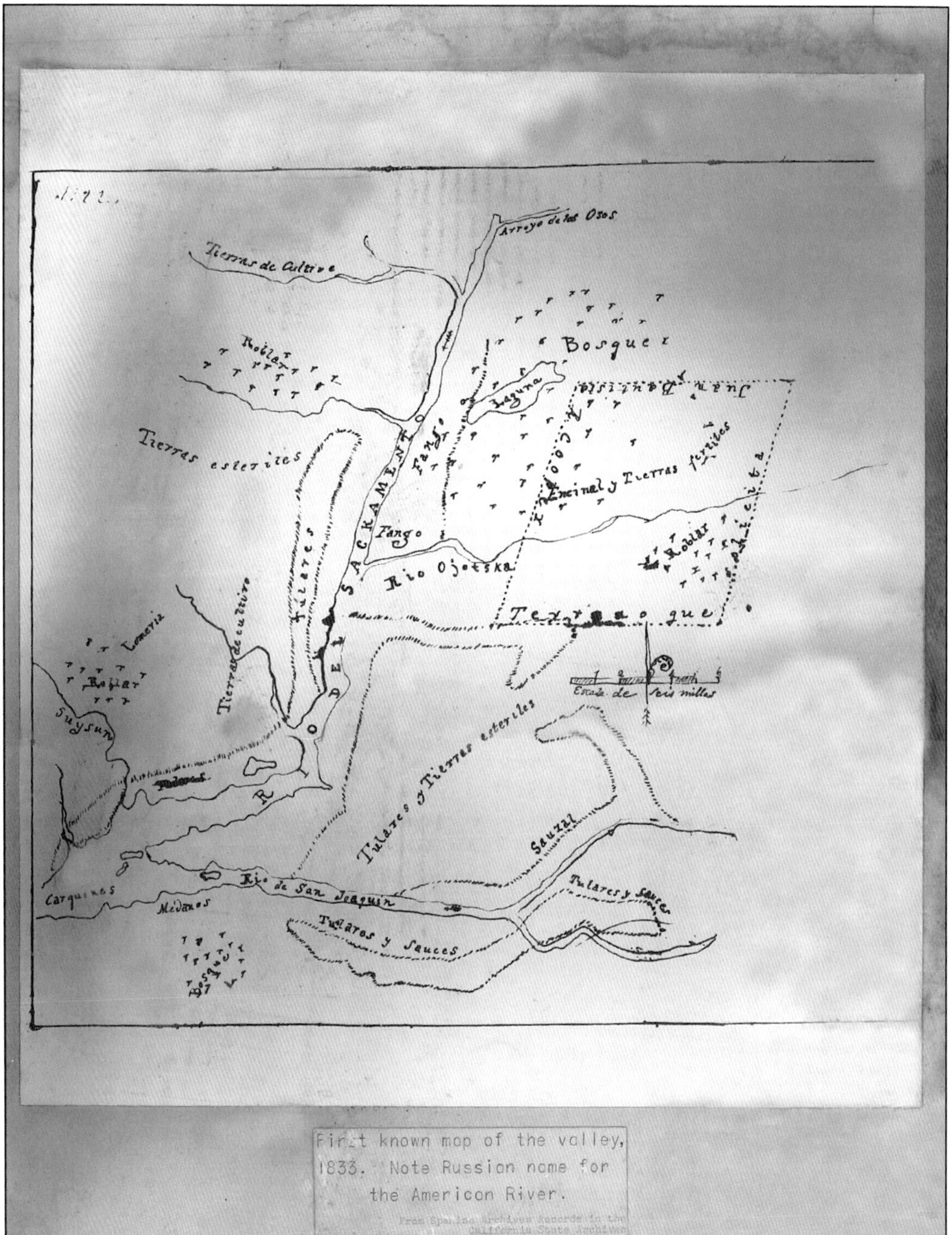

Oldest Map. Drawn by Spanish explorers in 1833, the first known map of the Sacramento River follows it from Suisun Bay to what became Sacramento, the capital of California. In seven years, Sutter's Fort would arise at the junction of the American and Sacramento Rivers. Spanish explorers were beginning to forge their way upriver but were frequently turned back by the maze of channels and islands. It took the Gold Rush in 1849 to begin to open river traffic. Flat boats, rowboats, and passenger ships brought gold seekers upriver to challenge everything from mosquitoes to high-priced gold pans. If you can read Spanish, this map may be of some help.

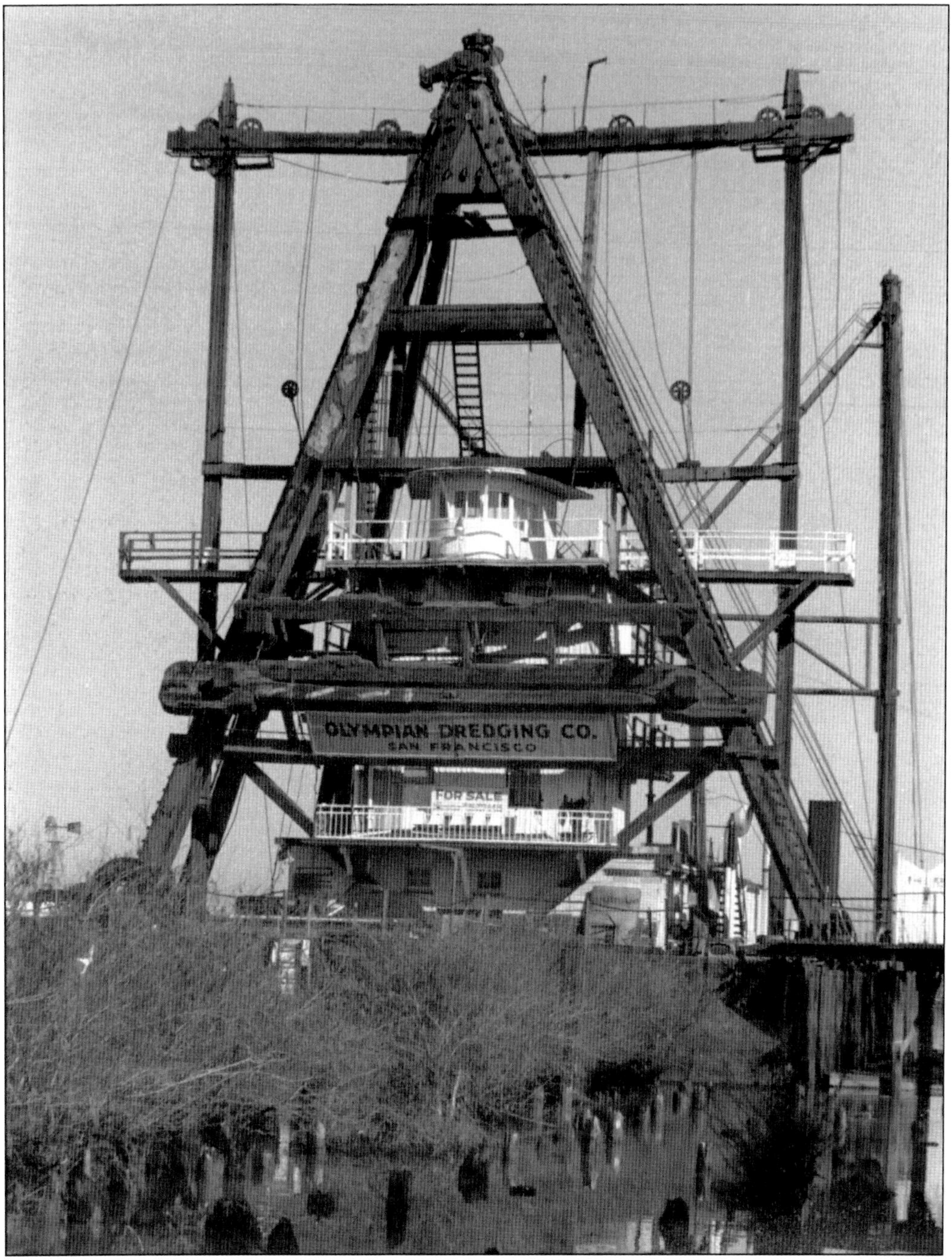

Olympia Dredge. Used on the rivers at the turn of the century, this particular dredge was owned by the Olympian Dredge Company of San Francisco. The Neptune, as it was named, suffered a broken boom during a storm. It had a long history of work, including stints as far away as Guam. Here it sits, in the 1930s, anchored at Isleton waiting for a buyer.

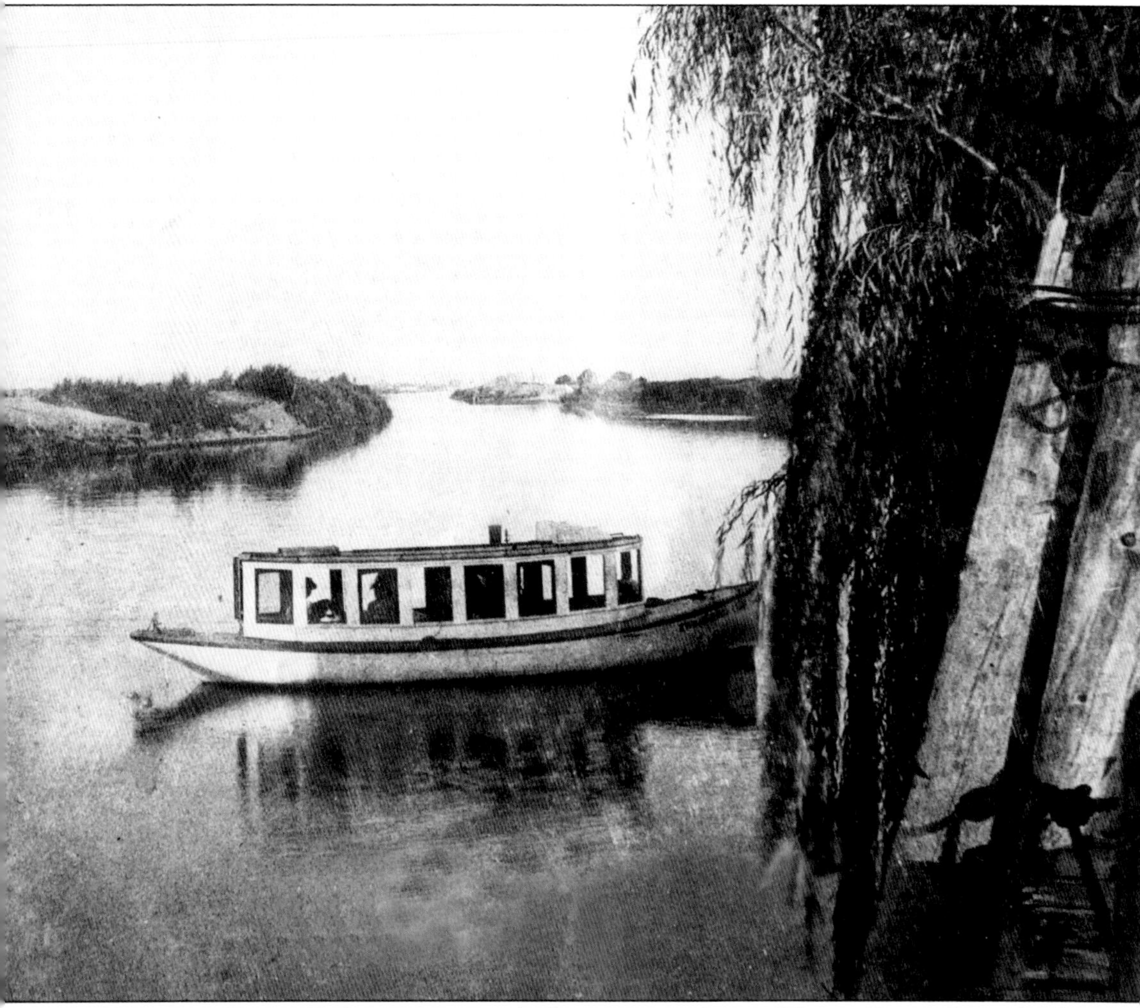

Passenger Boats. Early transport on the big rivers was by small boats. To get from island to island, or up and down the river, people either rowed, used a tether line, or had small motors. This passenger boat has neither oars nor motor, but is transporting people across the Sacramento River to Grand Island by tether. In this setup a cable is run across the river and the boat is pulled from one side to the other by steam power.

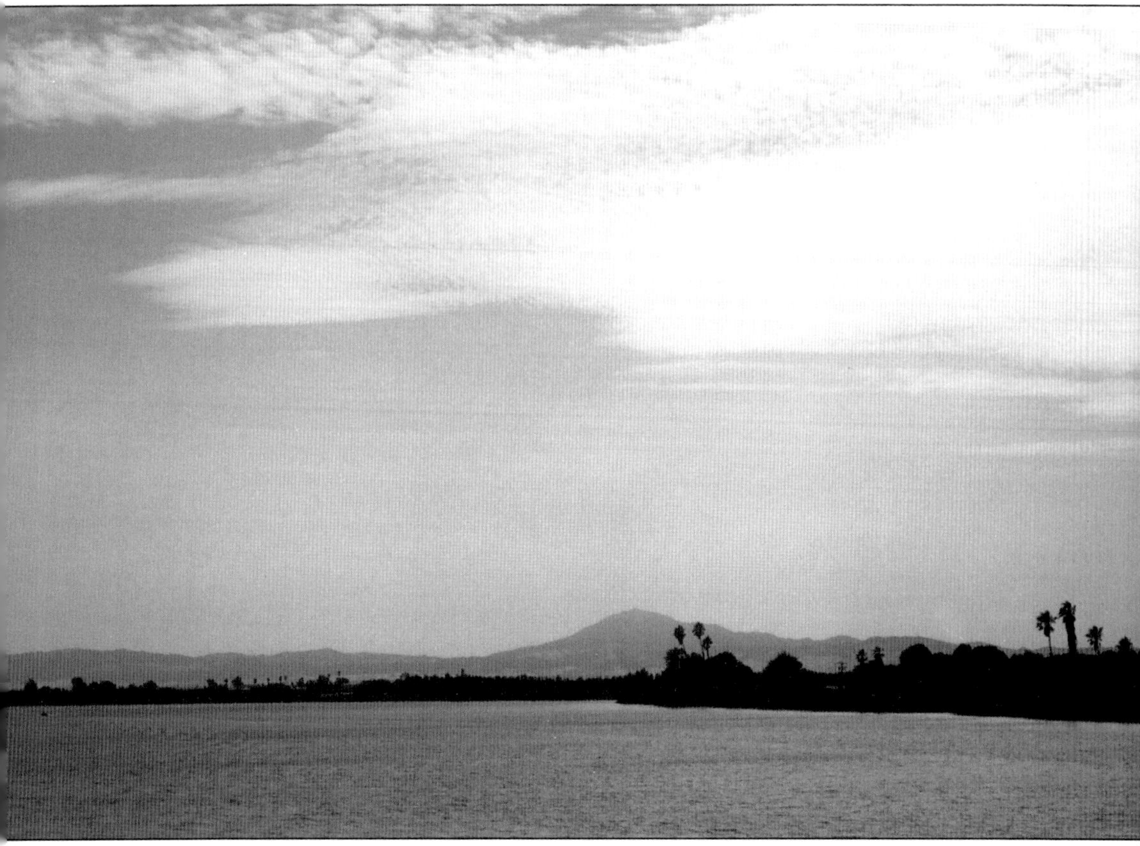

GEORGIANA SLOUGH. Sloughs are a major part of the Delta, and are used for several purposes. Most of the land is below river level so it must be drained using large pumps. Sloughs serve as drains and connections between major rivers, and also act as relief valves during floods. They are also excellent recreation areas. Many marinas are located on the sloughs where fishing, boating, berthing, water skiing, and swimming opportunities abound. This is the Georgiana Slough near Isleton. Mount Diablo acts as a landmark, as the Georgiana flows from the Sacramento to the San Joaquin River.

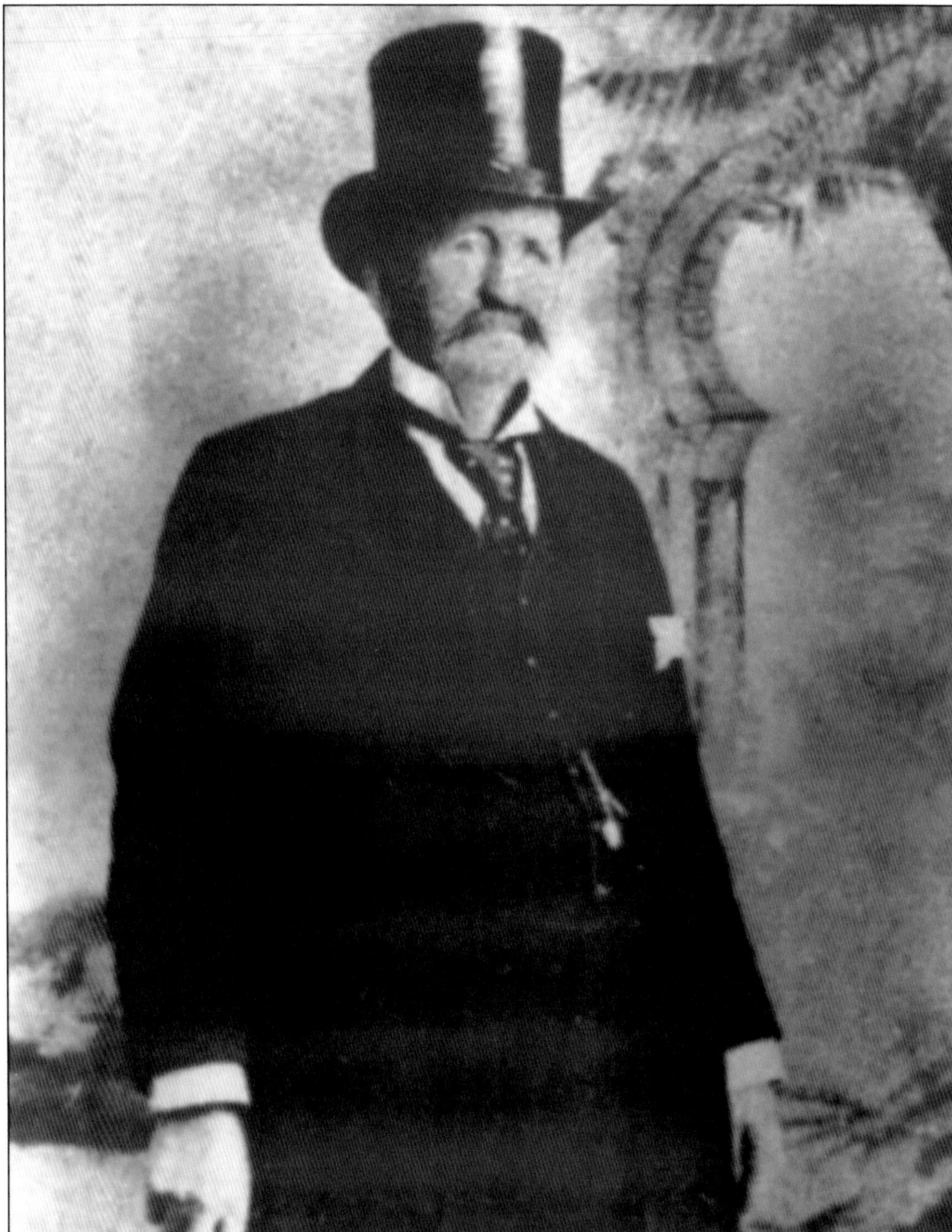

WILLIAM WILCOX. Building levees was no easy task. Besides hard work, it took organization and engineering skills. Wilcox was one of the early pioneers who brought Chinese workers to the Isleton area to build levees. Like Charles Crocker of railroad fame, it took an understanding of the culture, teamwork, wheelbarrows, shovels, and good planning to get the job done. The Chinese worker's physical stamina and ability to perform backbreaking labor was essential in the heat, fog, mud, mosquitoes, and wind in the Delta.

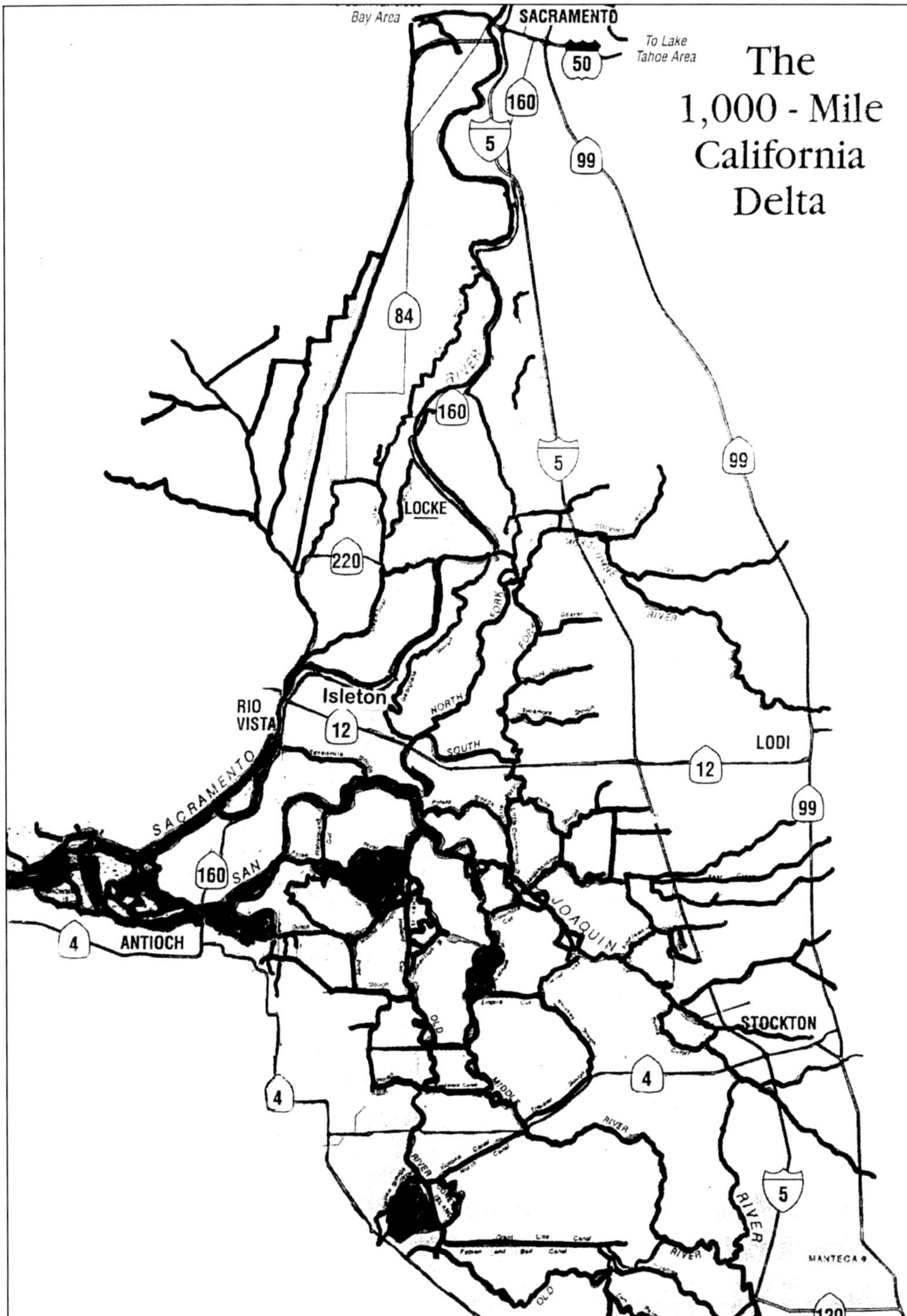

Delta Map. The 1,000-square-mile California Delta is hard to get around in without a boat. The water routes, roads, and islands have no symmetry. Old timers who know their way around have a definite advantage over the newcomer.

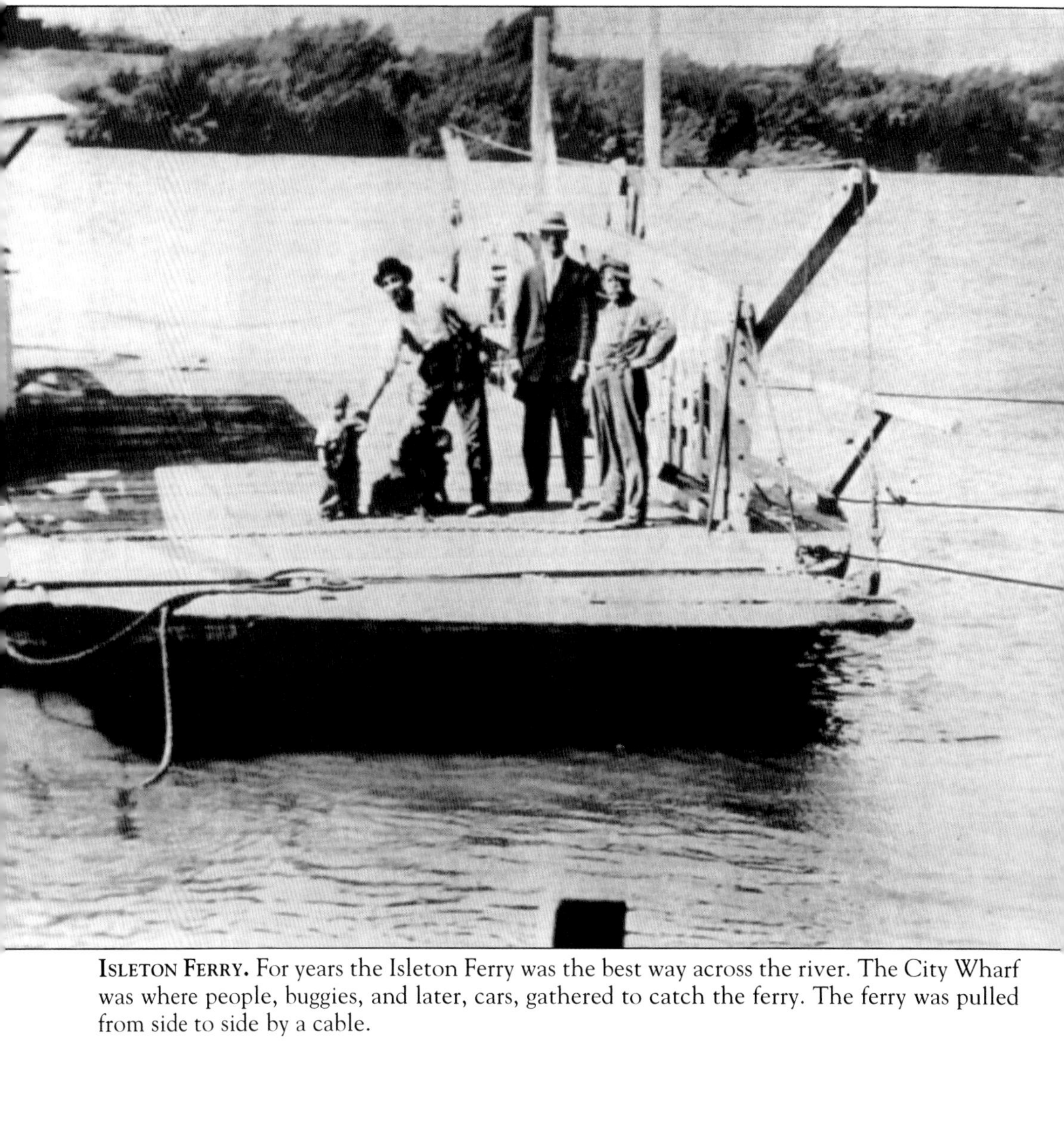

ISLETON FERRY. For years the Isleton Ferry was the best way across the river. The City Wharf was where people, buggies, and later, cars, gathered to catch the ferry. The ferry was pulled from side to side by a cable.

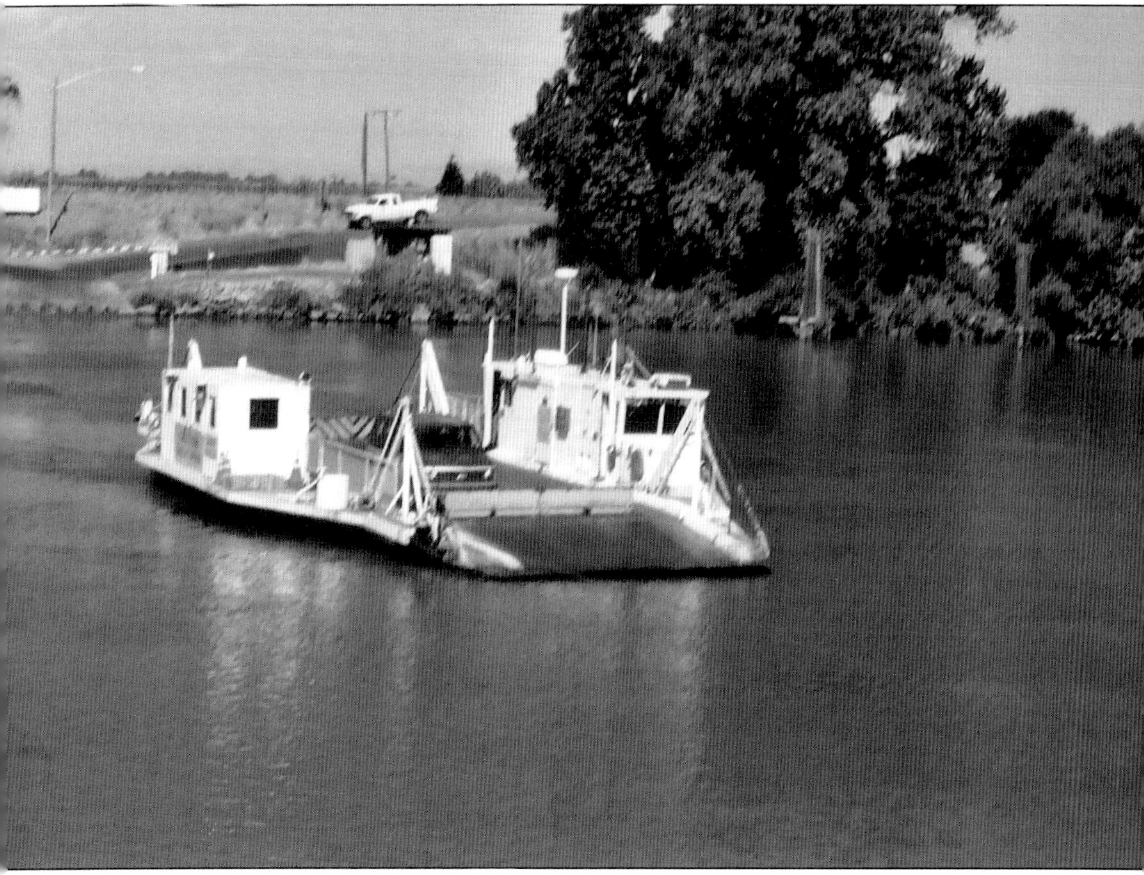

RYER ISLAND FERRY. If you want to go from Grand Island to Ryer Island the best and most enjoyable route is on the Ryer Island Ferry. Open 24 hours a day, 7 days a week, it is a free trip across the Sacramento River at a most colorful place. In operation for over 100 years, it's not only a step back into the past. It is near historic landmarks and some of the best farming land in the world. To get there, take Highway 160 to Ryde, turn onto Highway 220, and on to the ferry.

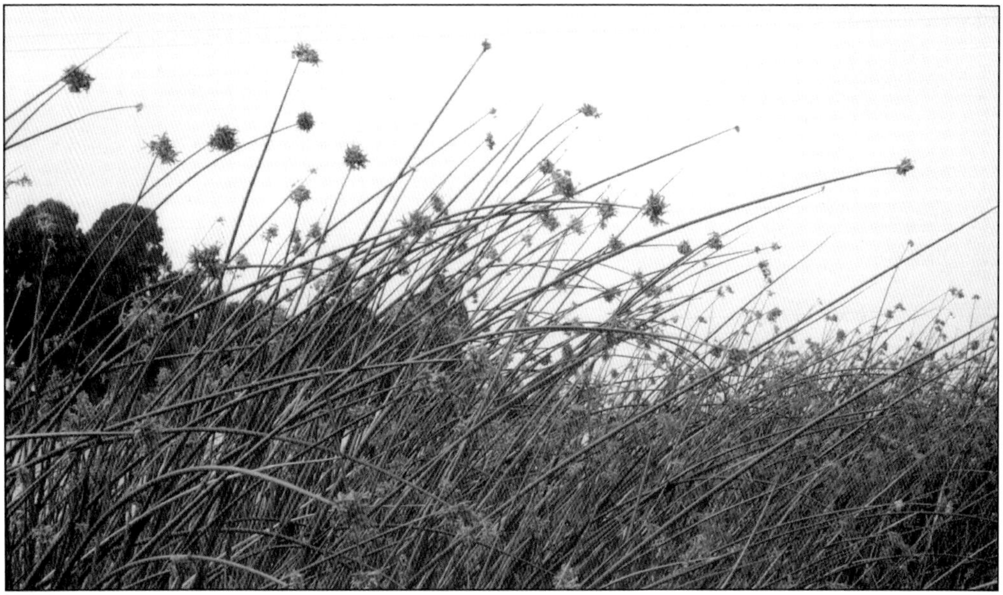

VIEIRAS ISLAND. Vieiras Island is just a couple miles downriver from Isleton. The old timers called it Idas Island. It is easily accessible from Highway 160 and has a marina, a boat ramp, a restaurant, and many permanent homes.

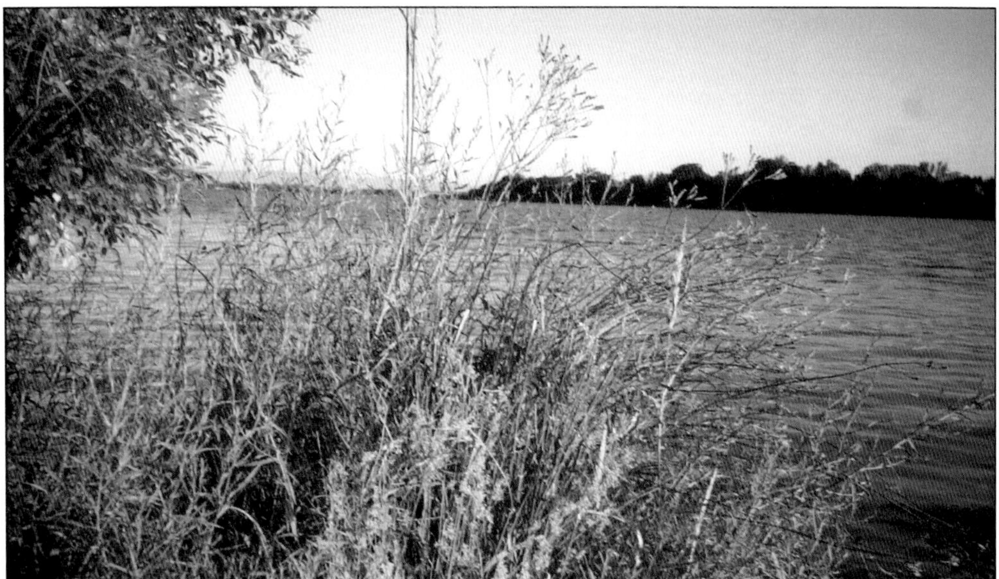

GRAND ISLAND. Islands are a major part of reclamation. This is the western end of Grand Island where the old and new channels of the Sacramento River join. Large ships headed to dock in Sacramento take the distant channel to the deep river channel. Grand Island was one of the first areas where levees were built. Some of the finest farmland in the world exists here. Grand Island was named by Spanish explorers who discovered a "grand" village of Native Americans who lived here. The Delta was a haven for mosquitoes and thus malaria, brought over by Europeans, soon infected the original inhabitants, who had no resistance and were soon decimated. Some "Indian mounds" still exist in remote areas.

Two

Early Families and Farming

As large numbers of unsuccessful argonauts returned from the Mother Lode, the memory of nuggets and quick riches were replaced by the challenges of beautiful California. For some, their future lay on the banks of the flooded farm lands of the Delta. The first successful farming was during the 1850s.

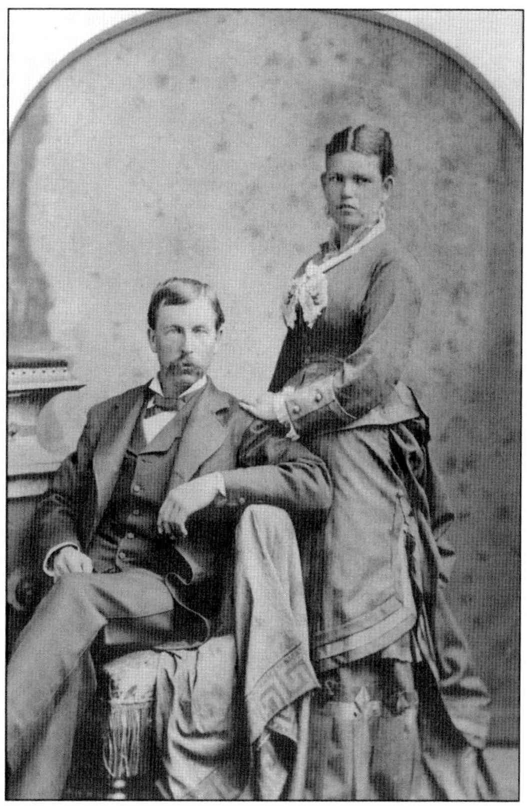

HOGATE AND IDA GARDINER. Potatoes were grown near Freeport and sold at a premium to gold-seekers. Soon sugar beets became the major Delta crop, followed by asparagus, wheat, corn, and pears. Special equipment was necessary to work the muddy fields, drain the land, and plow the deep soft peat. Farms developed in large plots while pioneer families and immigrant workers settled in Isleton in the 1870s. Josiah Poole was the first settler to farm the area today called Isleton. He raised sugar beets, but his crops were wiped out by floods. He sold his land to Hogate Gardiner who had married Pole's daughter. Hogate and Ida stayed on, raised a family, and established Isleton. Today, fifth-generation Gardiners still farm and are very active in community service.

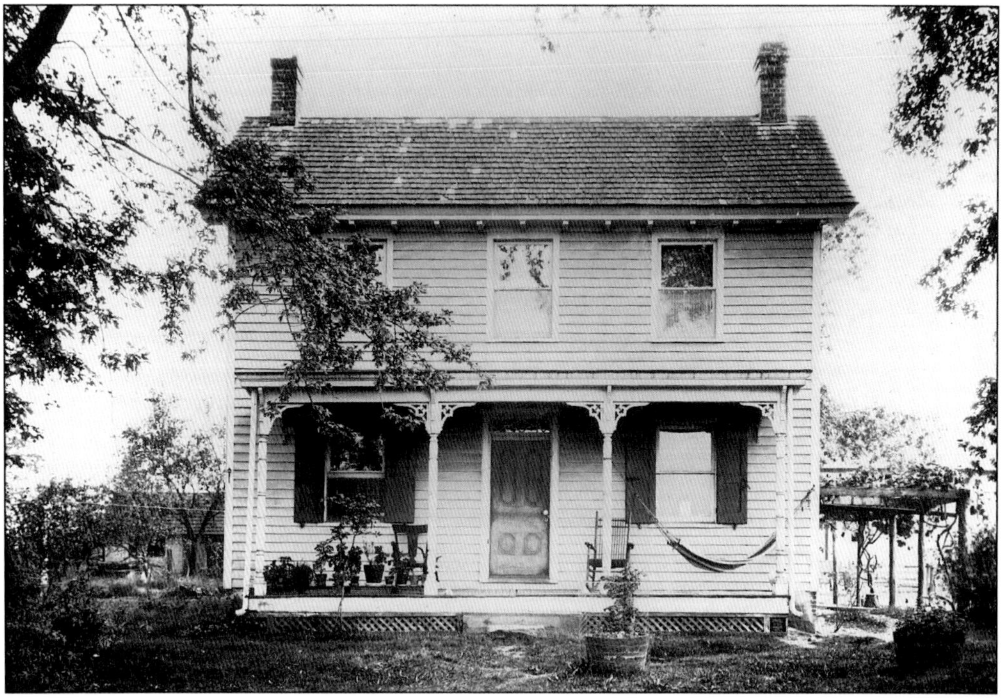

GARDINER HOME. The original Gardiner home on A Street was a small Victorian that was soon too small for the expanding family.

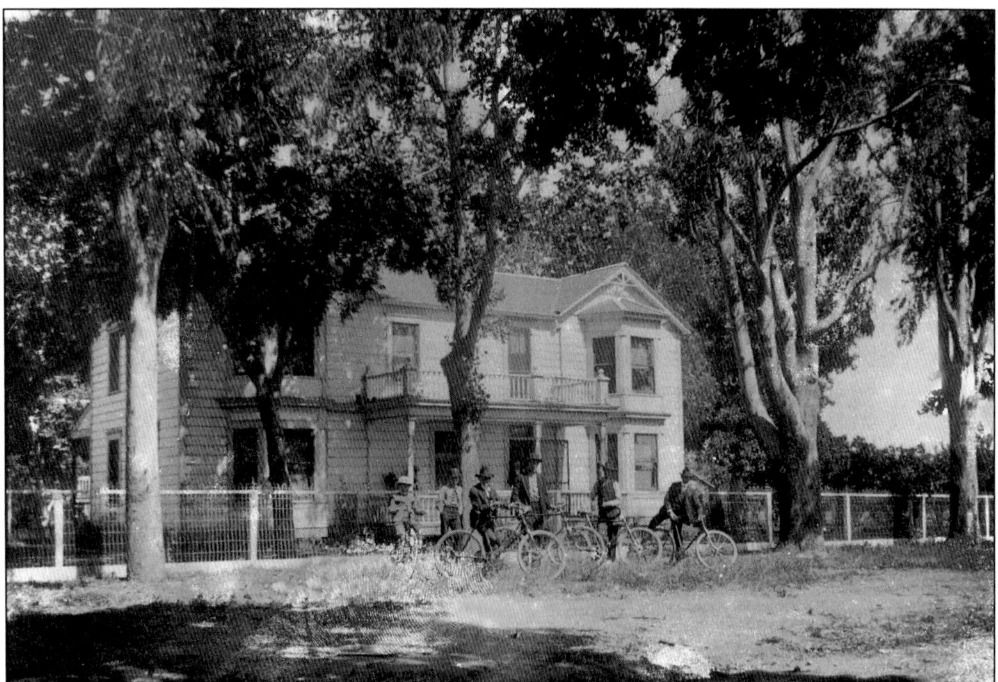

EXPANDED GARDINER HOME. By the turn of the century the Gardiner home was expanded. It is still located on A Street, next to the bank, and looks much the same as in this photograph.

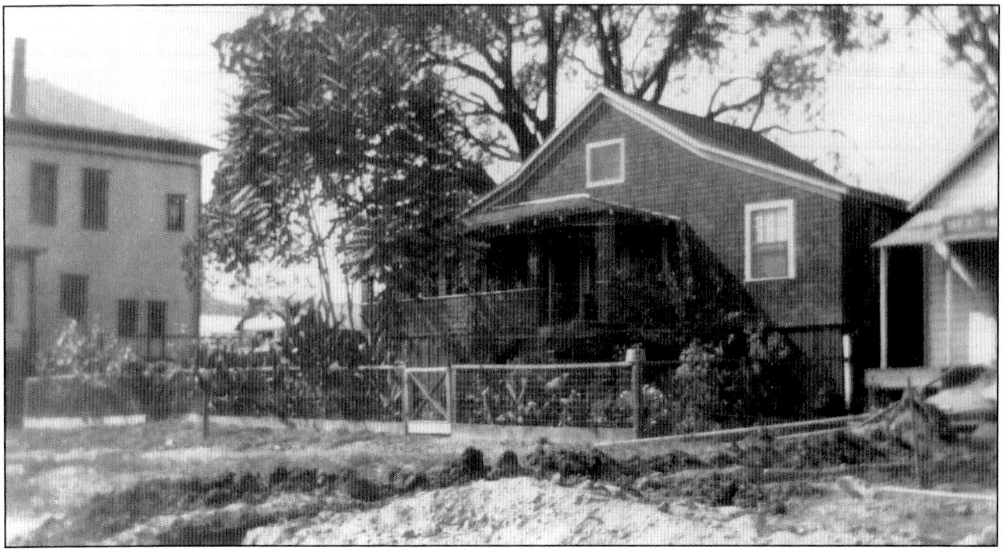

DEBACK HOME. The Deback home, done in the shingled, craftsmen style, was the home of one of the prominent families. The large building on the left was the Gardiner Improvement building. That building still stands, but the Deback home was replaced by Del Rio Real Estate and the Del Rio Restaurant and Hotel.

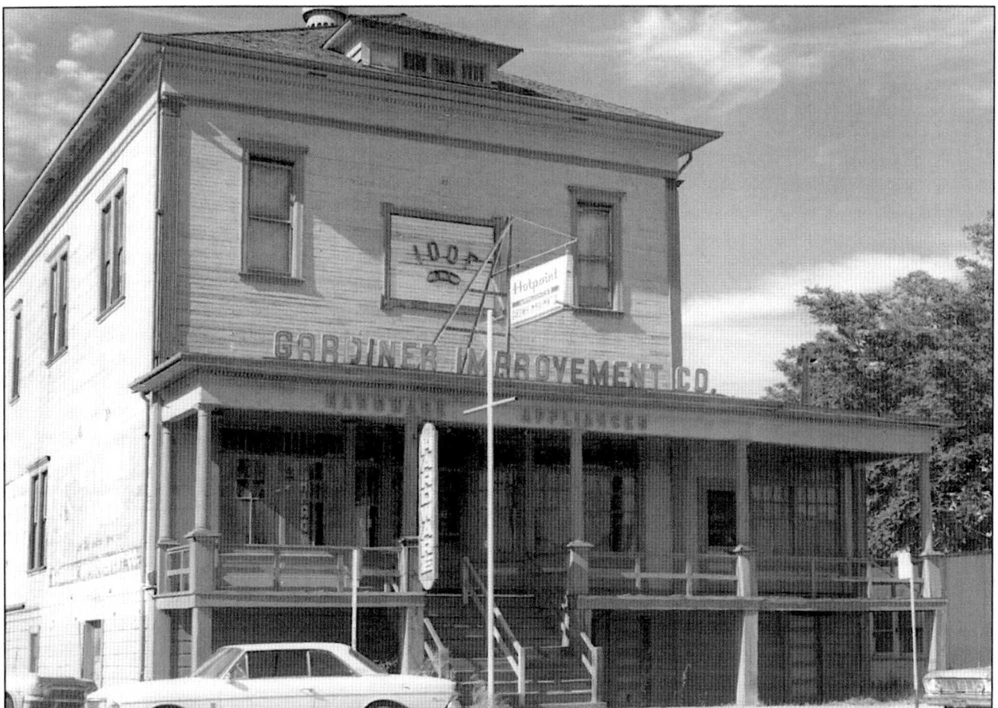

GARDINER IMPROVEMENT BUILDING. The large Gardiner Improvement Building is still standing. It is right below the levee and welcomes people into Isleton. It is a landmark that has served many different functions such as a post office and a hardware store. The large rooms have high ceilings and were used as meeting rooms.

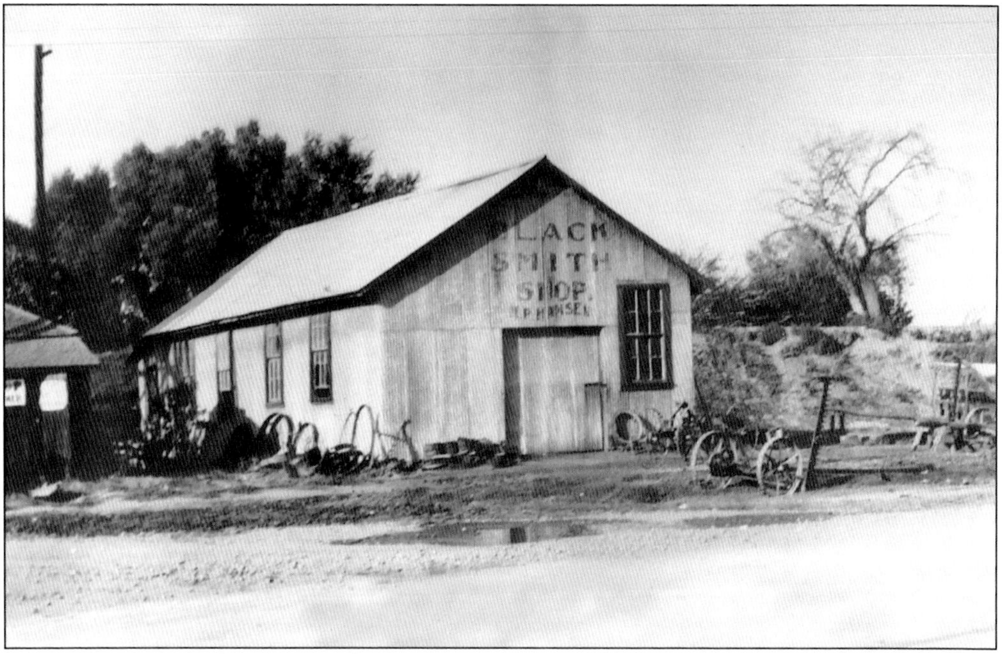

BLACKSMITH SHOP. The Blacksmith Shop was located on Second Street close to where Balsmeiers Plumbing and Sheetmetal is located today. Horses and carriages needed to be maintained in this growing agrarian community.

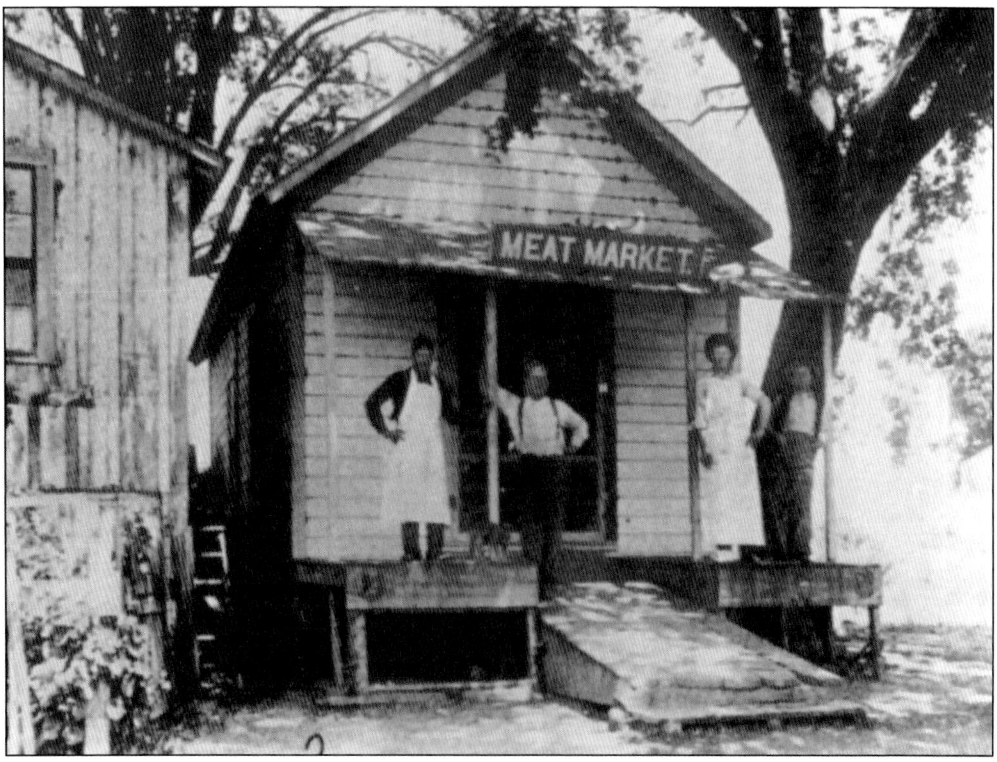

BUTCHER SHOP. The Meat Market was also on Second Street, near B Street.

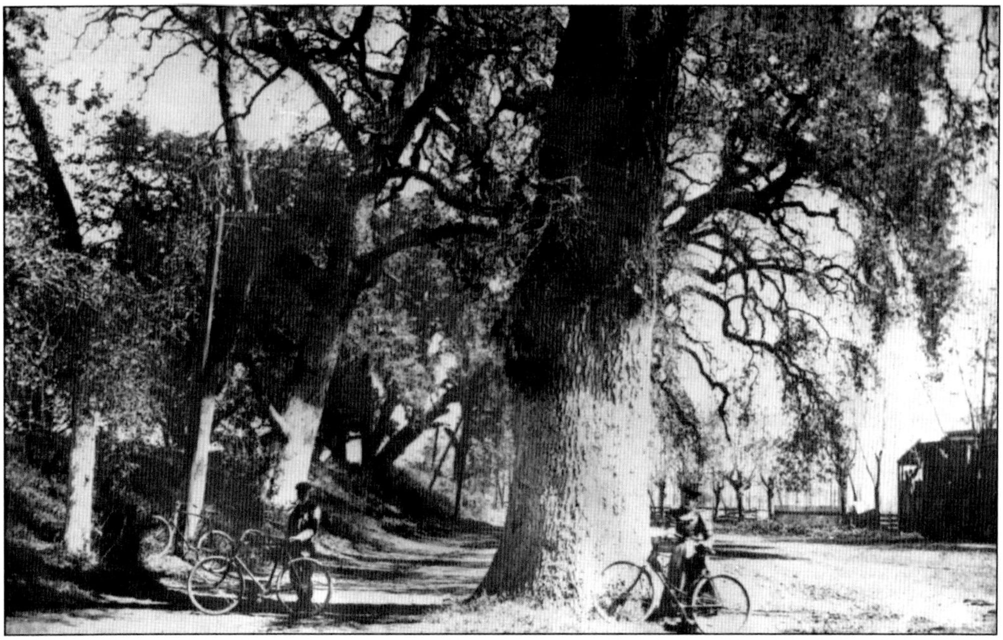

Riverside Road. The River Road wandered along the Sacramento levee. Bicycles and "fine carriages" were the means of locomotion in the 1890s. The natural levee, large oak trees, attractive friends, and farmhouse on the left created a beautiful spot for a picture by the third bicyclist.

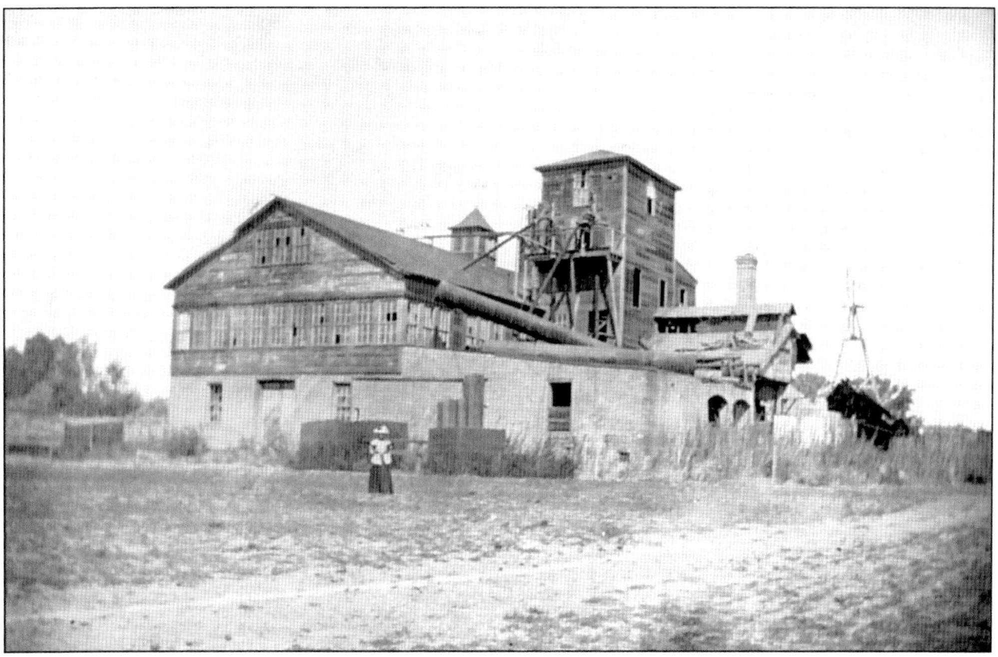

Sugar Beet Factory. Seen here is the first sugar beet factory in Isleton. The actual site is unknown, but the river or slough was nearby for transport. The woman in the center of the picture is dressed in 1890s style, and the state of the road dates this image to the turn of the century. Old newspaper accounts tell of a sugar beet factory destroyed by floods at the turn of the century; perhaps it was this one.

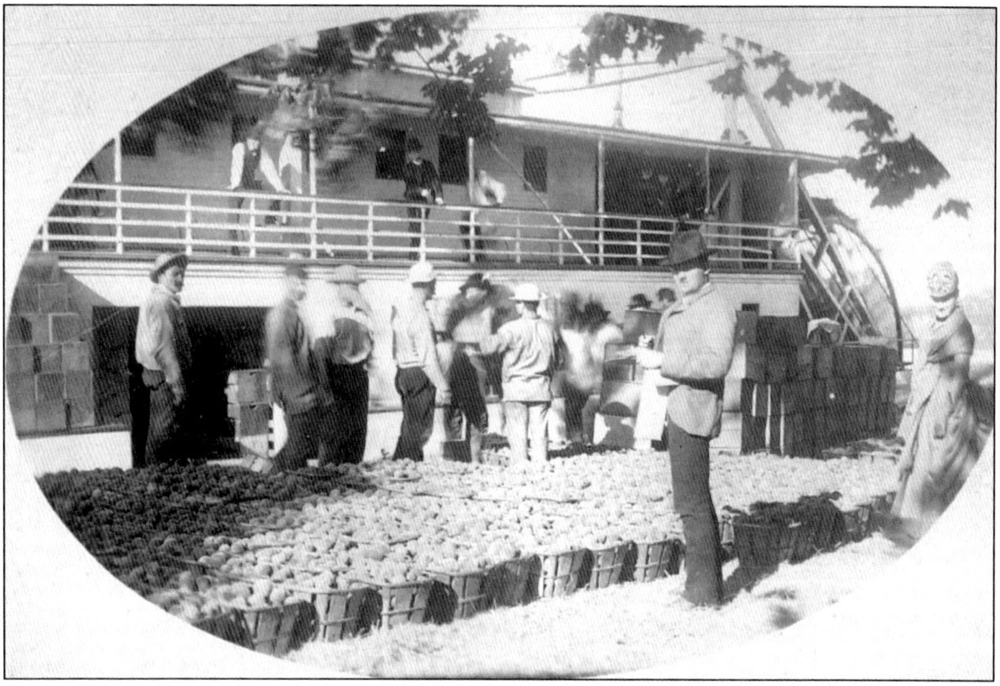

Sugar Beet Bushels. Riverboats supplied the best transport out of Isleton. Here is a dock filled with sugar beets in bushels headed for market. The boat is a paddle-wheeler that also provided passenger service to Sacramento and San Francisco. The woman on the left is dressed in 1890s style, and the paddle-wheeler and lined up bushels date this image to the late 19th century.

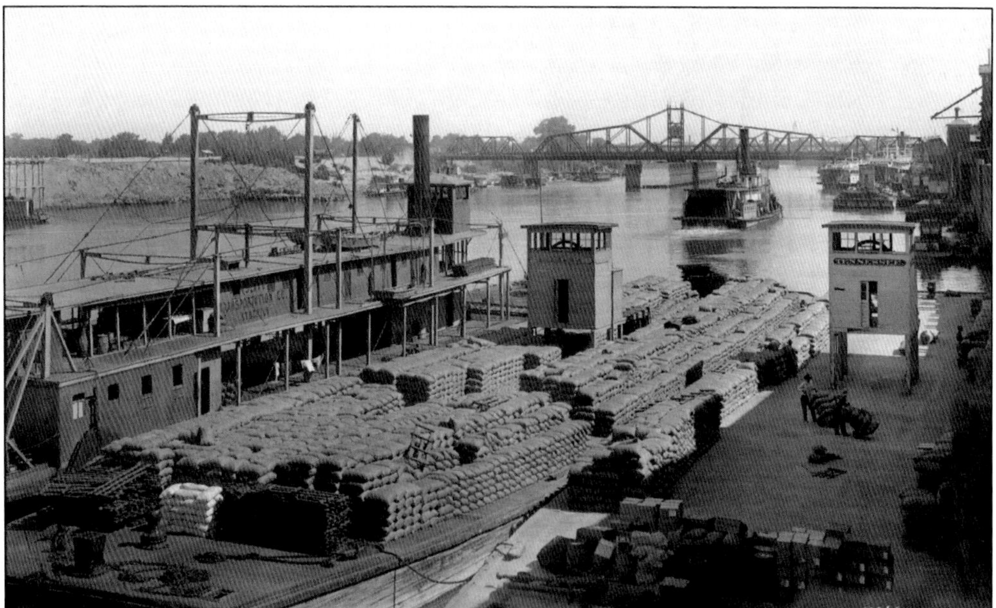

Sacks of Grain. From 1870 to 1940 goods were transported to Sacramento or San Francisco by way of barge. This laden ship is ready for pushing on the San Joaquin River. Note the paddle-wheeler in the background. This barge is carrying over 8,000 sacks of grain. That's a lot of bread!

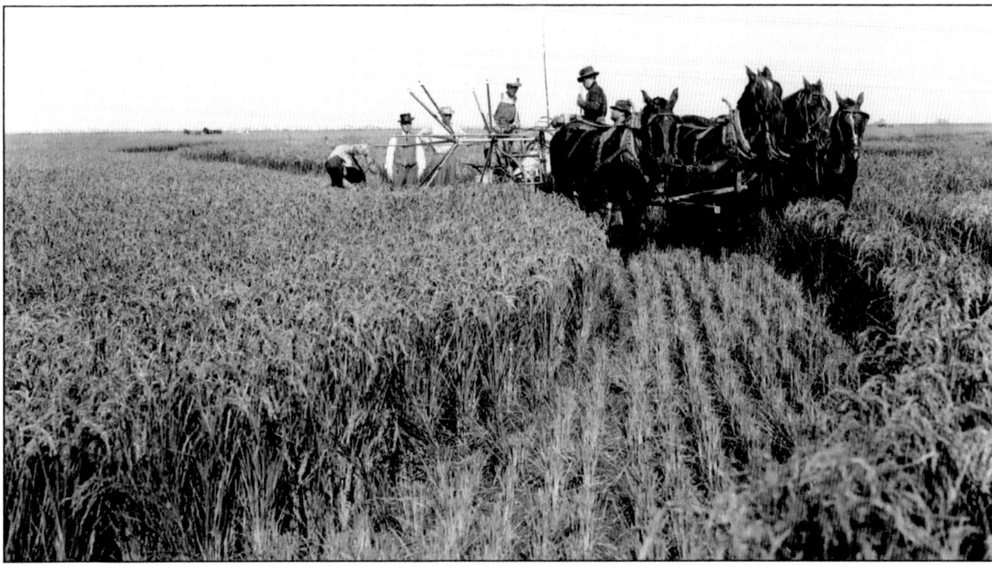

Harvester and Horses. Four large working horses pull this harvester thru the Delta peat soil before the turn of the century. The rake is near four feet and the cut less than two. These draft animals were a mainstay in early Delta farming. It is interesting to note the men and their dress on this particular day. Everybody has a hat, and either overalls or a vest and tie. Note the heavy horse collars.

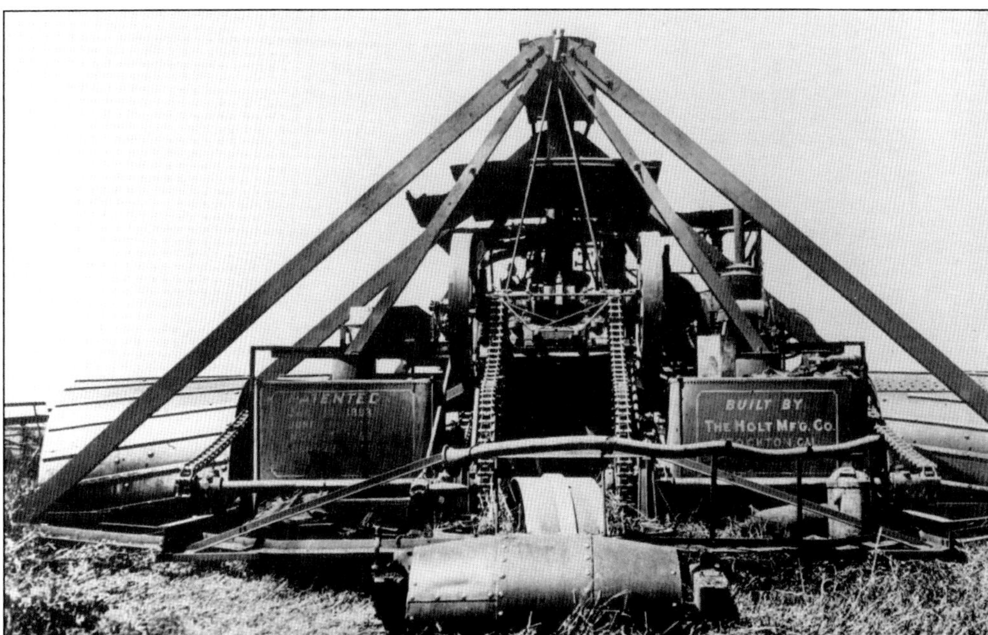

Holt Steam Harvester. The Holt Tractor Company of Stockton developed this wide based steam tractor for the Delta's porous peat soils. The wide base and the large treads were driven by steam over the marsh and soggy soil. The wheel base was almost 46 feet wide and the center of gravity distributed the weight over the base. Note the extremely wide treads and the booms that extend to the cutters.

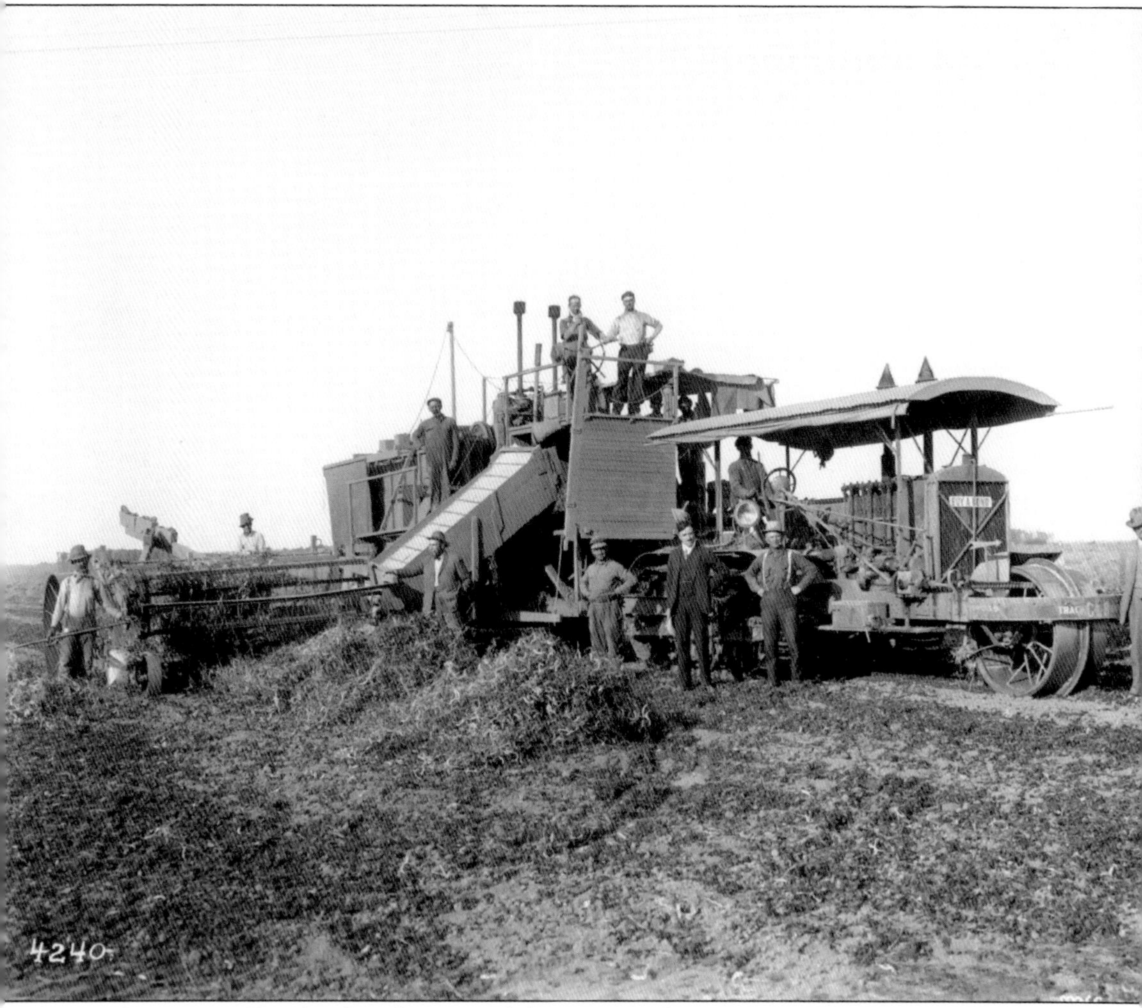

HARVESTER. Shortly after the turn of the century the stream engine was replaced by huge petroleum driven thrashers, harvesters, and tractors. This Holt 32 is pulled by a tractor. This combine did a lot of work but used extensive labor. Note that is took ten men to keep this rig on the mow; notice, however, that more than one are in suit and tie. The amount of rigging, lubrication, adjustments, and calculations must have kept everybody pretty busy. The sign on the radiator says, "Buy Bonds," which places the photo during World War I.

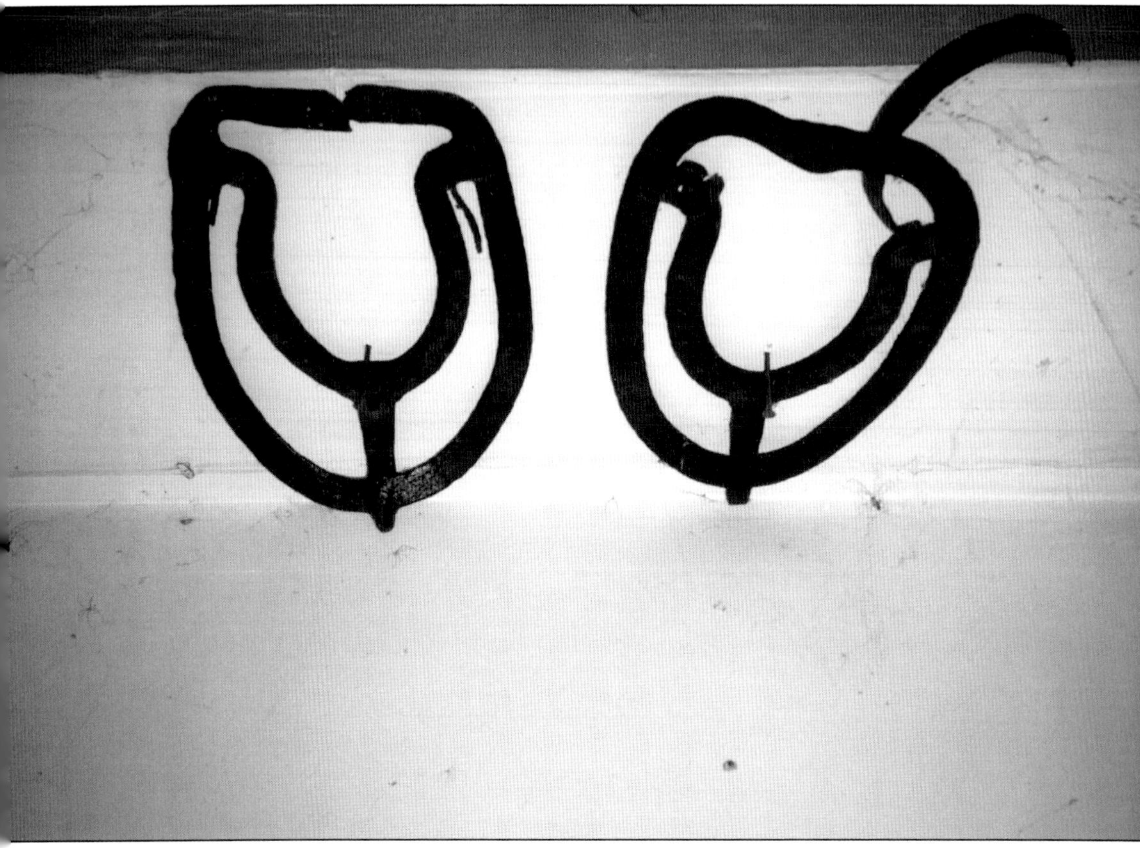

TULE HORSE SHOES. Tule horse shoes are a Delta innovation. This pair of horse shoes was adapted just for the soggy Delta farm lands. They were found in a barn on Grand Island. The wide footing worked the same as human snowshoes distributing a horses weight over a larger area. The large horses then had a chance to push themselves out of the thick peat bog.

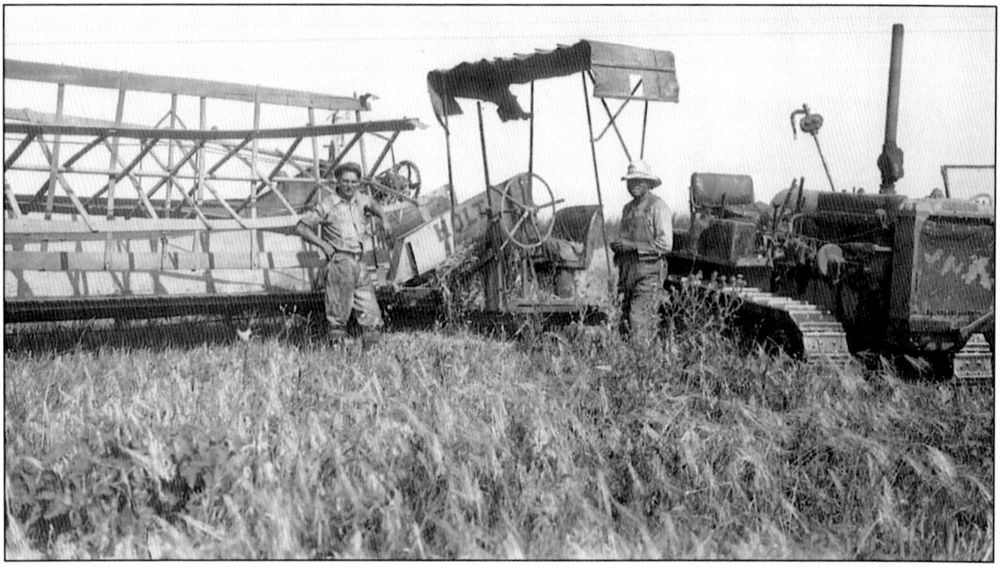

Holt Harvester. The Holt Tractor Company of Stockton built this harvester that was used on Twitchell Island near Isleton. Grain harvest usually takes place in early spring and the tracklayers must be strong and powerful to pull a wide harvester like this. The advantage for the farmer was a major cut in labor costs. The tractor appears to be either a Best or Caterpillar 30.

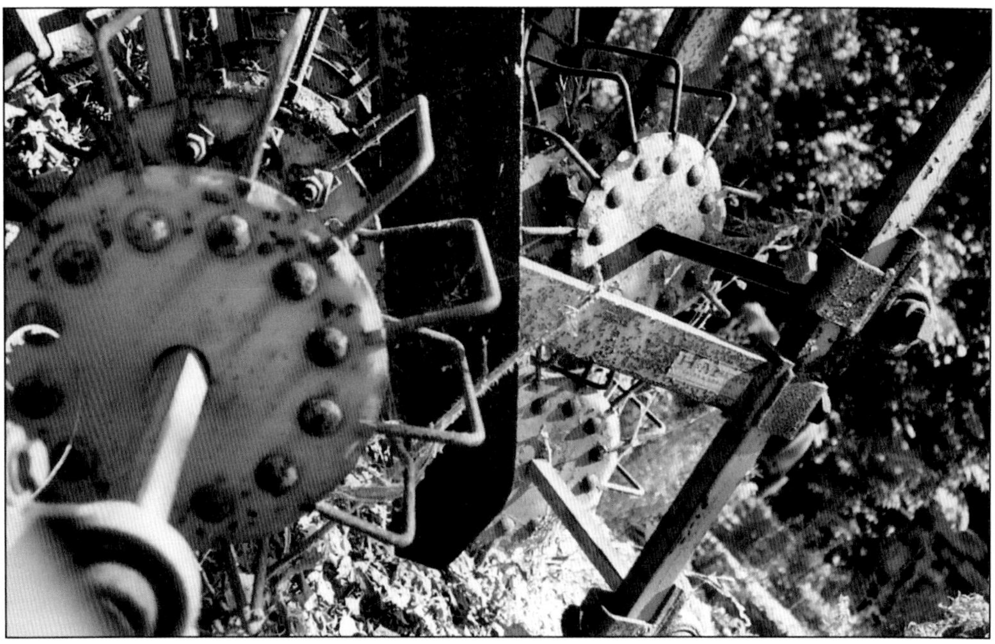

Blackwelder's Thinner. Prior to the invention of the sugar beet thinner, the work was done by hand. Sugar beet seeds were planted in large numbers and then later thinned. The Blackwelder Company manufactured this beet thinner in the 1960s to reduce the number of plants. Not long after the thinner was developed sugar beet seed was improved and thinning was no longer necessary. This thinner was found in the metal waste pile at the Silva Ranch.

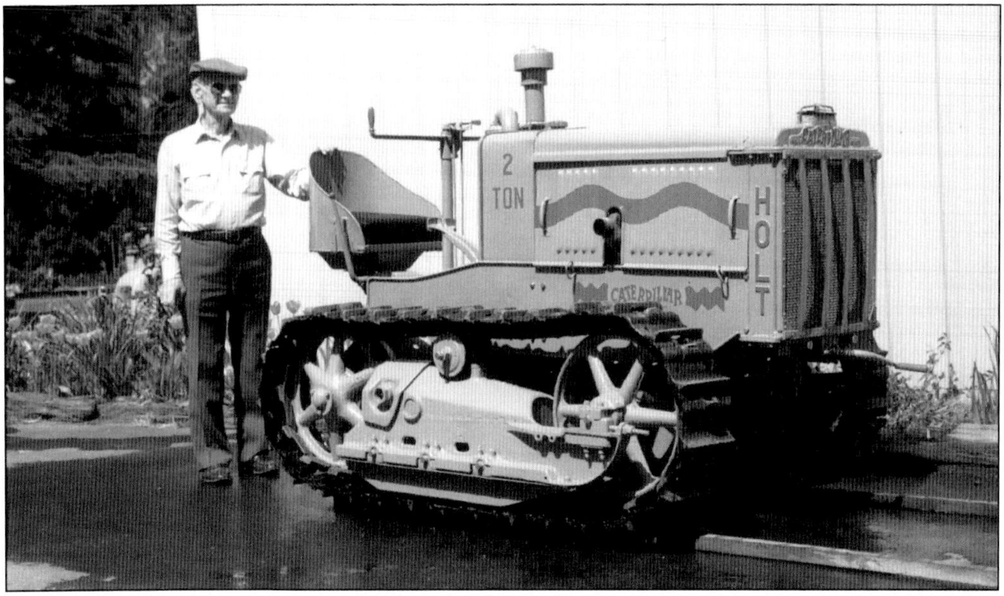

Holt 2 Ton. Hubert Van De Maele bought this Holt 2 tractor new in 1925. He farmed with it on Sherman Island, plowing, discing, pumping, and lifting beets. The air cleaner was changed to allow the operator to view his work and move around better. This tractor is retired on the Van De Maele ranch near Isleton. It has been restored by Denis Van De Maele

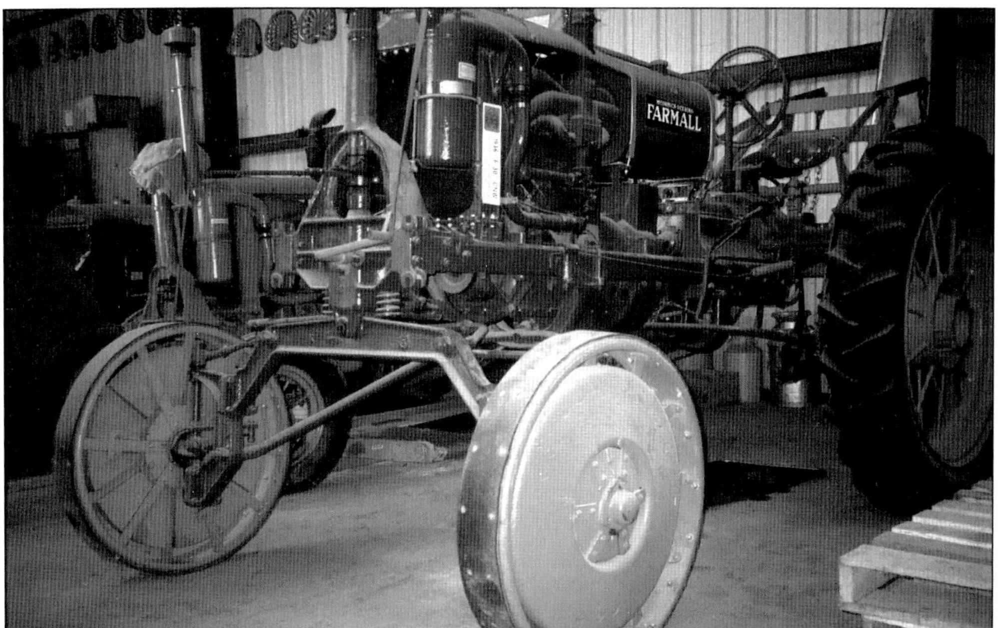

Farmall F 30. One of the "workhorses" of the Delta was the Farmall F 30. It was used for wheat, sugar beets, asparagus, and most farm work. Asparagus tractors had to have a wide front wheelbase to edge the asparagus row and extra weight to keep the front wheels tracking properly. For white asparagus the front wheel width had to be close to seven feet. Note the extra weights and width of the front tires on this Farmall F 30.

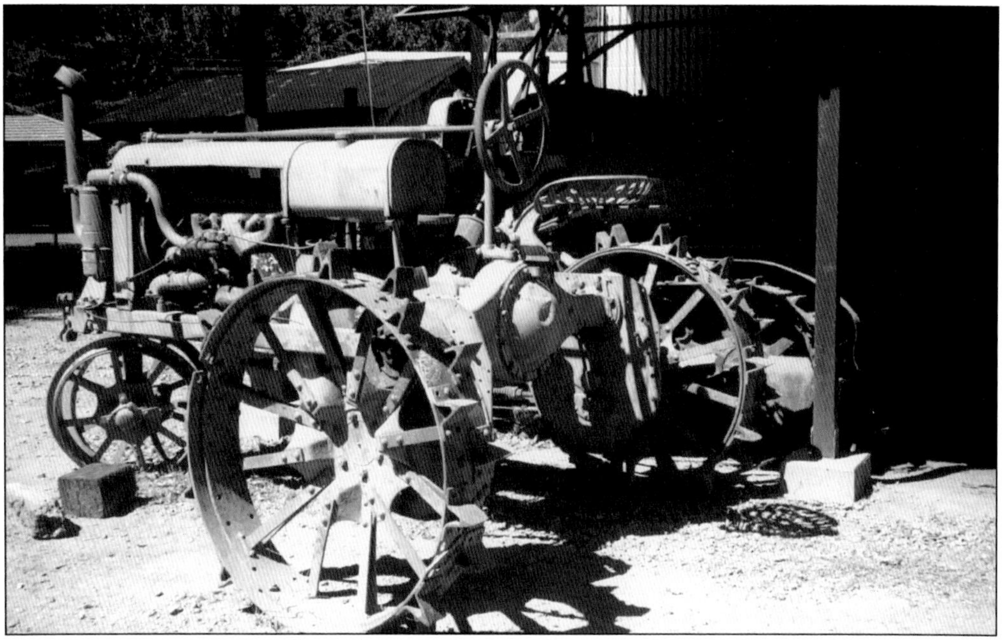

Steel-Rimmed Farmall. The earlier a farmer could get into the marshy peat fields the better. This Farmall F 30 is equipped to facilitate this. The wide rear rims were equipped with spikes to push through the soggy soil. Note that the front wheels are close together, not equipped for asparagus, but ready for sugar beets.

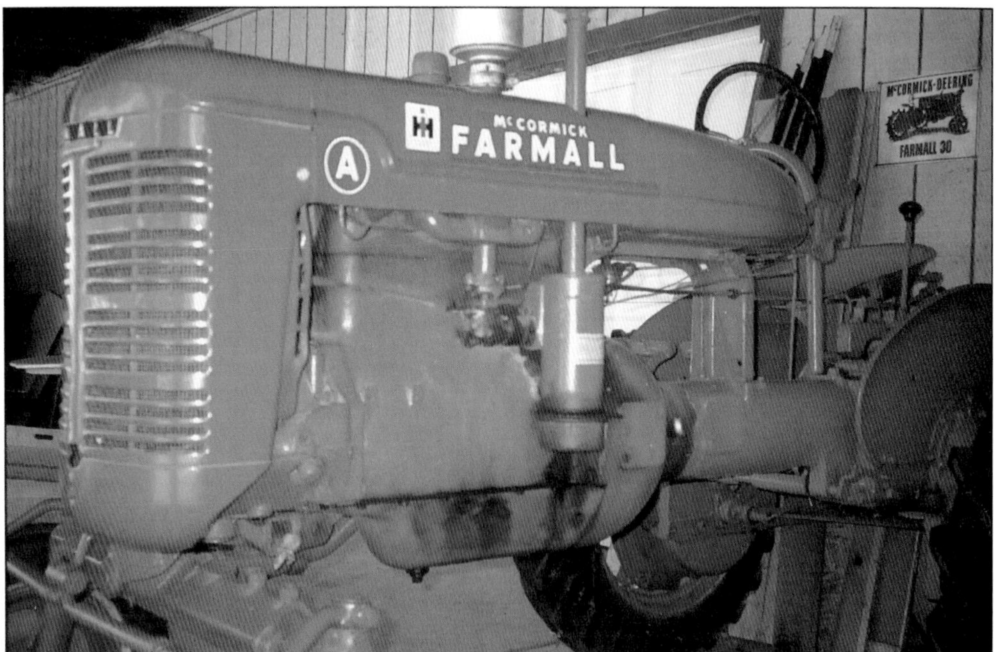

Farmall A 1. A coveted piece of farm equipment in the Delta was the A 1. This Farmall kept many farms going during the Depression and many kids busy after school on the ranch.

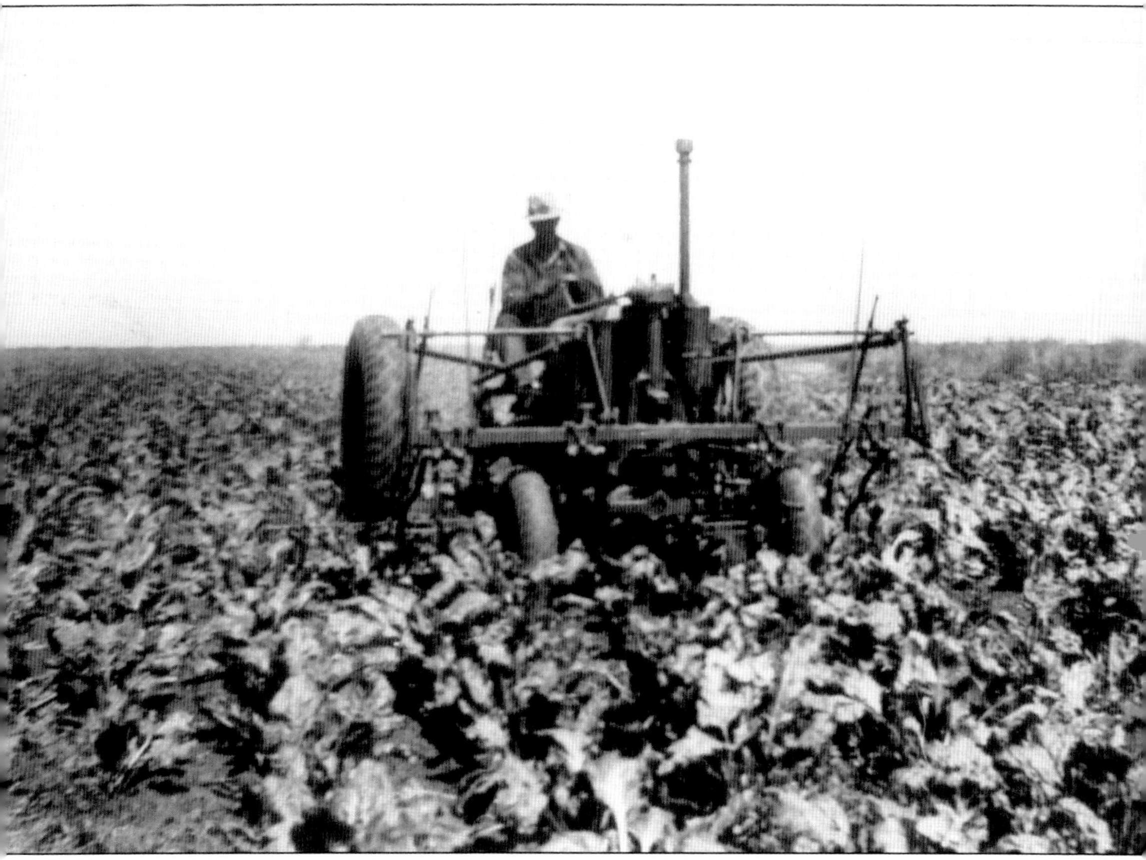

FARMALL F 12. Hubert Van de Maele cultivates his beet field on a Farmall F 12.

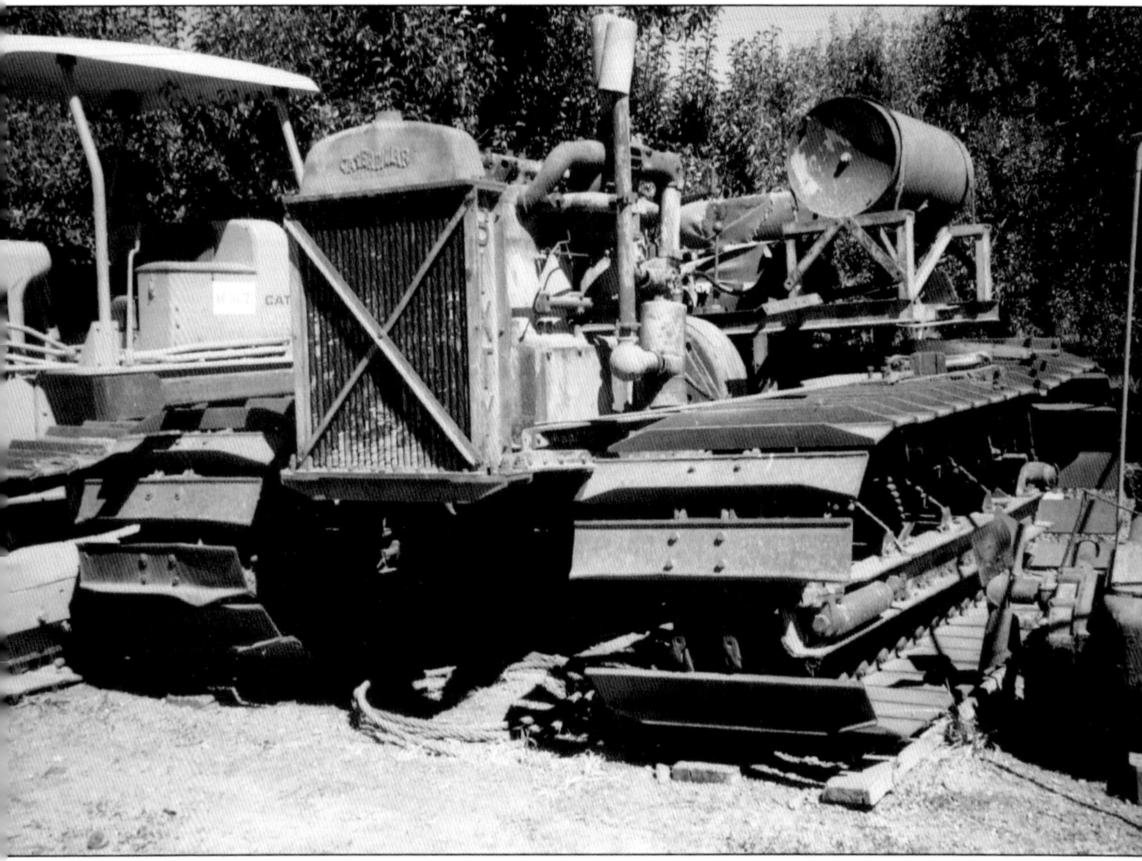

CAT 60, WIDE. This Caterpillar 60 has been modified to work in the Delta. The width has been extended as has the length. The tracks have been widened a great deal to give it better traction. Old timers said that it could almost "walk on water, but it used a lot of fuel." Note the very wide tracks!

Three

Steamboats and Commerce

After blasting, laying track, and removing mountains of sledge, Cantonese workers migrated to the Delta. The Chinese came to the Isleton to build levees and to work in agriculture. Seeking to establish a home away from home, a strong sense of community developed. Fires and prejudice didn't keep this ancient culture from establishing their homes, businesses, and institutions.

The rich peat soil, reclamation, hard work, technology, and abundance of water soon created bumper crops around Isleton. The Sacramento River was the natural route to new bustling population centers in Sacramento and San Francisco. Continuous dredging, levee management, and water control helped to manage the rivers. Successful marketing, sales, and transport depended upon river boats. Large steam ships were soon bringing passengers and cargo to and from Isleton, and the city began to develop.

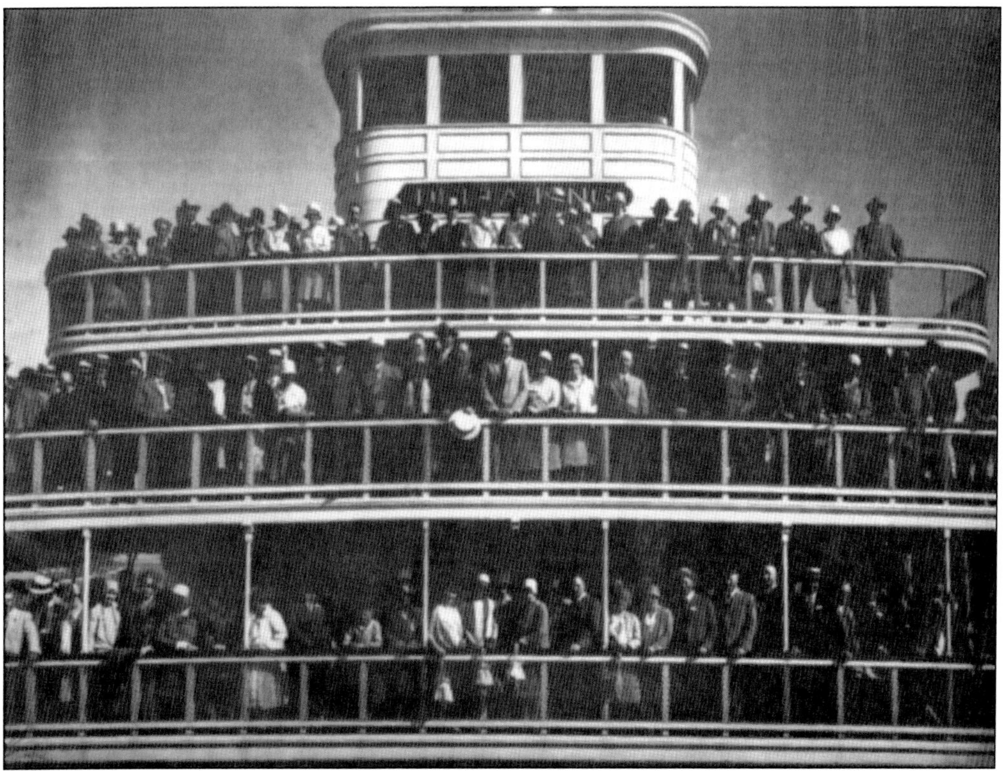

Delta King Passengers. The last steamboats to carry freight and passengers on California waters were the *Delta King* and *Queen*. During the Roaring Twenties river-side speakeasies and bordellos kept the ships loaded with passengers. It looks like they are having a good time!

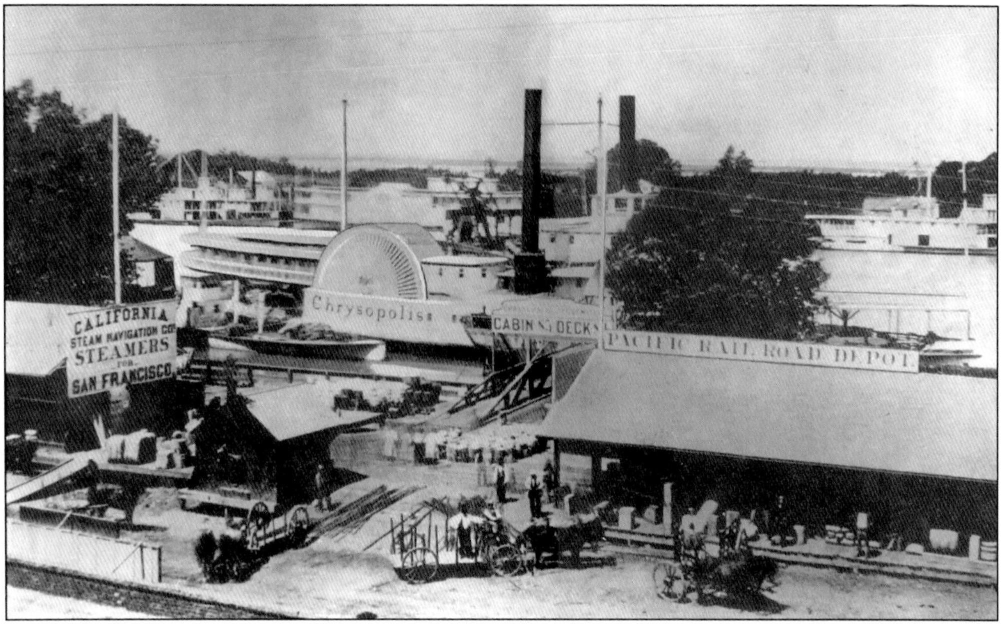

CHRYSOPOLIS. This sleek side-wheeler was one of the first and best liners in the Delta. Its dual smokestacks streaked the skyline at nearly 25 miles per hour with Victorian elegance. It was built in San Francisco, launched in 1860, and ended its service on San Francisco Bay as a double-ender ferry named the *Oakland*.

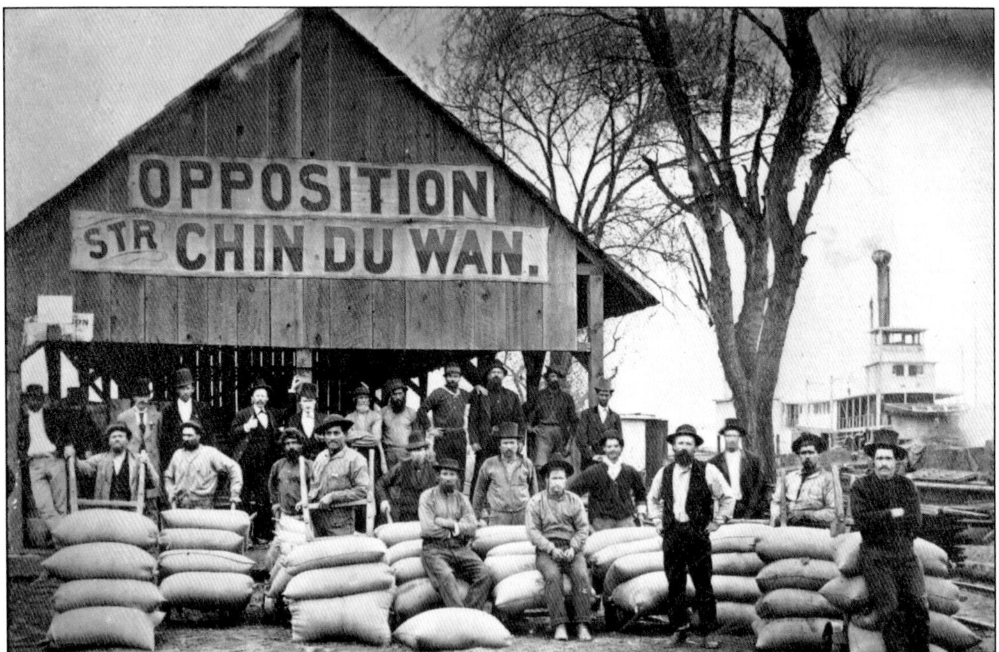

VARUNA CREW. Isleton was not much more than a wharf in 1876. The Civil War was over, Reconstruction was taking place in the South, and California was just starting to develop. The steamer *Varuna* is in the background and her crew, probably a few '49ers, has sacks of wheat to load for a trip past Isleton on the Sacramento River.

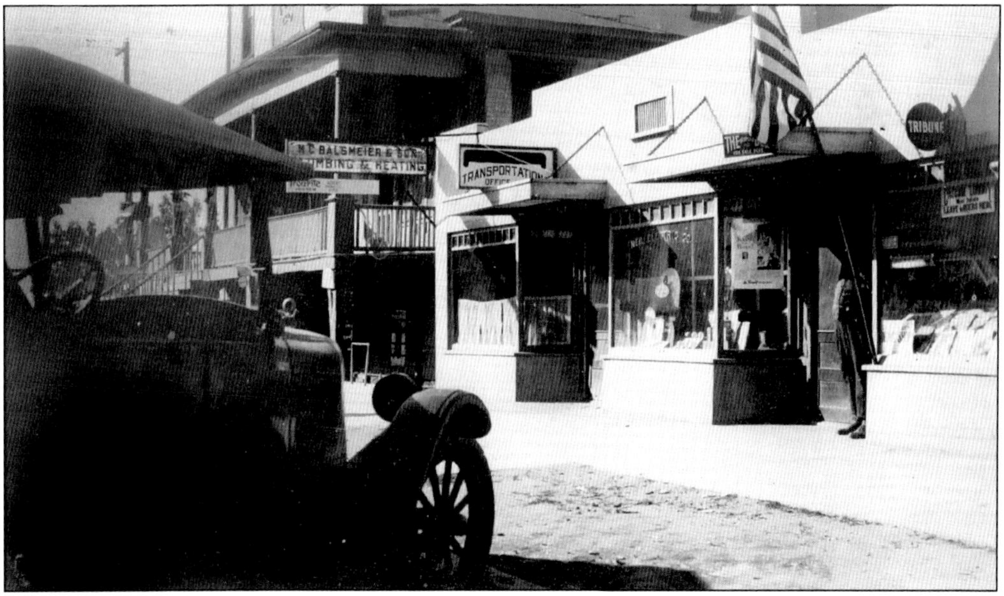

BALSMEIER SHOP. Second Street was a dirt path when Balsmeier used the Gardiner Building as his shop. As homes were being built, water and sewer lines were providing all the modern comforts. The buildings in the foreground selling the *Tribune* and bus tickets are located where the Del Rio Real Estate is located today. Balsmeiers is today located just a few doors up river and is still installing and repairing plumbing lines.

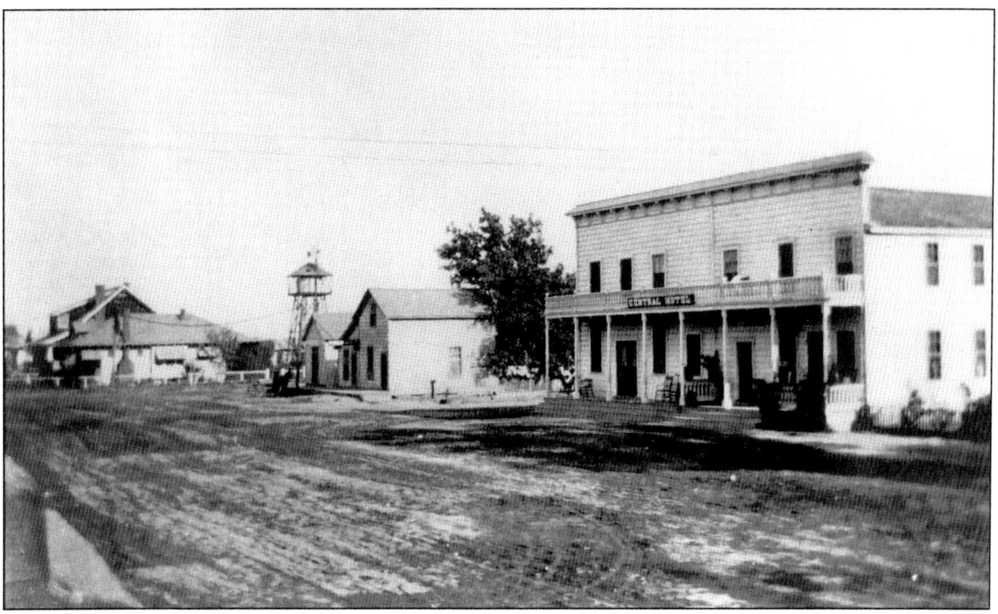

SECOND STREET UNPAVED. Victory Highway, as Highway 160 became known, was just a dirt road at the turn of the century, and the Central Hotel, where Ernies restaurant stands today, was the major stop over. The present-day water tower is close to the water tower shown here, but the current post office has replaced the white home that sits in the mid-left corner. The home behind it still stands.

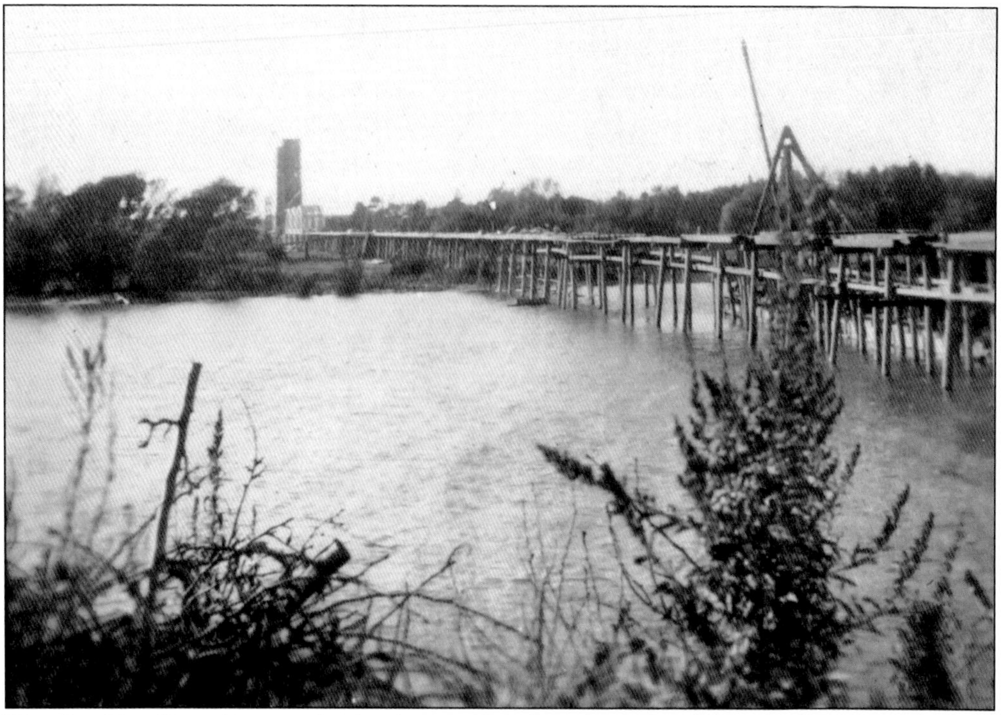

The Old Rio Vista Bridge. In the distance, on the other side of the island, are the towers of the draw bridge. The ship channel was located on the Rio Vista side of Wood Island. Traveling across the bridge was an exciting experience, especially if the water was high and the current swift.

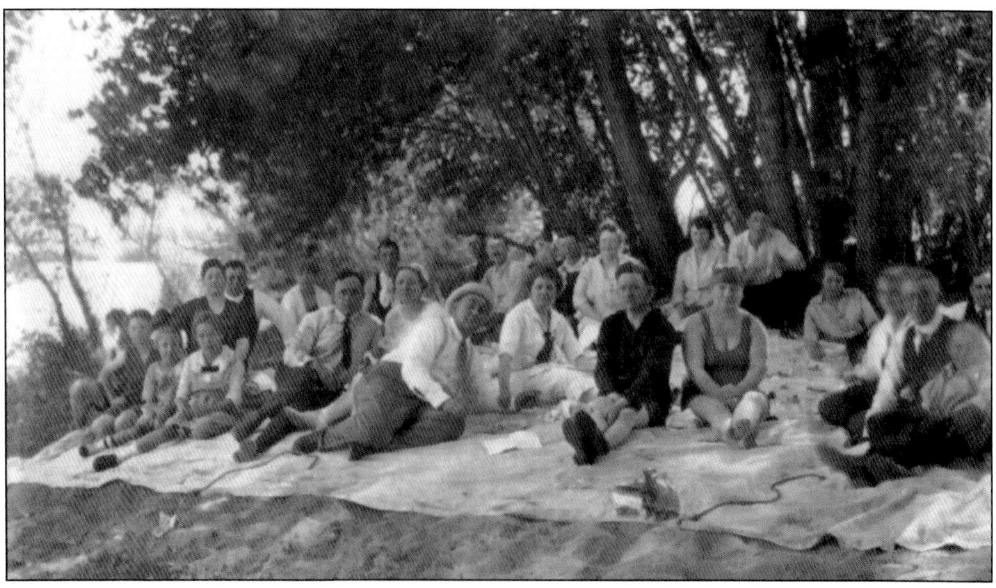

Wood Island Picnic. The Balsmeiers were a prominent family in Isleton at the turn of the century, and they are shown here at a picnic in 1922 on Wood Island. This island no longer exists, but the Balsmeiers do. Wood Island was eliminated to deepen the river channel. The Balsmeiers have been major community leaders for years.

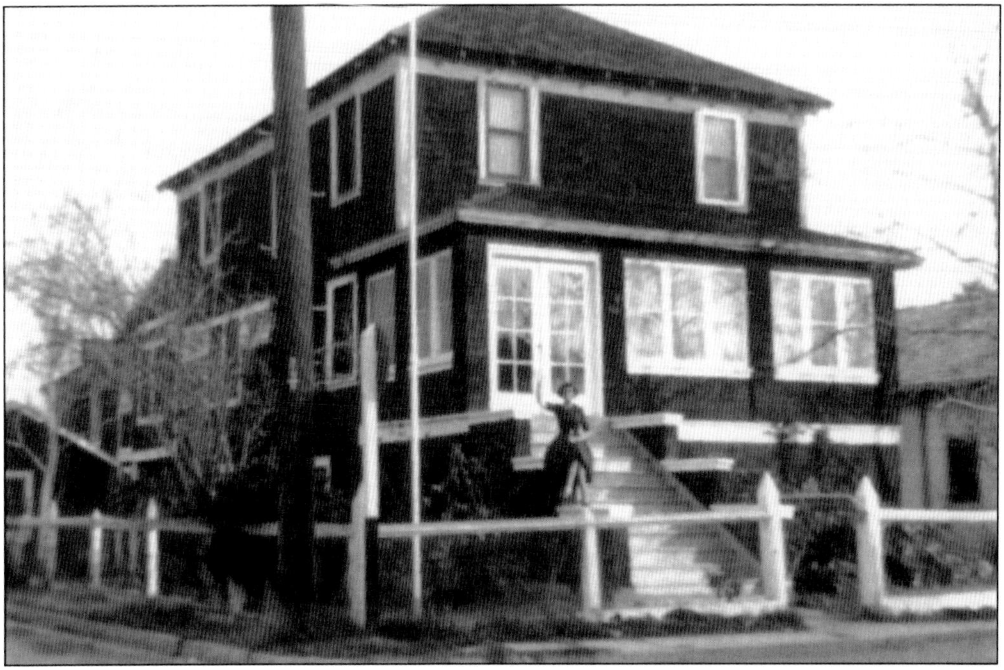

PERKINS HOME. The Perkins house at the corner of Second and B Streets was the home of another prominent family. Charles Perkins was a produce buyer for a San Francisco firm and was instrumental in getting the Bank of America to Isleton. He owned the first car in Isleton, a Cadillac. His wife Lena was a well-known teacher and his two daughters also were involved in education. Alice Perkins married Fred Heimbaugh, who later became the mayor.

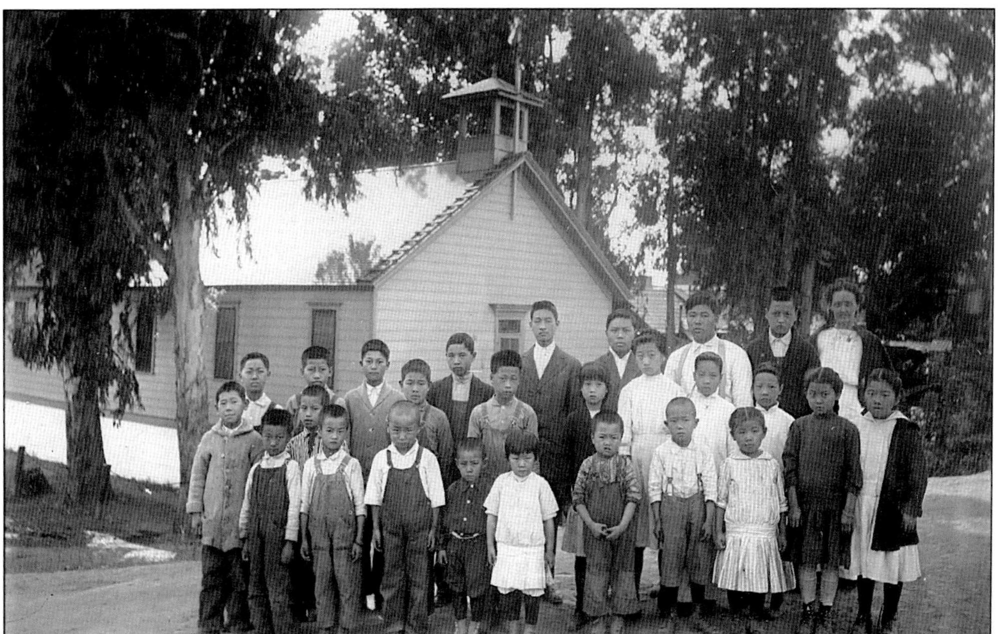

ORIENTAL SCHOOL. Lena Perkins guides her students through the paces at the Oriental School in the 1920s. There appears to be a big age range.

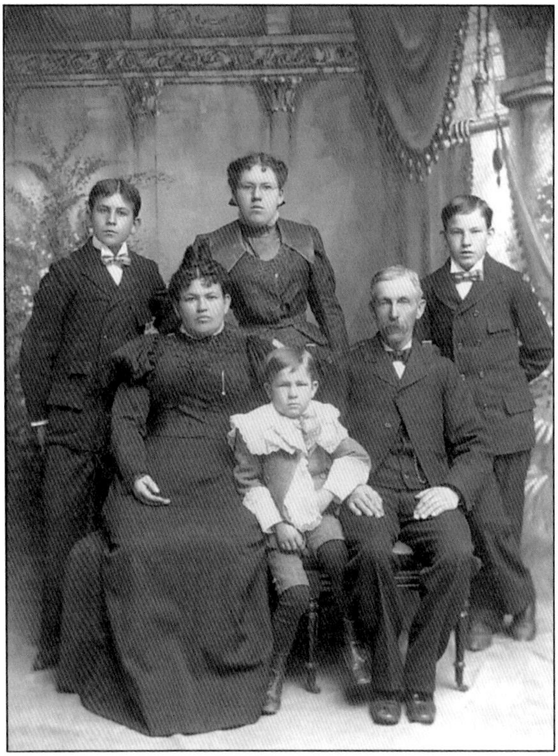

John Gardiner's Family. John Gardiner was one of the three children of Hogate and Ida Gardiner. Here the family gathers for the photographer. John was a business leader, banker, councilman, farmer, postmaster, and leader of the World War I bond drive.

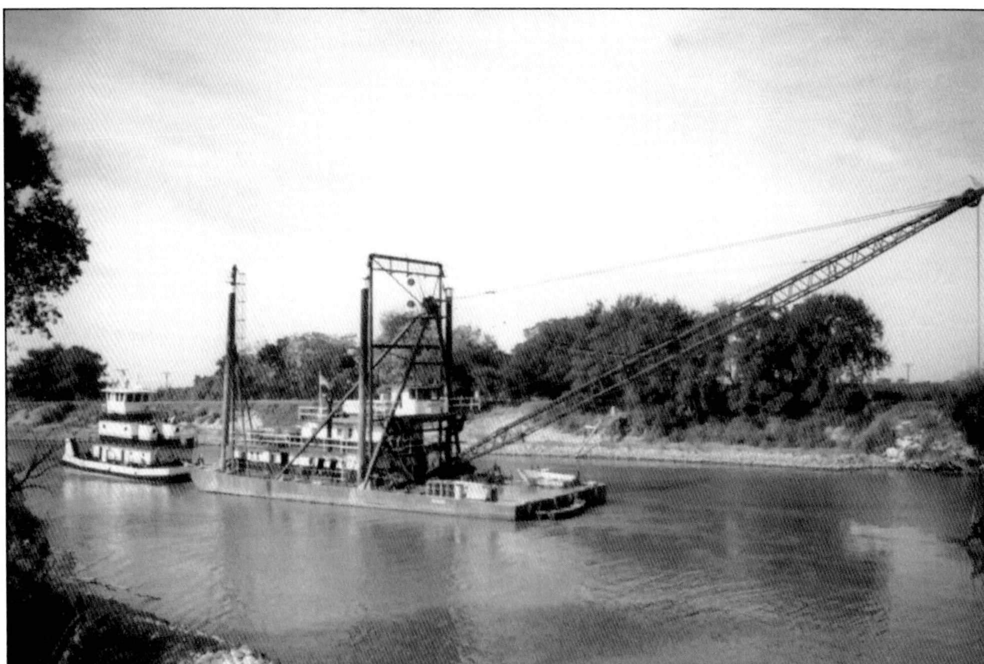

Dutra Dredge. A modern Dutra clamshell dredge came through every year to dredge out the river bottom. The fine silt that has been washed into the river for hundreds of miles is capable of raising the river a great deal. Dredging is a must to prevent flooding.

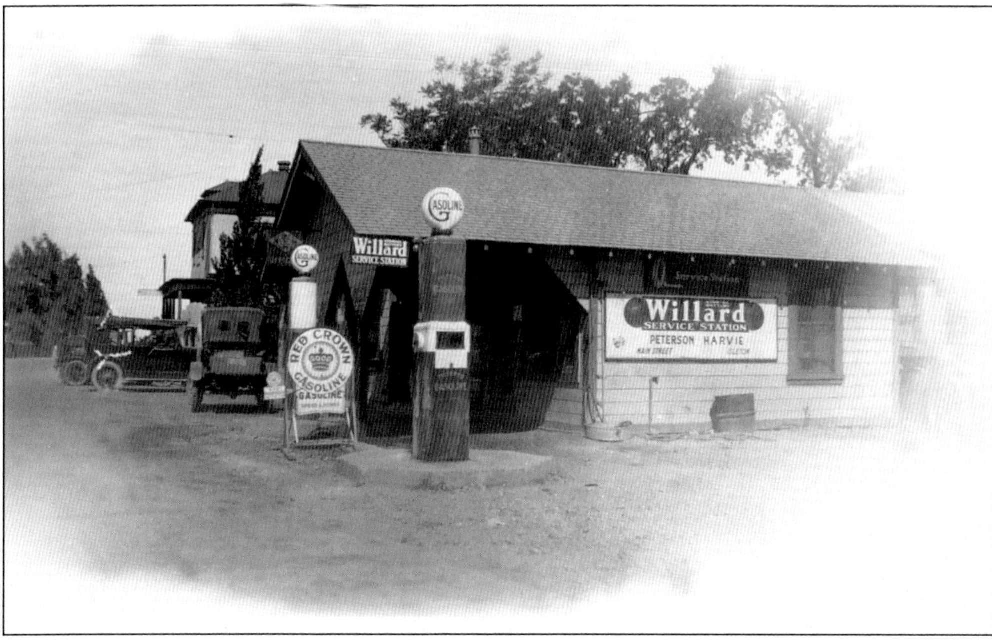

PETERSON HARVIE. This 1924 photograph on the Victory Highway, across from Dunn's, shows the Peterson Harvie station and repair. Notice the Gardiner Improvement Building in the background.

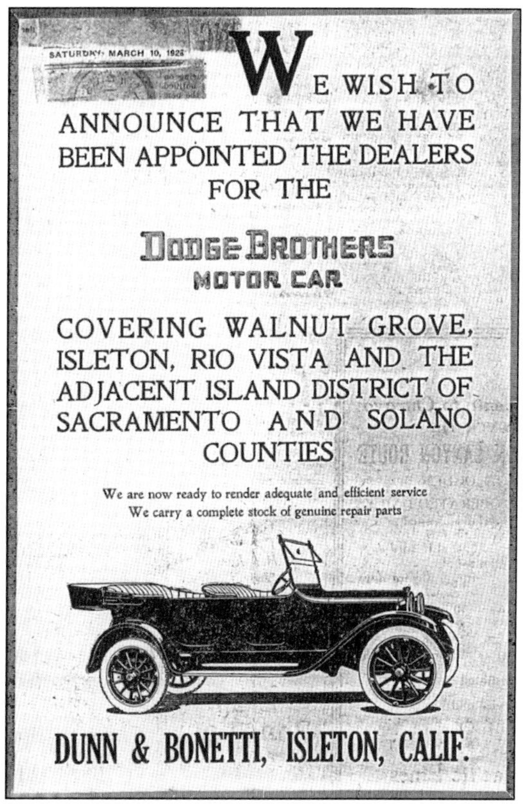

1923 DUNN AD. A 1923 Dodge Phaeton with the top down advertises the grand opening of the Dunn and Bonetti Dodge Dealer in Isleton.

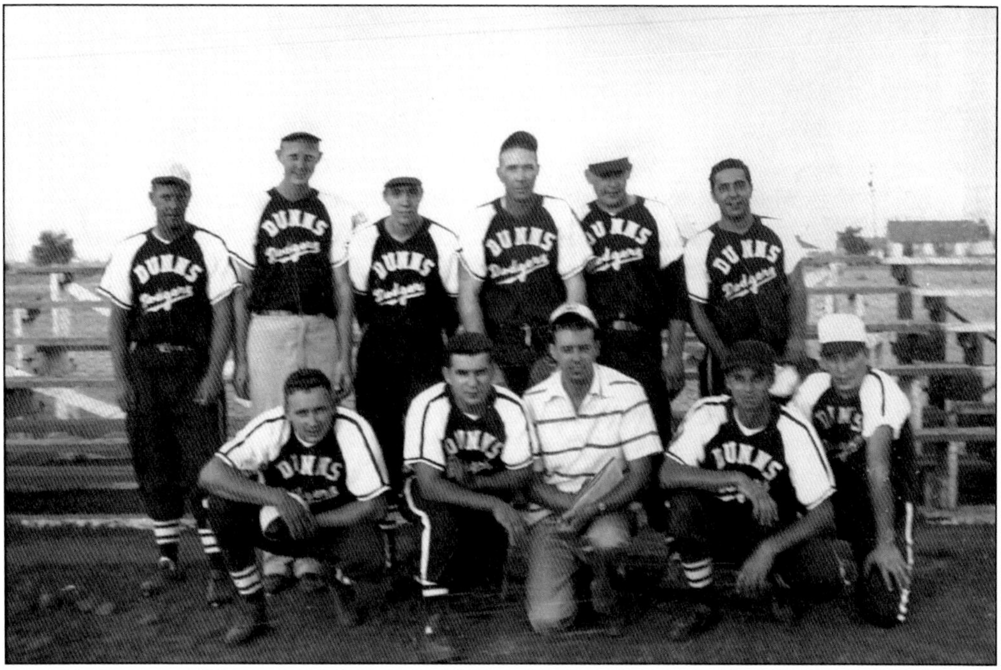

DUNN'S DODGERS. Every year Isleton was able to recruit a darn good baseball team. Supported by Dunn's Dodge, they competed up and down the Delta. Some of these players have been on the team for years.

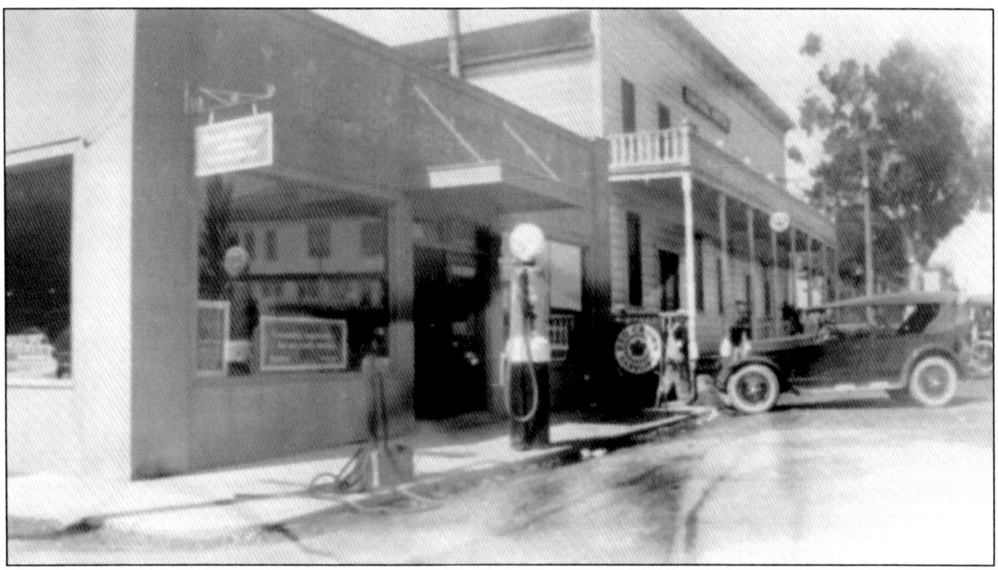

CENTRAL HOTEL AND DUNN. This photo shows the commercial street of Isleton in the 1920s, with the Central Hotel in the background and Dunn Dodge in the foreground. The street was paved by this time and the gas pumps are ready for those new Dodge automobiles, sold by one of the earliest Dodge dealers in California, Dunn and Bonetti at Second and B Streets.

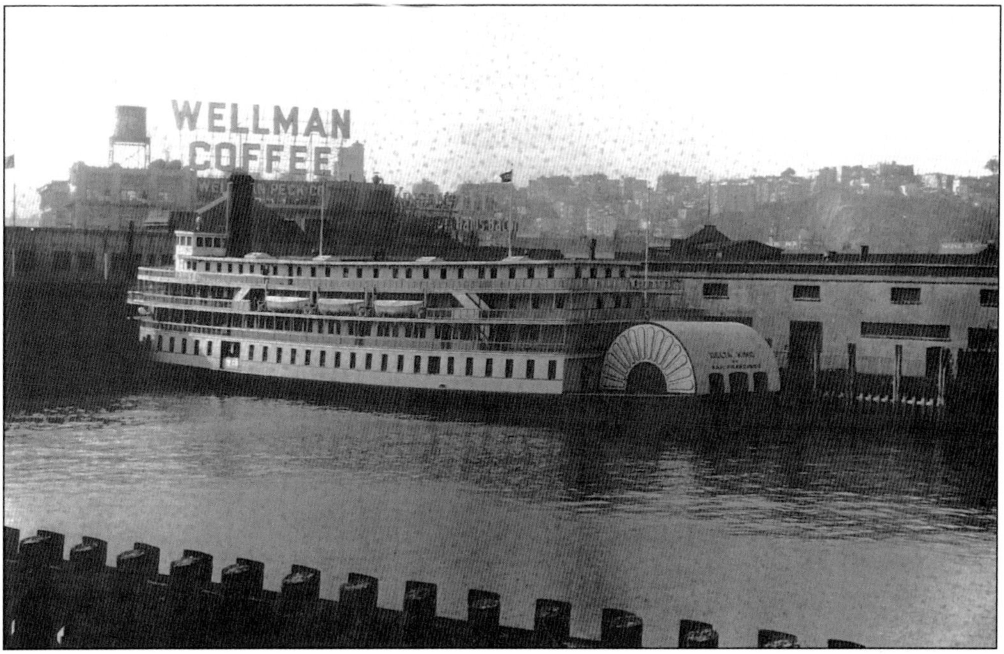

DELTA KING. The sternwheeler *Delta King* docks in San Francisco after cruising the Sacramento River. It was a valued piece of transportation and a beautiful ship. It hit on hard times and was almost abandoned, but has been restored as a restaurant on the Sacramento River in Old Sacramento. The *Delta King* made regular stops at the Isleton wharf.

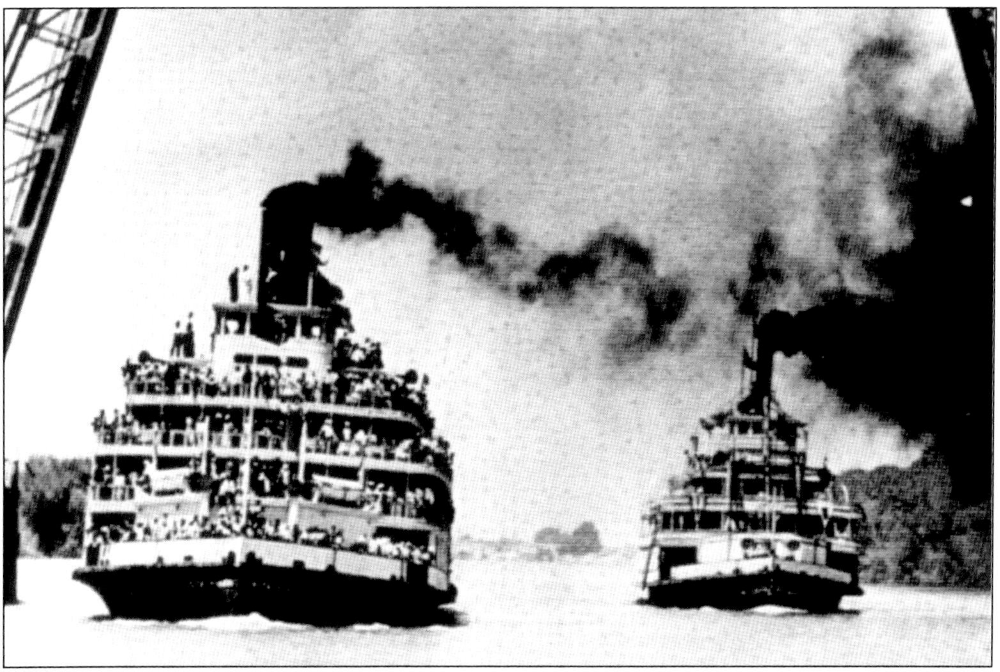

DELTA KING AND QUEEN. The *Delta King* and *Queen* are shown here under a drawbridge on the Sacramento River. The *King* is in the background. The two ships raced on April 22, 1939, each with 600 to 900 passengers. The *King* won by less than a boat length.

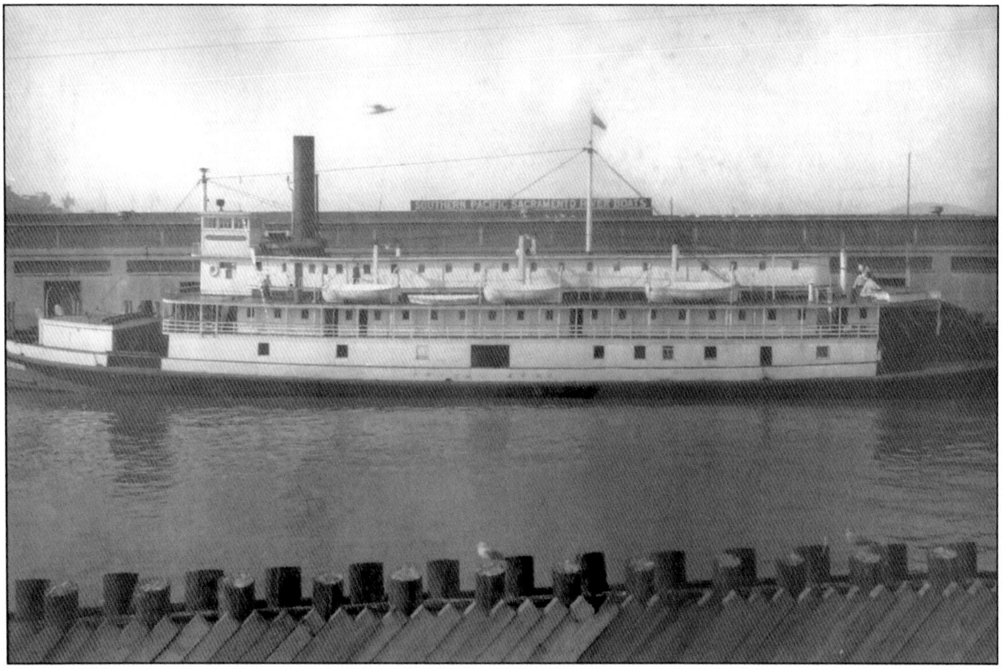

STEAMSHIP *J.D. STEVENS*. This lady of doubtless virtue not only took off, but she changed her name and found happiness with some "reservation." Her real name is *J.D. Peters*, and she, along with the *Navajo*, was used in 1938 to save Mandeville Island. They were floated to a major break in the levee to block the San Joaquin from flooding the island. Once the levee was partially restored the *Peters'* paddle-wheel was used to force water off the land. Once the water was off the ship was dry-docked and ended up as a bunkhouse for farmhands.

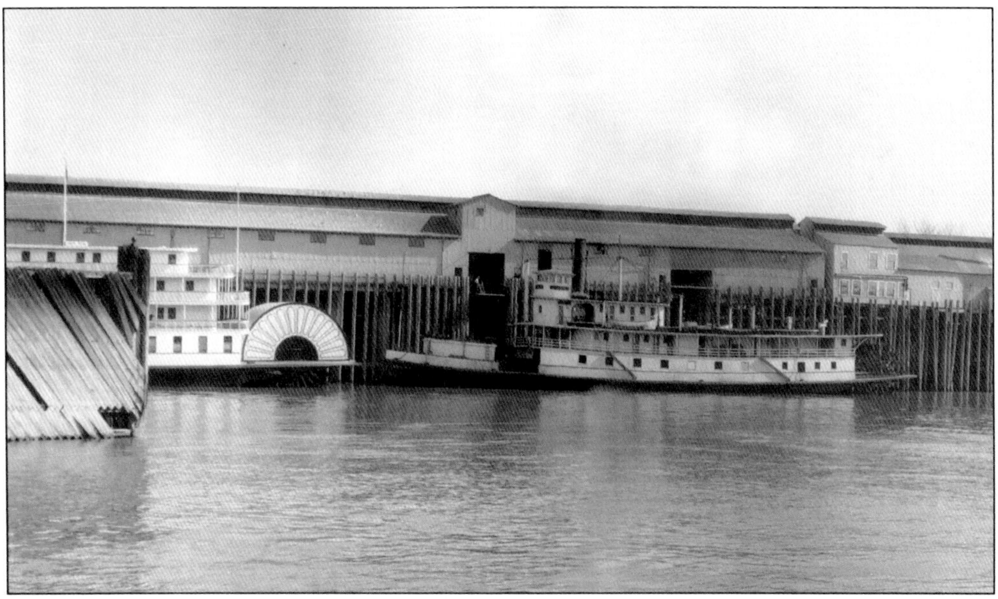

STEAMBOAT *LEADER*. This beautiful steamboat, the *Leader*, was cast in a movie in 1935 called *Steamboat Round the Bend*. The movie was shot in the Delta, but the script was all Mississippi. Will Rogers was the star, and the *Cherokee Steamboat* was also in the film.

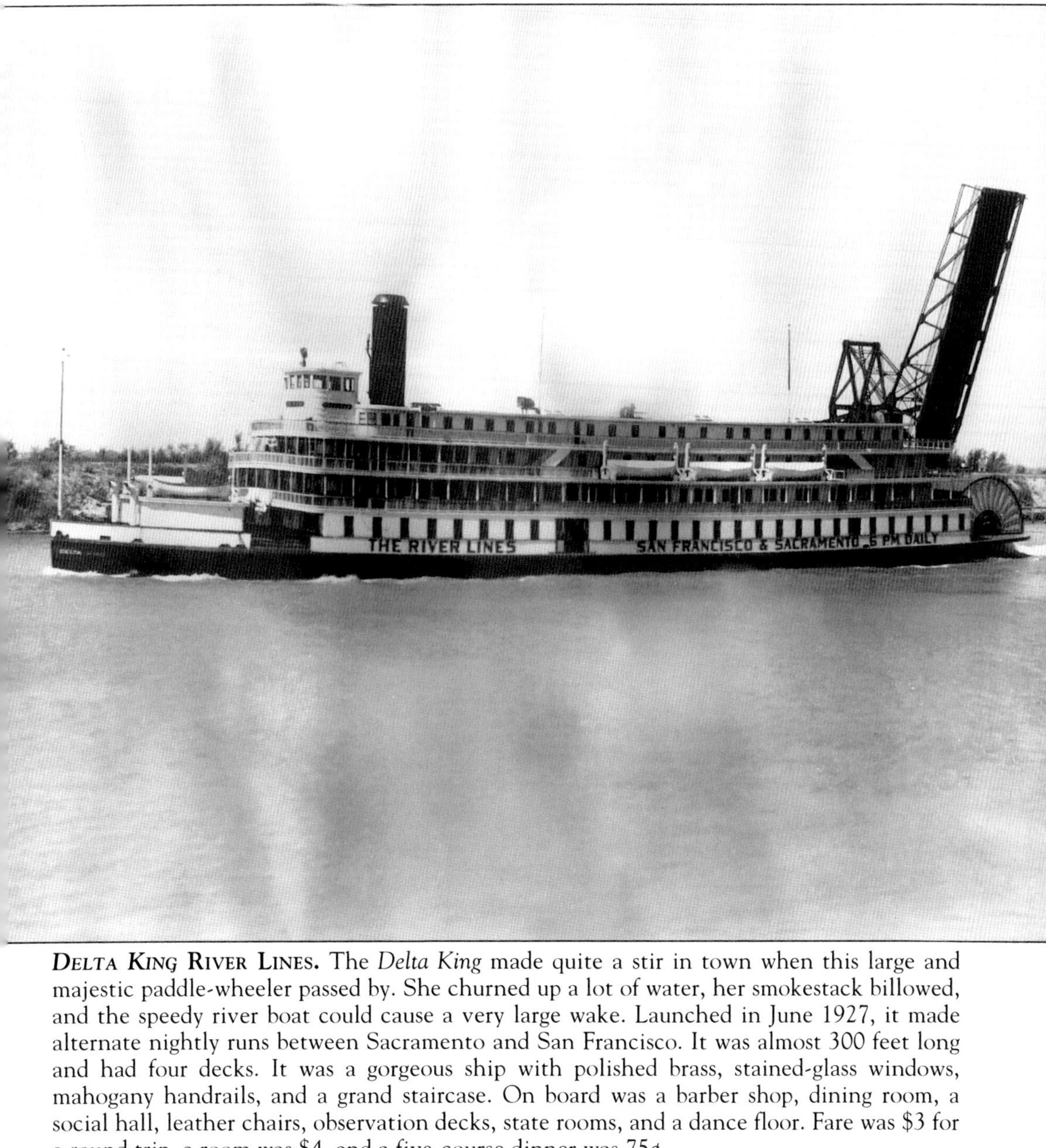

DELTA KING RIVER LINES. The *Delta King* made quite a stir in town when this large and majestic paddle-wheeler passed by. She churned up a lot of water, her smokestack billowed, and the speedy river boat could cause a very large wake. Launched in June 1927, it made alternate nightly runs between Sacramento and San Francisco. It was almost 300 feet long and had four decks. It was a gorgeous ship with polished brass, stained-glass windows, mahogany handrails, and a grand staircase. On board was a barber shop, dining room, a social hall, leather chairs, observation decks, state rooms, and a dance floor. Fare was $3 for a round trip, a room was $4, and a five-course dinner was 75¢.

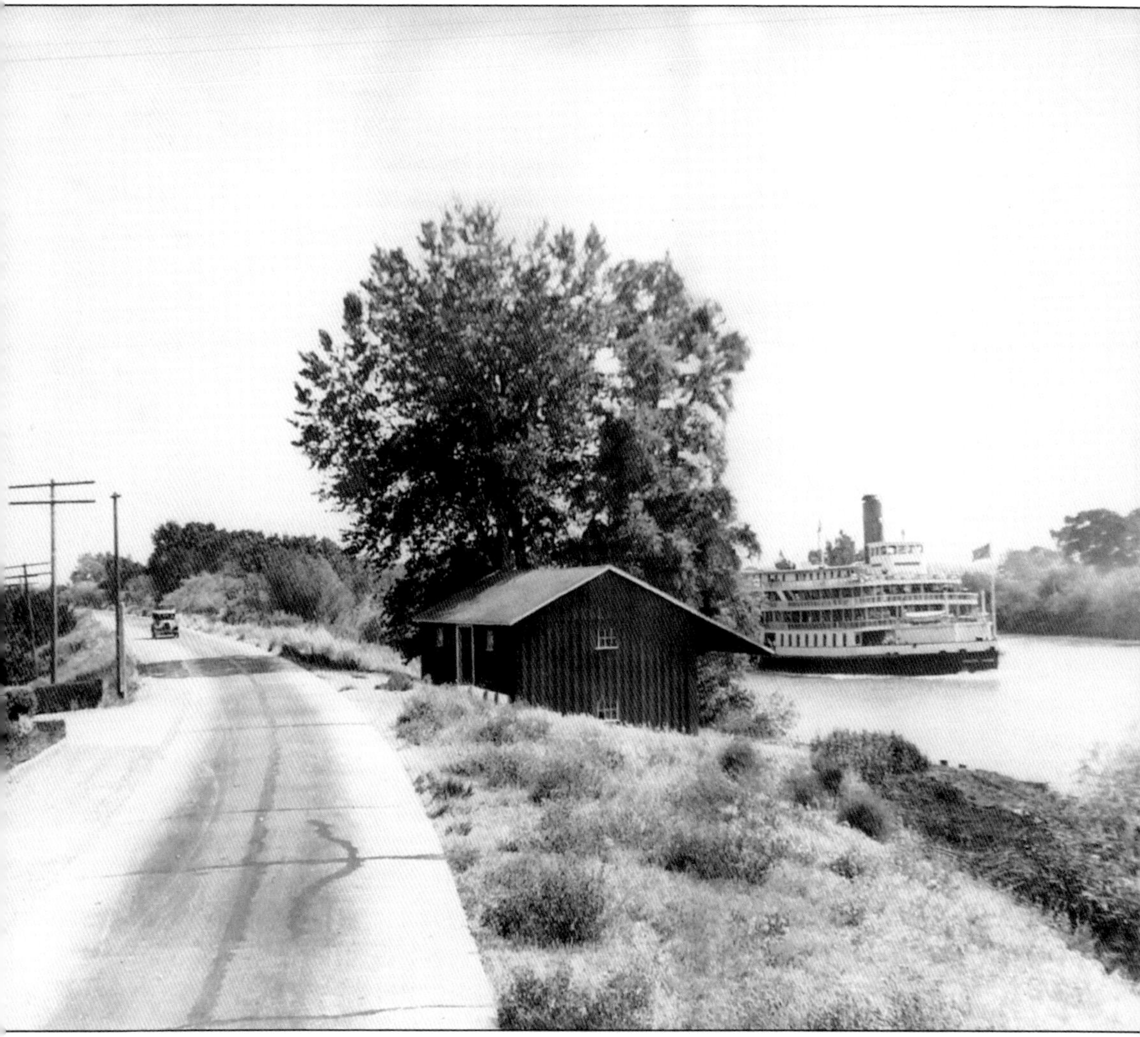

DELTA QUEEN. The *Delta Queen* makes its way along the Sacramento River near Courtland. The road and levees put this photo in the 1920s. This paddle-wheeler is still in operation on the Ohio and Mississippi Rivers. More than passengers made the trips up and down the river. Up-river freight included equipment, machinery, hardware, parts, and cars. Down-river freight included rice, canned goods, and other farm products of the Central Valley. The paddlewheel was over 25 feet in diameter and 20 feet wide. It was pushed by a 1,500-horsepower steam engine that had a maximum of 15 miles per hour.

The Cherokee. This elegant vessel, which appeared in the movie *Steamboat Round the Bend*, served the Southern Pacific Company for years until it was sold to the California Transport Co. It operated on both the Sacramento and San Joaquin Rivers until river trade "dried up" with dock strikes, rate wars, and the 1929 stock market crash.

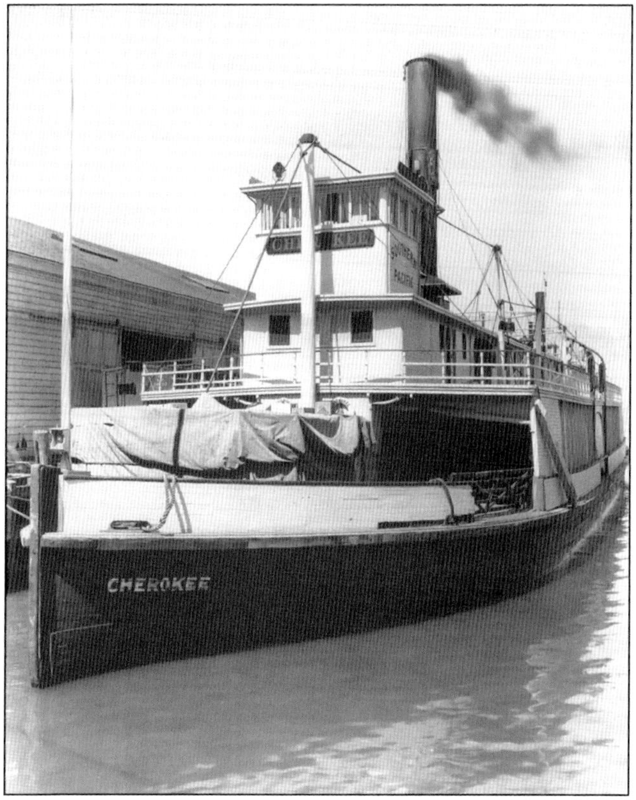

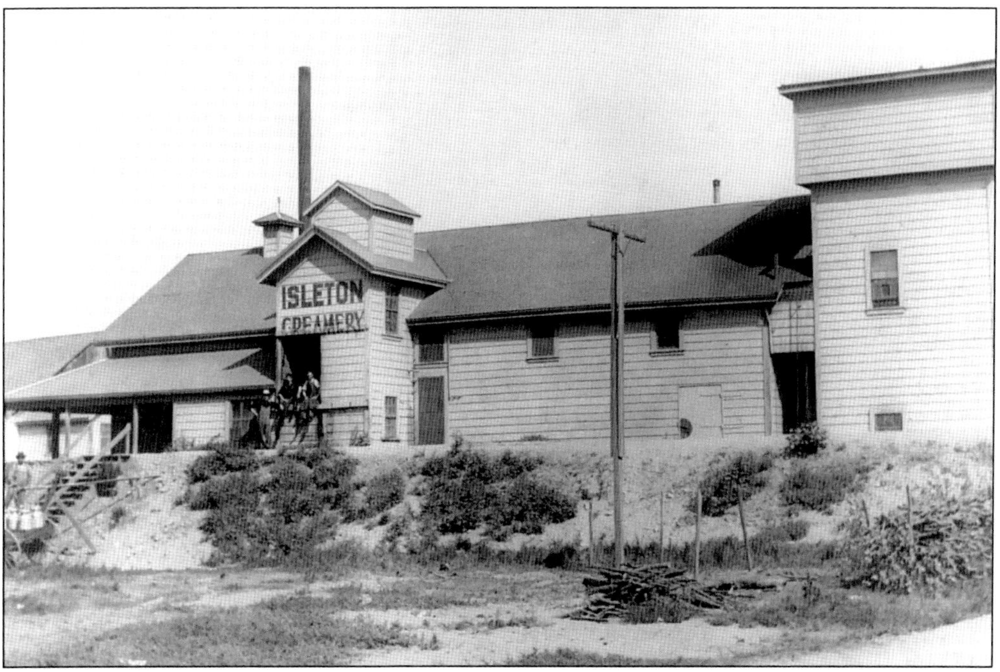

Isleton Creamery. The Isleton Creamery was located near the river and suffered the torment of many floods.

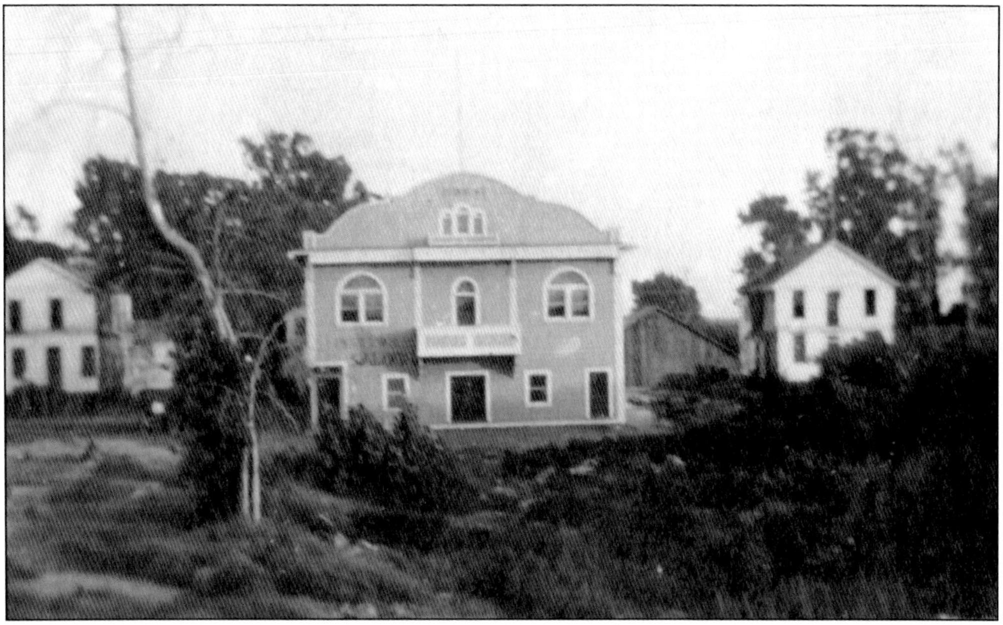

Sonny's Bakery. This familiar building looks misplaced by itself. Today it is the home of Sonny's Bakery and apartments. The building today is across from Dejacks Market on Second.

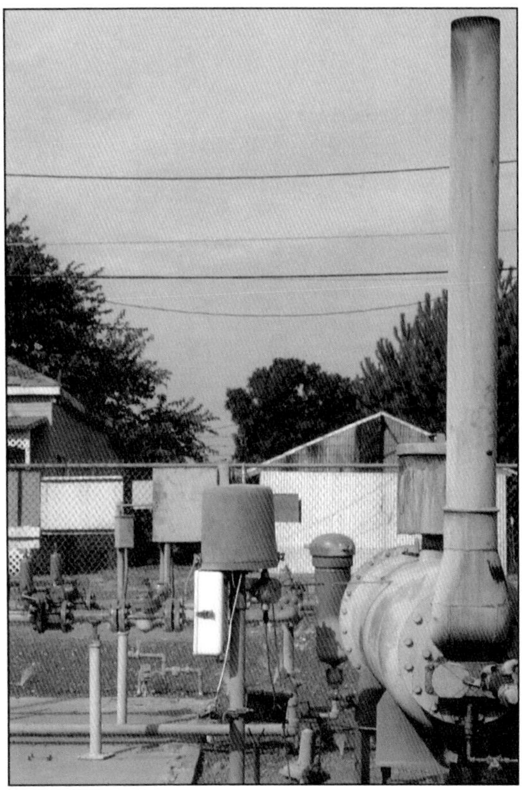

Isleton Gas Well. One of the natural resources of the Delta are the large deposits of natural gas. Isleton has its own near the corporation yard on Sixth Street. Royalties and exploration has benefited the entire region. New wells are being drilled daily, especially in the Montezuma Hills near Rio Vista.

World War I Parade. The liberty bond drive parade makes its way down Second Street. World War I was supported by boy scouts, girl scouts, veterans, and city officials. There must have been some excellent "victory gardens," and plenty of enlistments. Note the classic poster, "Keep these off the U.S."

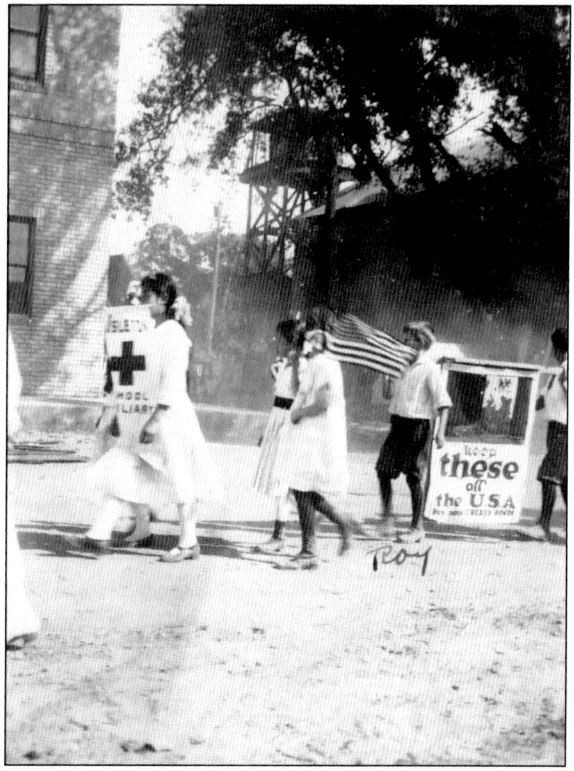

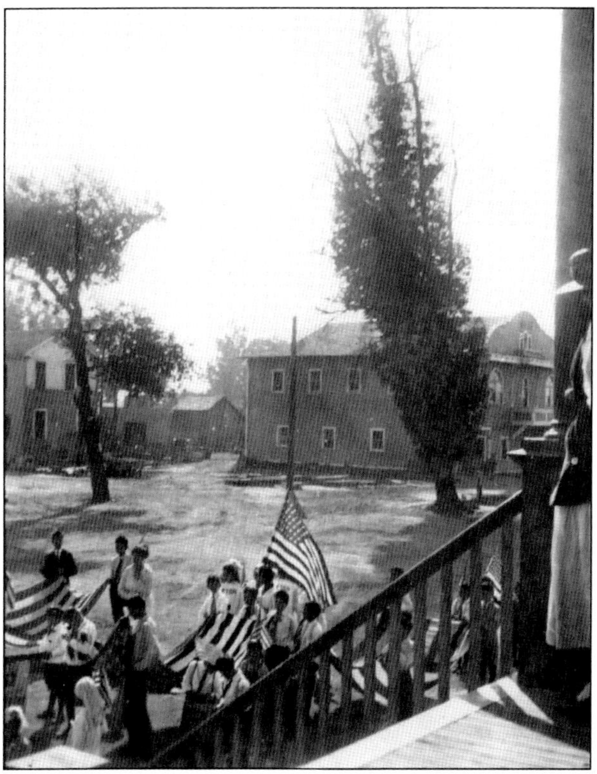

World War I Liberty Bonds. Isleton residents get ready for the parade for Liberty Bonds. This view is from the porch of Gardiner Improvement Building on Second Street. The move to stop "the Huns" was shared throughout the United States, along with "Liberty Cabbage" and "Daylight Savings Time." Everybody did their "bit."

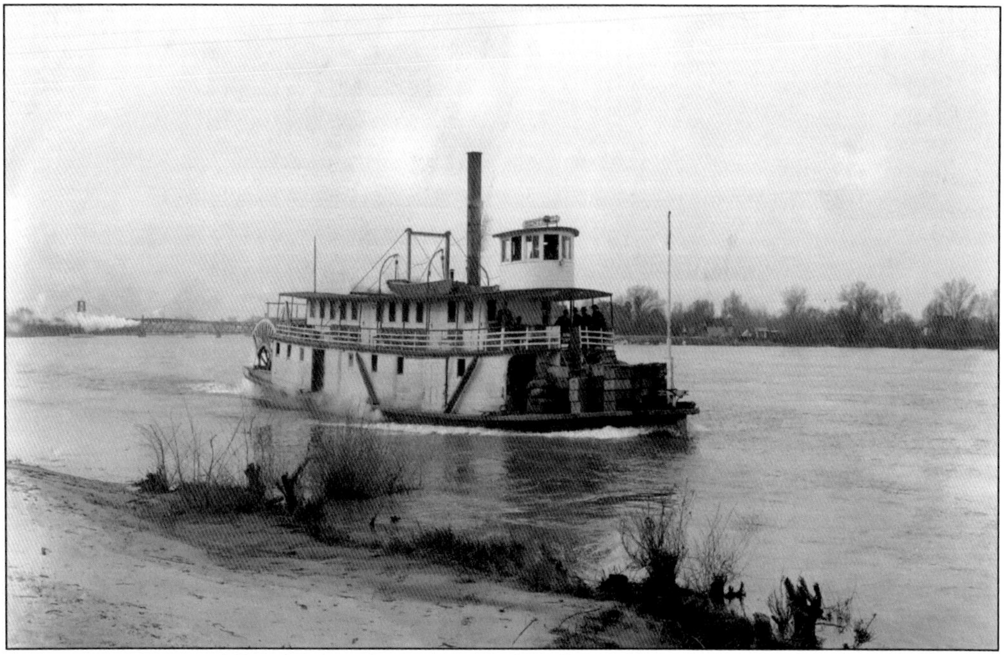

CONTINENTAL. A paddle-wheeler, the *Continental*, makes its way up river. This was the best way to get from Isleton to Sacramento, Walnut Grove, or Freeport. Both passengers and cargo keep this steamboat close to the water.

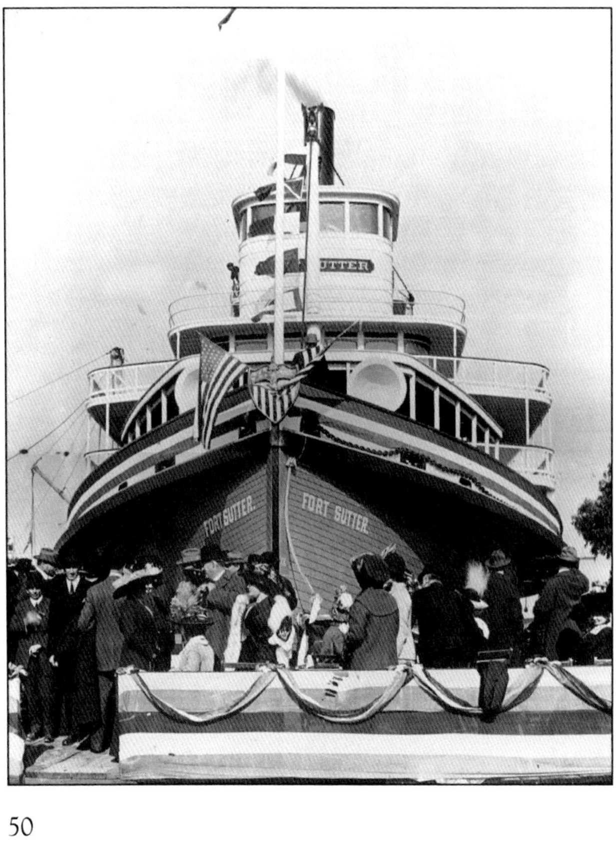

THE *FORT SUTTER*. This boat, owned by the California Transport Co., began service in 1912 with classic steamship design and hot and cold running water in every stateroom. It was a popular overnight trip from San Francisco to Sacramento with two "very good" meals. During World War II the boat was commissioned by the U.S. military to transport personnel on San Francisco Bay. It was destroyed by a mysterious fire in Stockton in 1952.

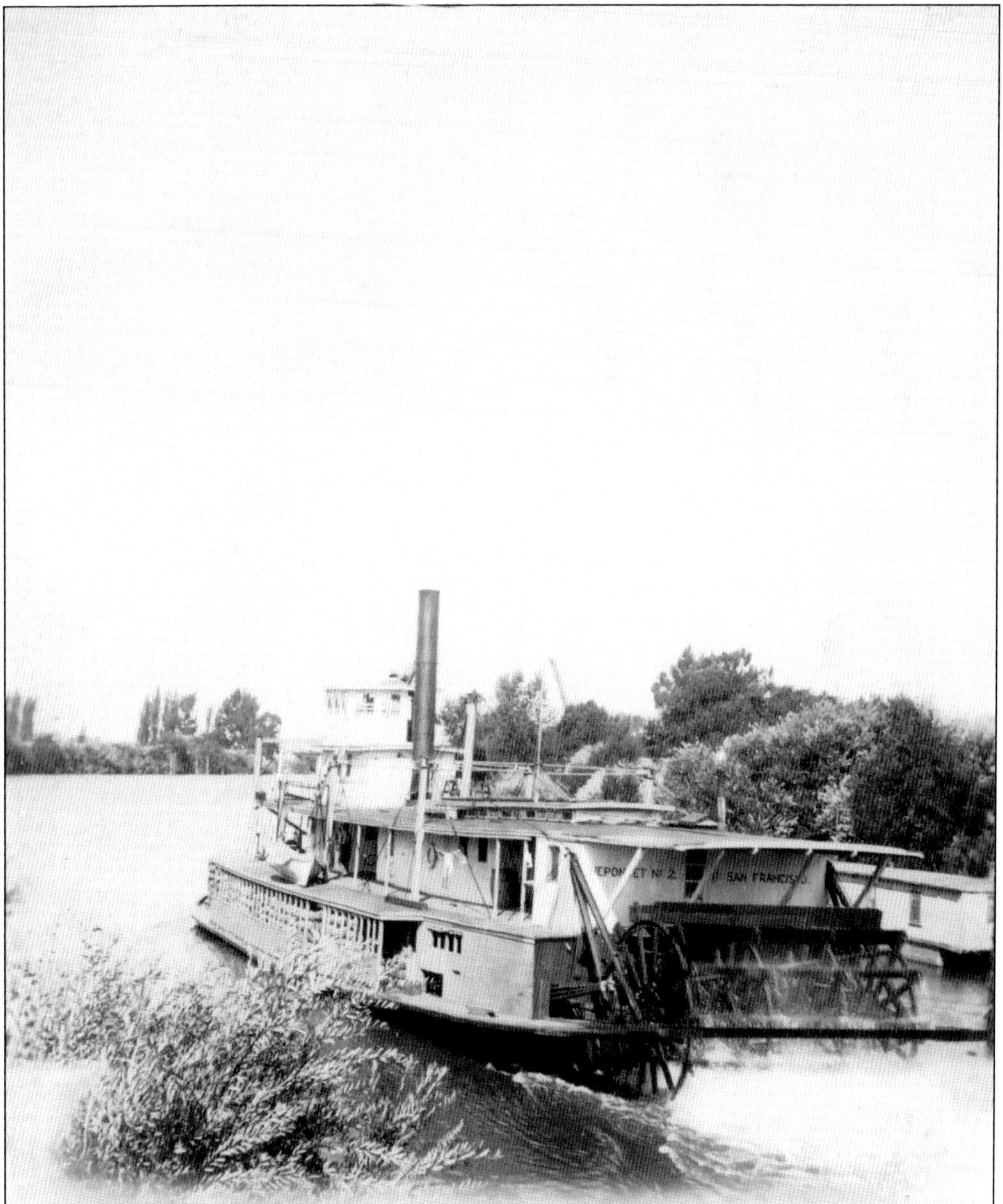

PADDLE-WHEELER TAKING OFF. The Isleton wharf was one of the frequent stops on the river route. Here a paddle-wheeler from San Francisco pushes out of its moorings. The force of the wheel and the sound of the paddle certainly caught this cameraman's attention. This may have been the *Isleton*, a favorite of the growing city.

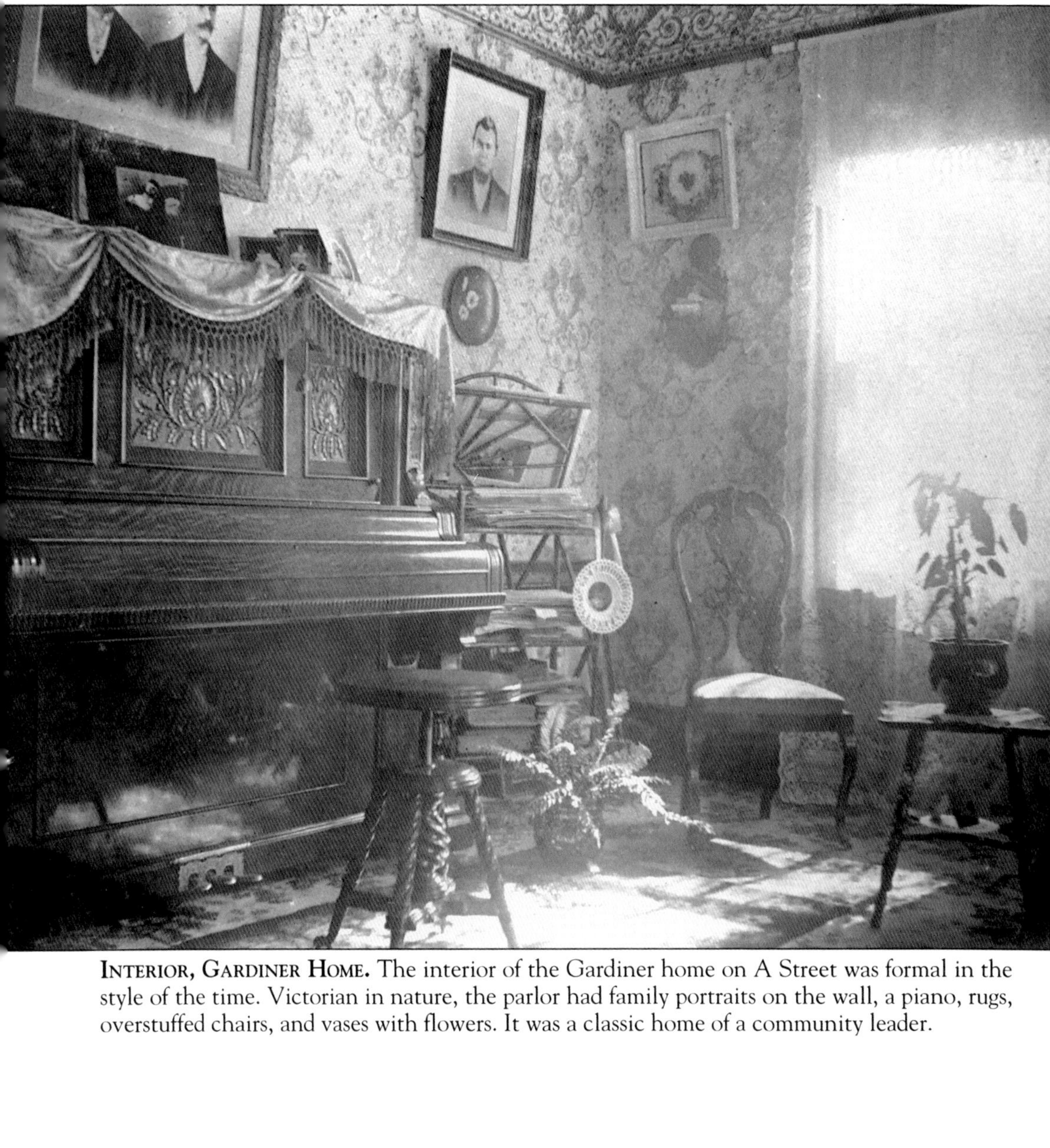

Interior, Gardiner Home. The interior of the Gardiner home on A Street was formal in the style of the time. Victorian in nature, the parlor had family portraits on the wall, a piano, rugs, overstuffed chairs, and vases with flowers. It was a classic home of a community leader.

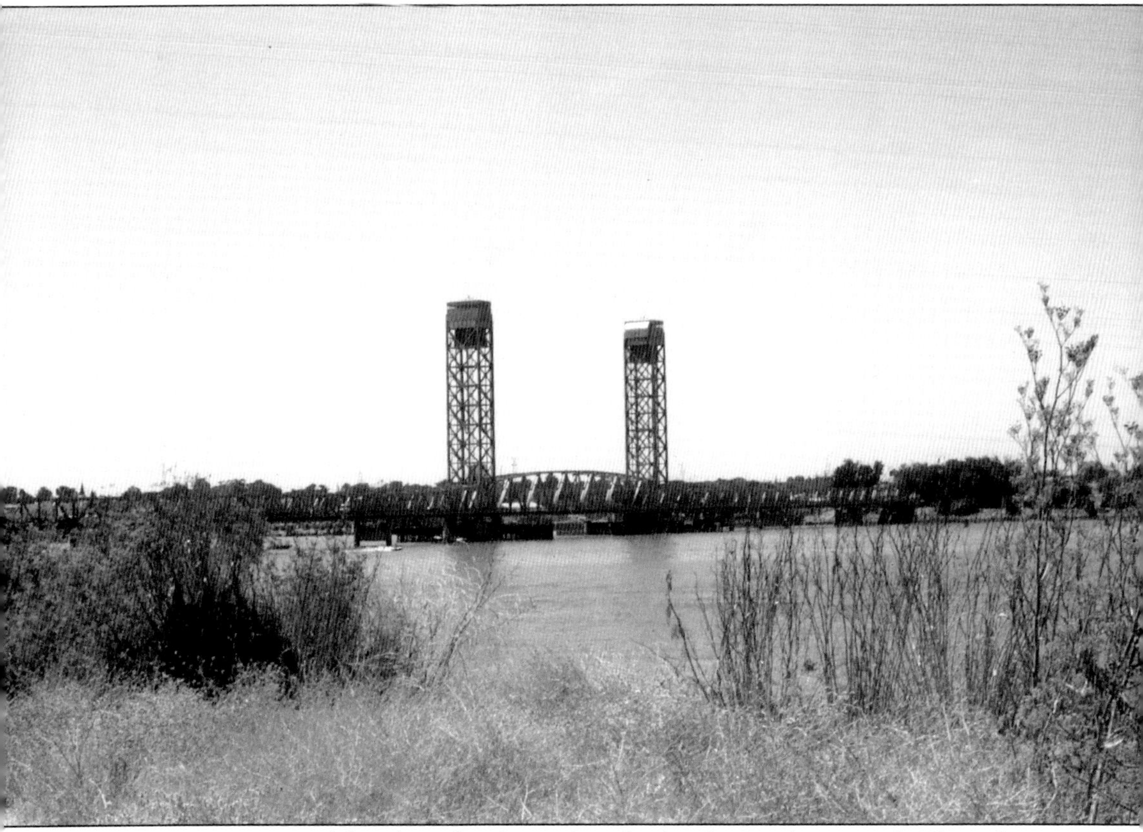

DRAWBRIDGES. A river craft has the right of way when the drawbridge alarm sounds. Throughout the Delta, over sloughs and rivers, the drawbridge is a traffic stopper. There are three types: a cantilever bridge, a swing bridge, and a tower bridge. The cantilever bridge has two large weighted ends that, when activated, pull the shore end of the structure down and the middle parts to let ships through. The tower bridge has two towers that are elevators operated by large chains that pull the center section of the bridge up. The Rio Vista Bridge, pictured here, is a tower bridge. The towers are very high because large ocean ships pass through here in the deep river channel to Sacramento. The swing bridge is on a large center piling that has a track that swings the bridge outward to become perpendicular to the existing road.

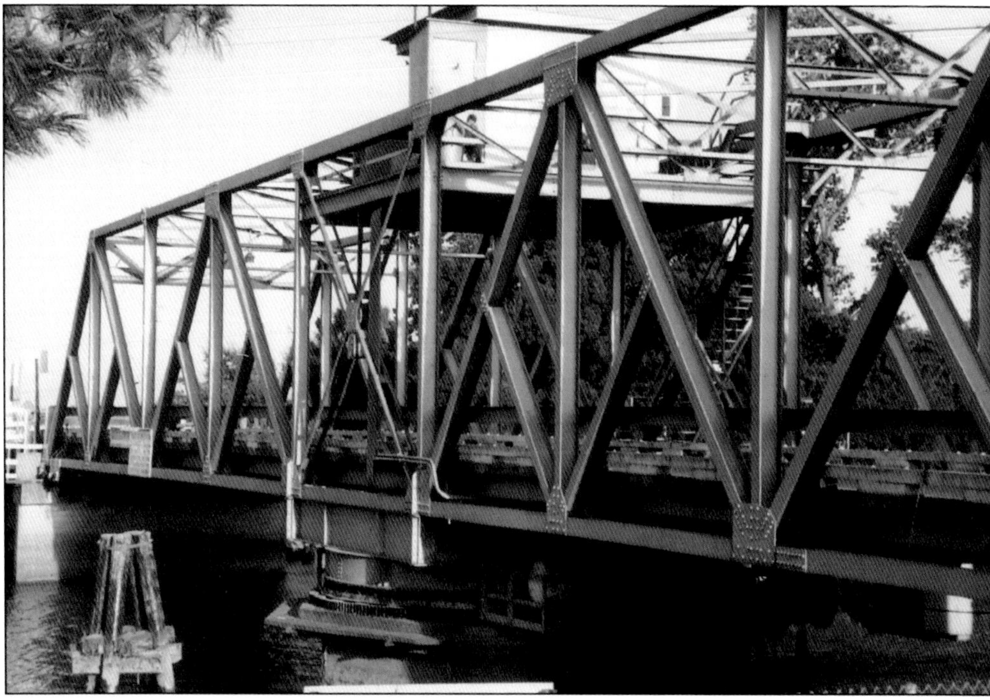

Tyler Island Bridge. The Tyler Island Bridge, just outside Isleton, is a swing bridge. It is operated from 6 a.m. to 10 p.m. daily, 7 days a week.

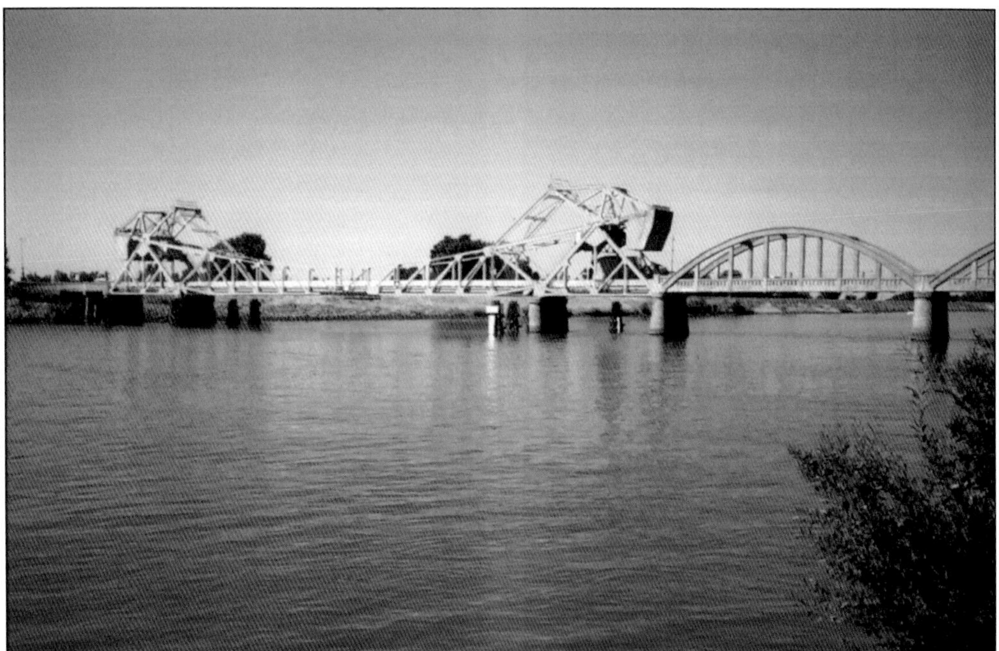

Isleton Bridge. The Isleton Bridge is a cantilever bridge, and it makes a spectacular sight when the bridge rises.

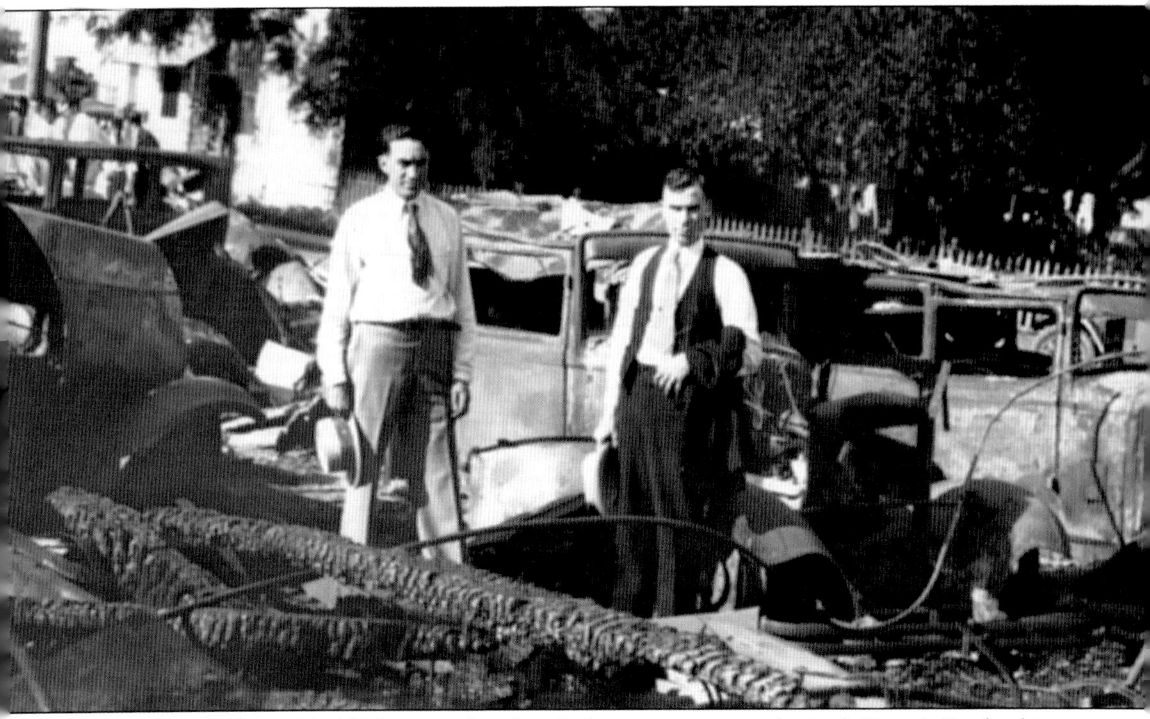

DUNN FIRE. On June 30, 1930, just a few days before an asparagus festival, Dunn's Dealership was gutted by a very hot fire. The owner and city official inspect the damage, including new cars and structure. It was cleaned up before the festival began.

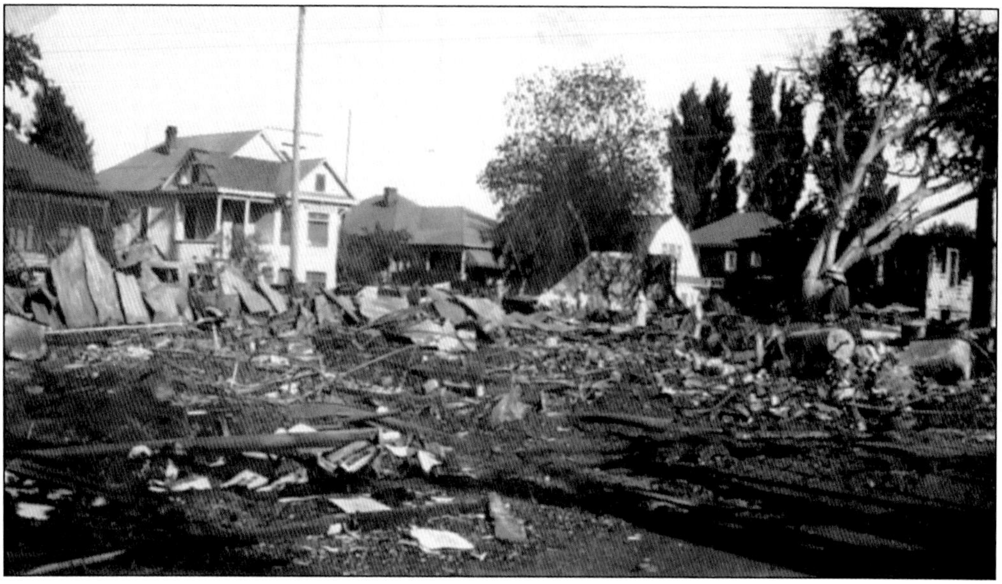

Dunn Fire and Damage. The fire also completely destroyed the Central Hotel next door and did over $100,000 damage. That was a large sum in the Depression era.

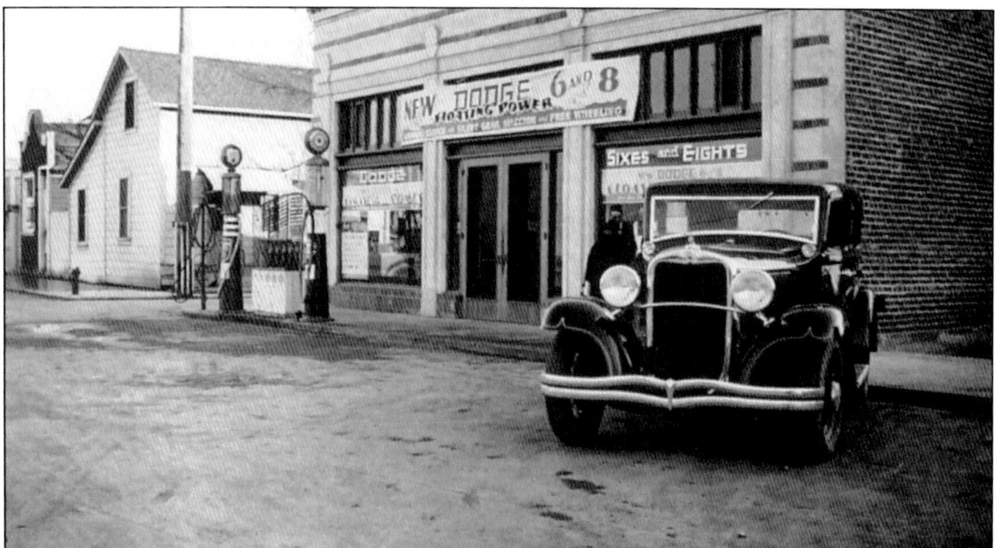

Rebuilt Dunn. The Dodge Dealership is shown here rebuilt and ready for business. The new 1932 Dodge had an automatic clutch, silent gear selection, and was free wheeling. It came with either a six- or eight-cylinder engine.

Four

Hard Work and the Tong

The center of immigration for the Chinese was San Francisco, but they soon established themselves throughout the West. The Six Companies kept exclusive control until 1882 when they were replaced by several different Tongs. Notorious for extortion and the control of opium, gambling, and prostitution, the Tongs became major blood-curdling stories in the "yellow journalism" of the West. The Hearst papers were no exception and the "Tong Wars" became a major fixture in California history. The Tong gangs were severely damaged by the 1906 earthquake and their role in history slowly changed. In Isleton the Bing Kong Tong became a benevolent society to help the community.

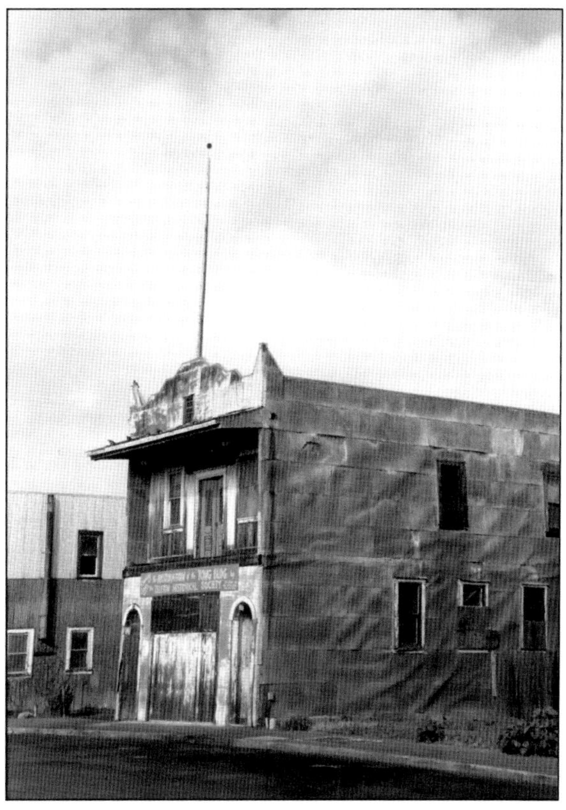

Tong Building. The Bing Kong Tong Building is a registered National Historic Building. It was built in 1926 by Chinese workers and designed by leaders in the community. It is almost 70 feet long, 25 feet wide, and 35 feet tall. Because it is higher than it is wide, and because of its long exposure to the northwest wind and rain, it has suffered some structural damage. The Tong Building has been stabilized by its owners, the Isleton Historical Society, and they are currently seeking to match a grant for its restoration. The metal embossed siding is original and was an attempt to make the structure fireproof.

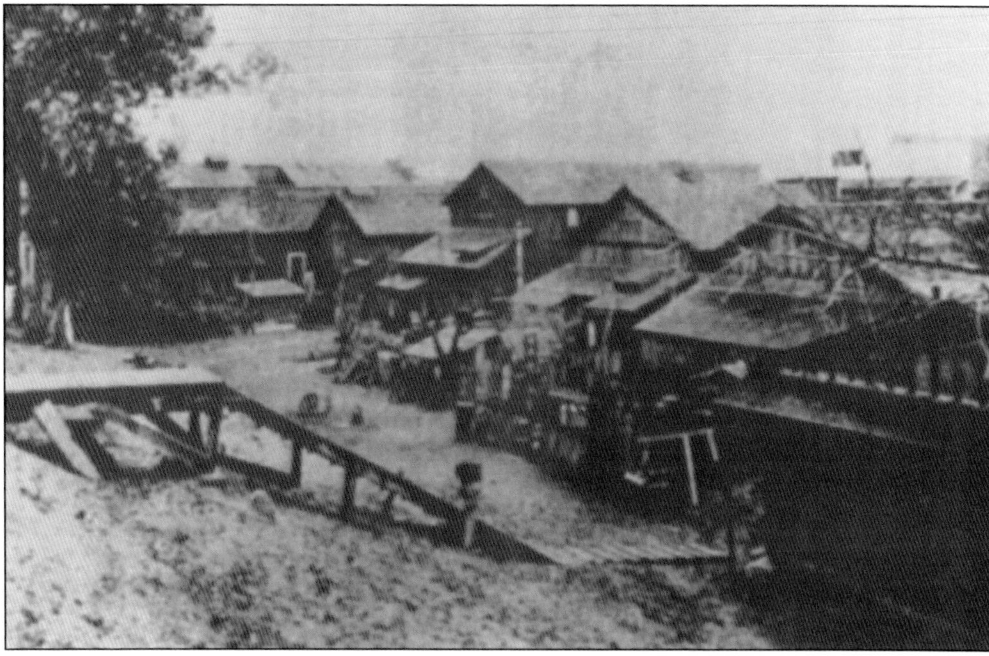

CHINATOWN, PRE-1915. The first Chinese community was located on Jackson Slough, near the locations of the city hall and Wilson Park. It was destroyed in 1915 by fire. John Gardiner offered the Chinese the property up-river on what is now Main Street to rebuild. By that time the U.S. Supreme Court had ruled that the children of the immigrant Chinese were natural born citizens. Since their parents could not legally own land, the new property was registered to the children.

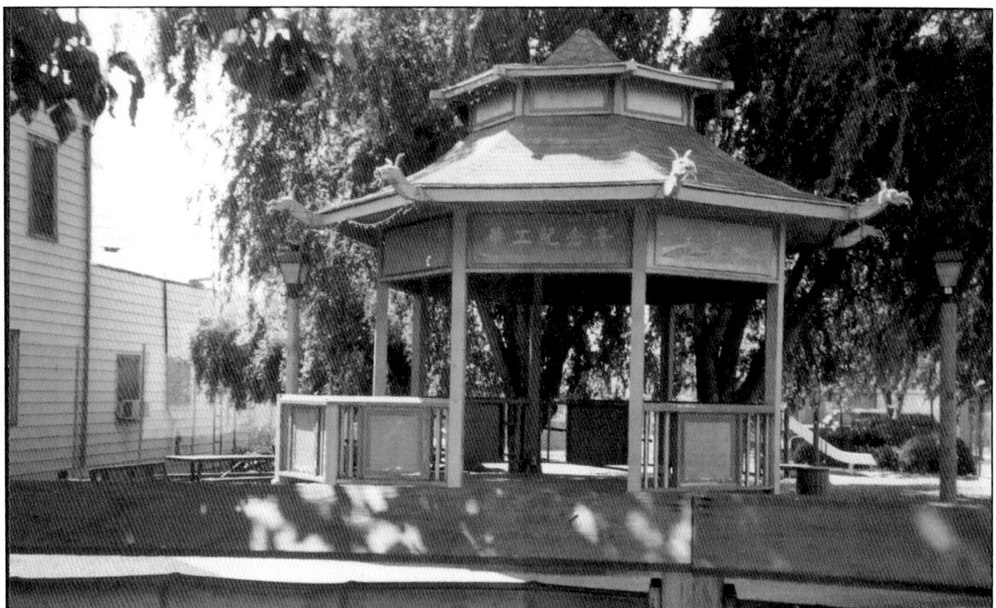

CHINATOWN PARK. This view shows the city park on the second block of historic Main Street. Built by the City of Isleton and volunteers from throughout the community, it is a park that remembers the Chinese community and their contributions.

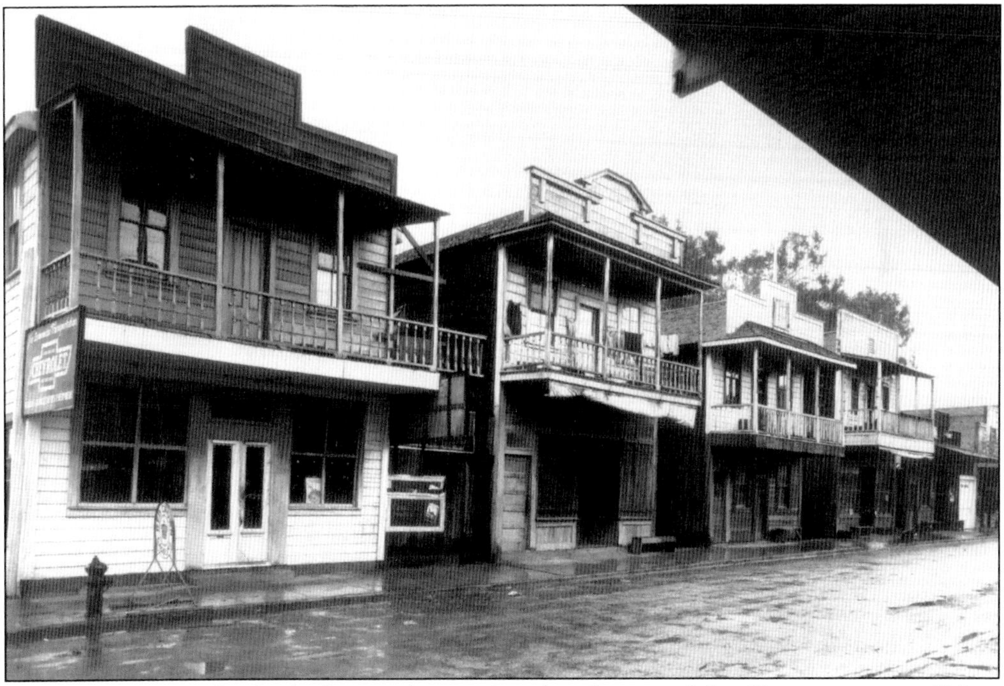

Four Balconies. The fire hydrant indicates that this photo is of the Chinese section of Main Street prior to the 1926 fire. The hydrant is still standing at the corner of Main and E Street. Note how close the buildings are together, and that they are built right up to the sidewalk with overhanging balconies. The Tong Building appears to be just beyond the white façade.

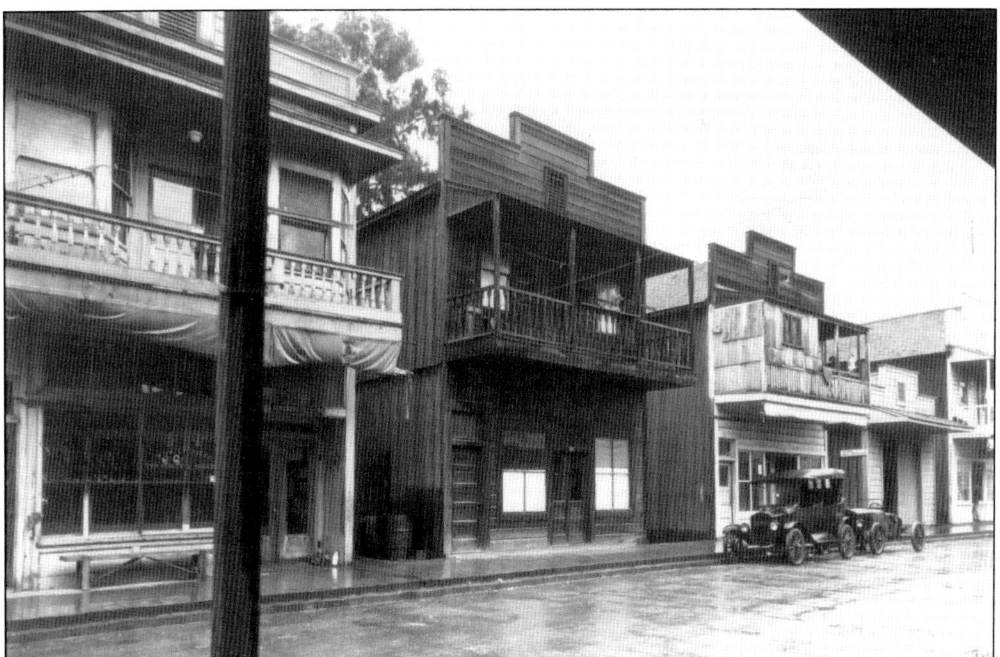

Chinatown, Pre-1926. Architecture in the Chinese section had both design and character. The parapets, balconies, and front façades were maintained after the fire of 1926.

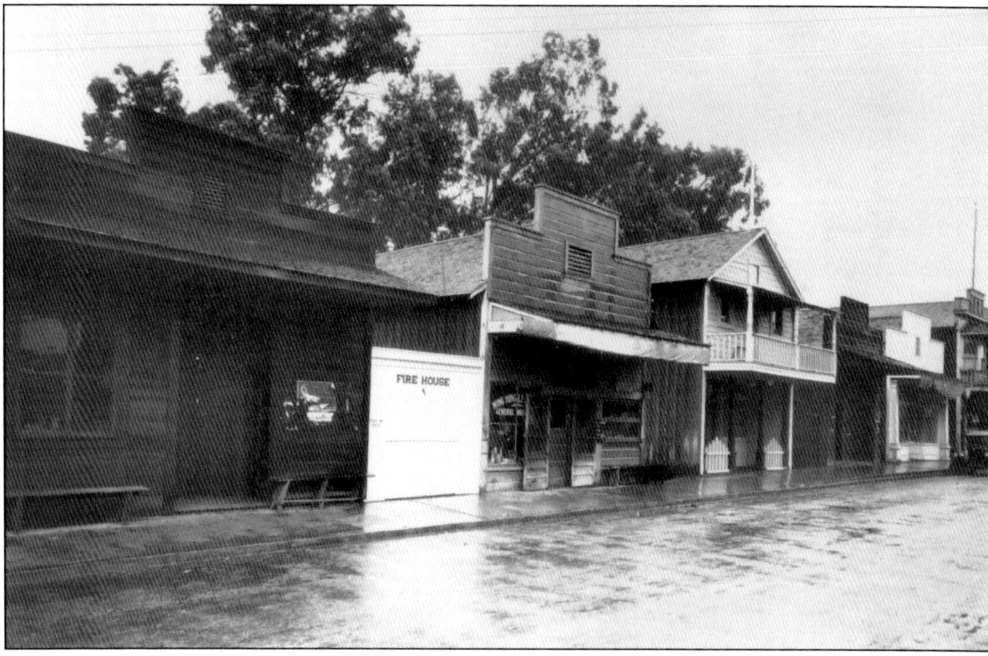

Fire House. Next to the fire station is a hardware store. Rebuilt and still standing, it has only two stories today. The last building in this picture (with the flag pole) is the Bing Kong Building with its more elaborate façade.

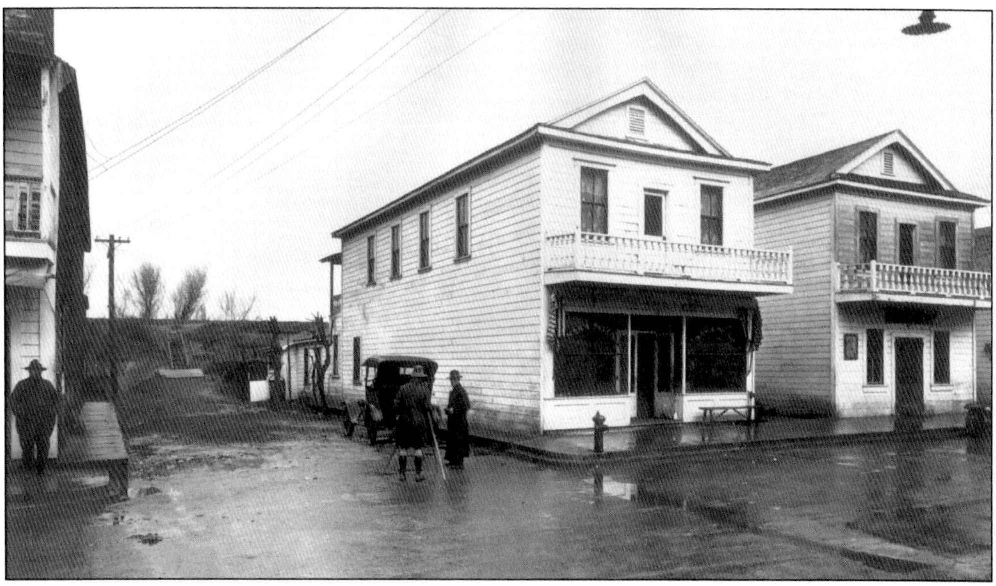

Japanese Main Street, Pre–1926. This is the corner of F and Main Streets in the Historic District. F Street was the dividing line between the Japanese and Chinese sections. This division was not a discrimination issue but only one of language and culture. The buildings on the right side were built and maintained by the Japanese culture. The buildings on the right side were built and maintained by the Japanese residents of Isleton; they were all destroyed in the 1926 fire. The post-1926 building on the left side that replaced the burned Chinese building has been carefully restored.

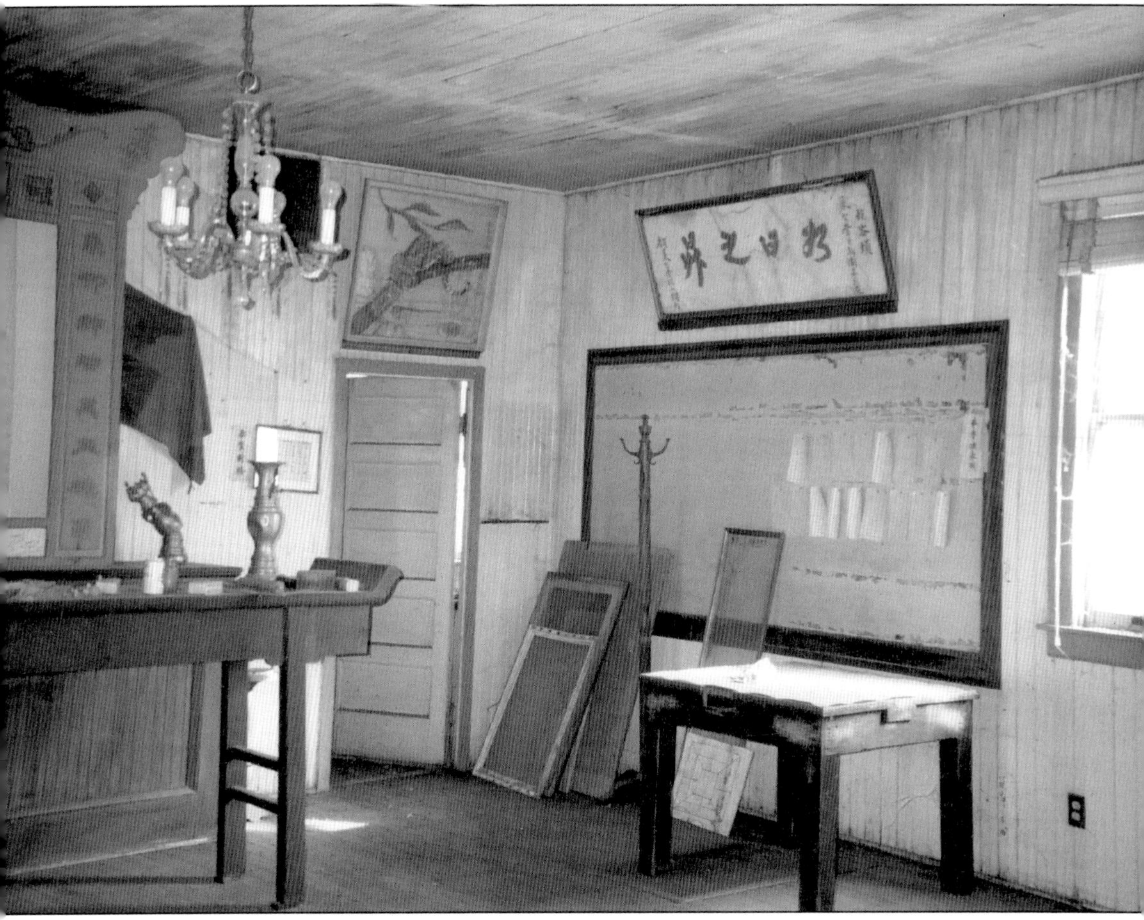

TONG INTERIOR. The interior of the Tong Building is functional and straightforward. Used as a meeting hall, game room, and school, it has two large rooms, one upstairs and one down. Stairs from both the front and back lead to the upstairs game room. Here a large bulletin board, mirror, altar, and flags of both Nationalist China and the United States were on the walls. Game tables and chairs were placed throughout the large room. The upstairs also had a small kitchen and bathroom facilities with an office and some storage space.

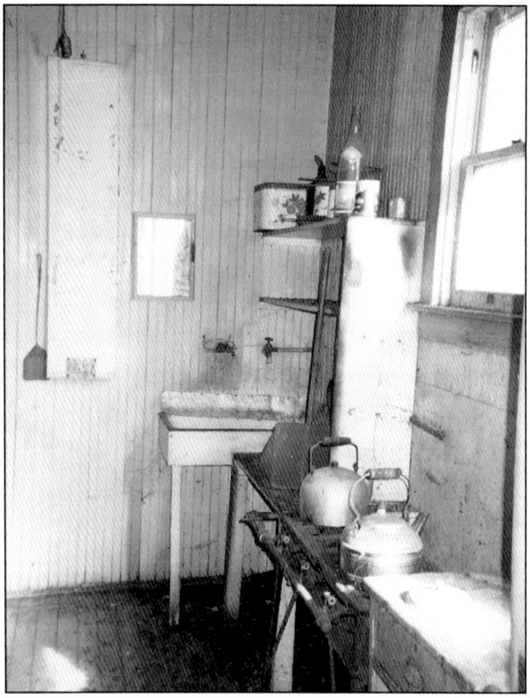

TONG COOKING. Like all fraternal associations, the Tong provided food for dinners and special occasions. This may not look like much of a kitchen, but it was used extensively for all types of preparation. Sometimes food was brought in and kept warm here, but there is plenty of room for a wok, vegetables, and rice.

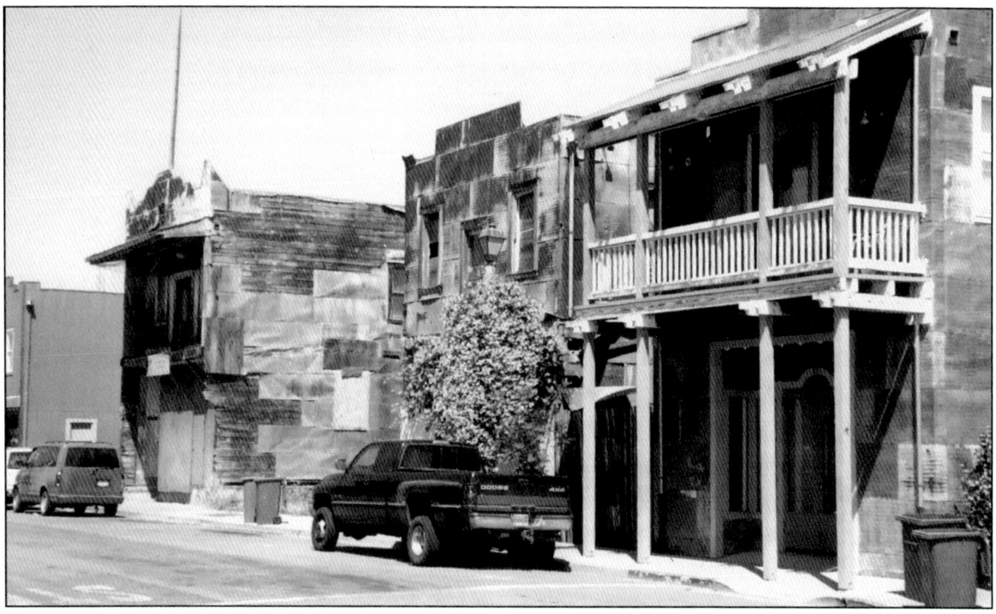

MAIN STREET CHARACTER. Many of the buildings have two stories, with a large balcony. Most were used both as residences and businesses. Today many of the businesses have left, and some have been turned into apartments. The Main Street buildings are unique in many ways. The parapets vary from store to store, most have attic vents in the front, a few are of brick construction, some have flagpoles on the roof, and the window and door treatments all have recessed openings with large front windows. Many have small windows over the large display area. Interiors are fairly sparse retail areas with living areas behind and above. Some of the buildings were never intended to be residences, but served as bordellos, gambling halls, or rooming houses.

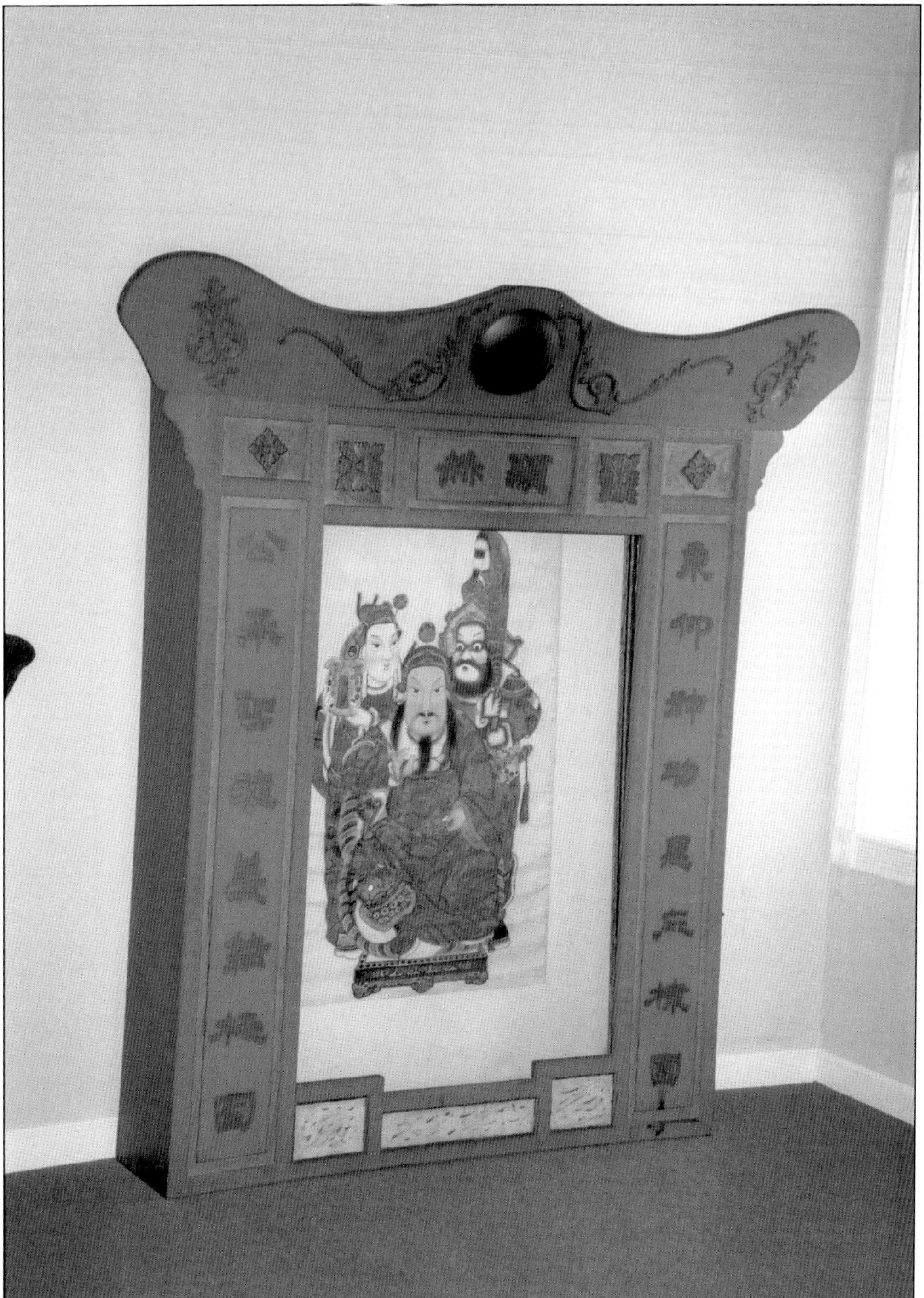

TONG ALTAR. This altar was on the second floor of the Tong Building. The deity in the center is Kuan Kung, patron of business, associations, and secret societies. Generally his face appears to be red colored and his clothing green. He is accompanied by Shou-ts'ang, his bodyguard, and Kuan P'ing, his son who holds the seal to heaven's authority.

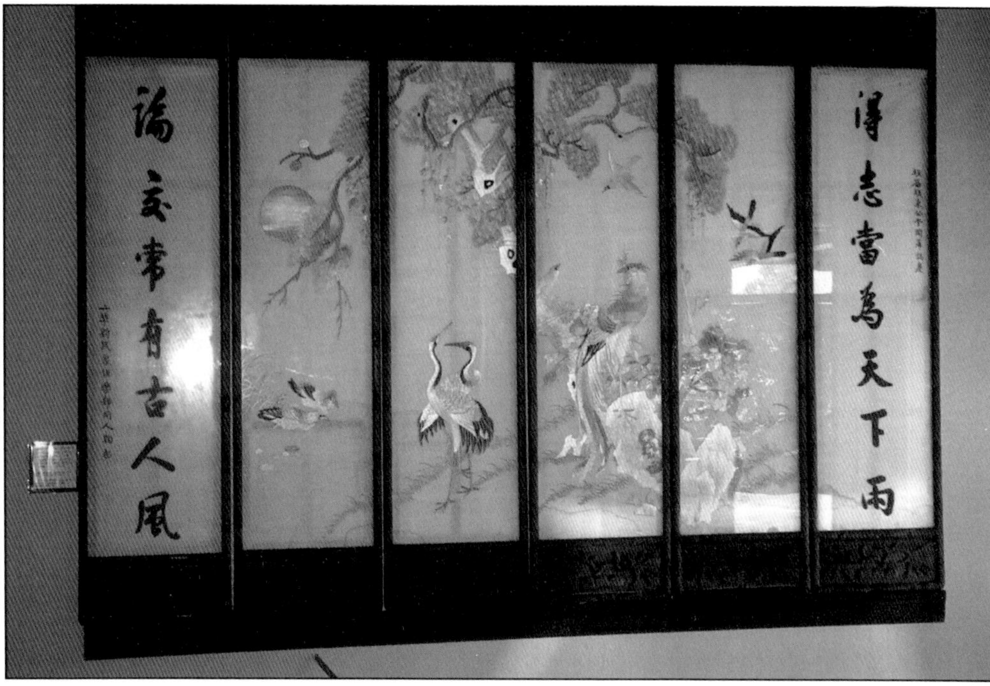

SIX PANEL EMBROIDERY. This beautiful six panel embroidery was a gift to the Tong at their grand opening in 1944. Despite a little water damage, it is in excellent shape. The inscription on the sides explains the nature and purpose of the gift.

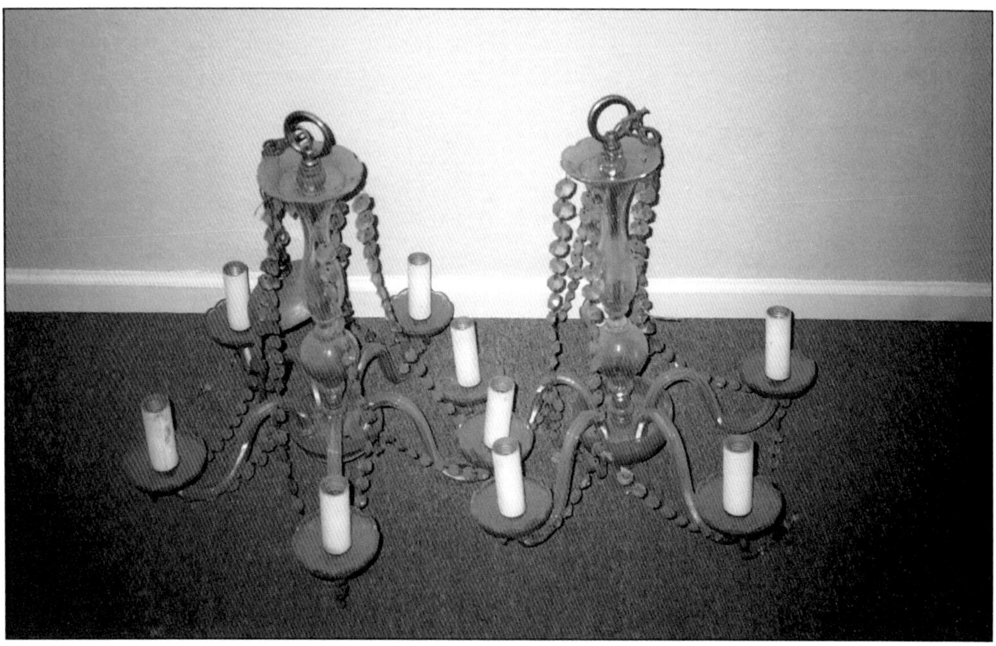

TONG CHANDELIERS. These beautiful crystal chandeliers were on both the first and second floors of the Tong Building. Some have been kept in the museum, while a few broken ones are still in the building. The other ceiling lights were white globes.

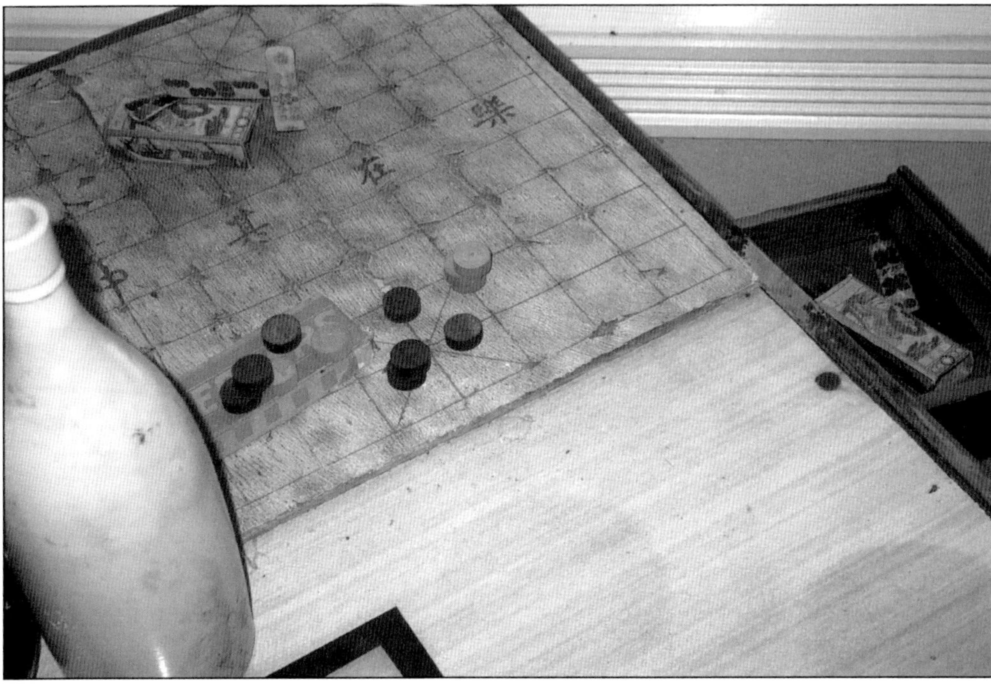

Checkerboard. Checkers was one of the more popular games played on the second floor.

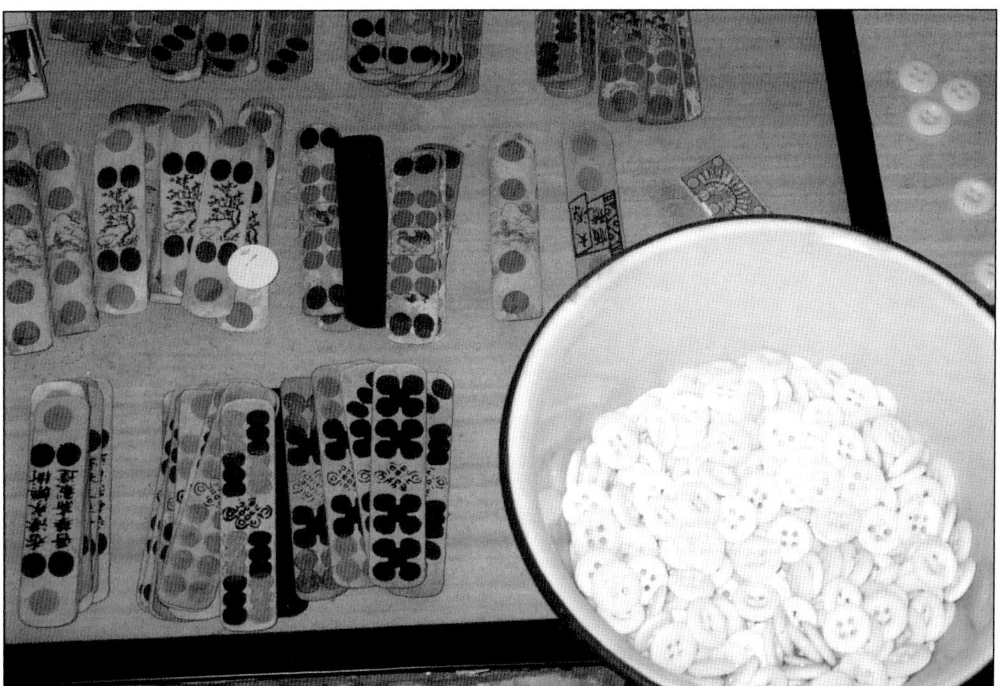

Mah-Jongg. Shown here is a Mah-Jongg board from the Tong. This game was played by four people with 136 or 144 tile pieces similar to dominoes. The tiles are marked in suits. The object is to build sets or combinations by drawing, discarding, or exchanging tiles.

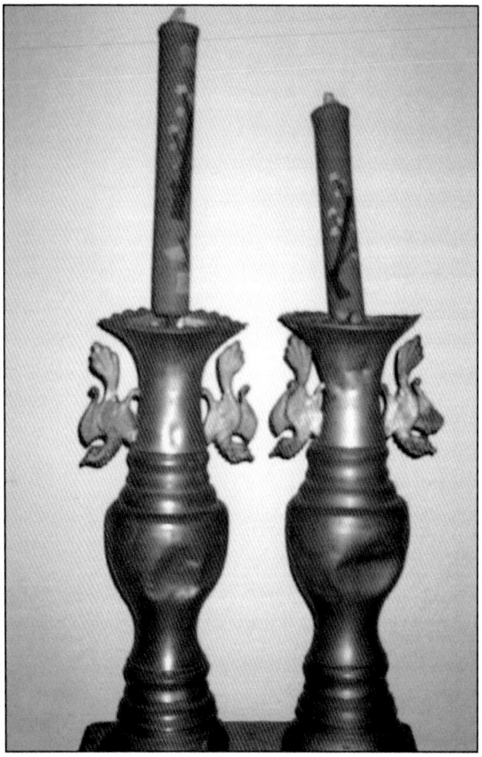

Metal Vase with Firecrackers. Chinese mythology is a mixture of elements from three religions, not all intact in the transfer. The peach is a symbol of longevity, the peacock a symbol of the queen mother, and the hare a symbol of inverts. Firecrackers drive off evil spirits and ritual vessels were for libations to the gods.

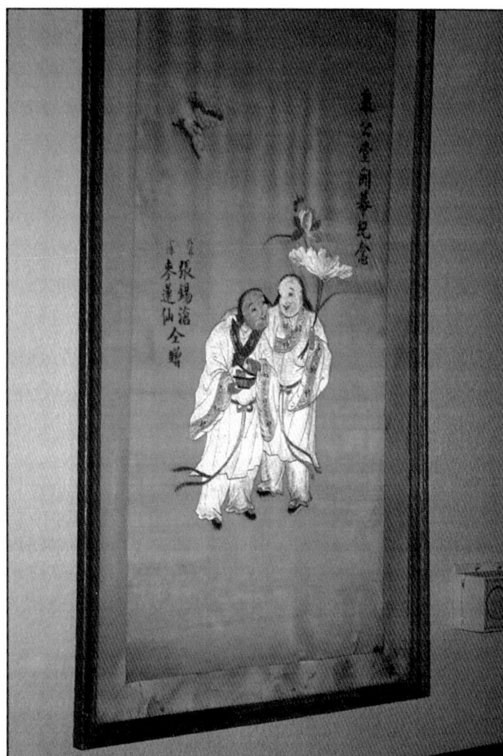

Two Gods Embroidery. This embroidery was one of the many panels on the wall in the Tong Building. It was a gift when this Tong was founded. It is the God of Wealth, Ts'ai-shen, who also brings good fortune. He is offered gifts by those who claim to be nonbelievers. He is the most popular of all Chinese gods.

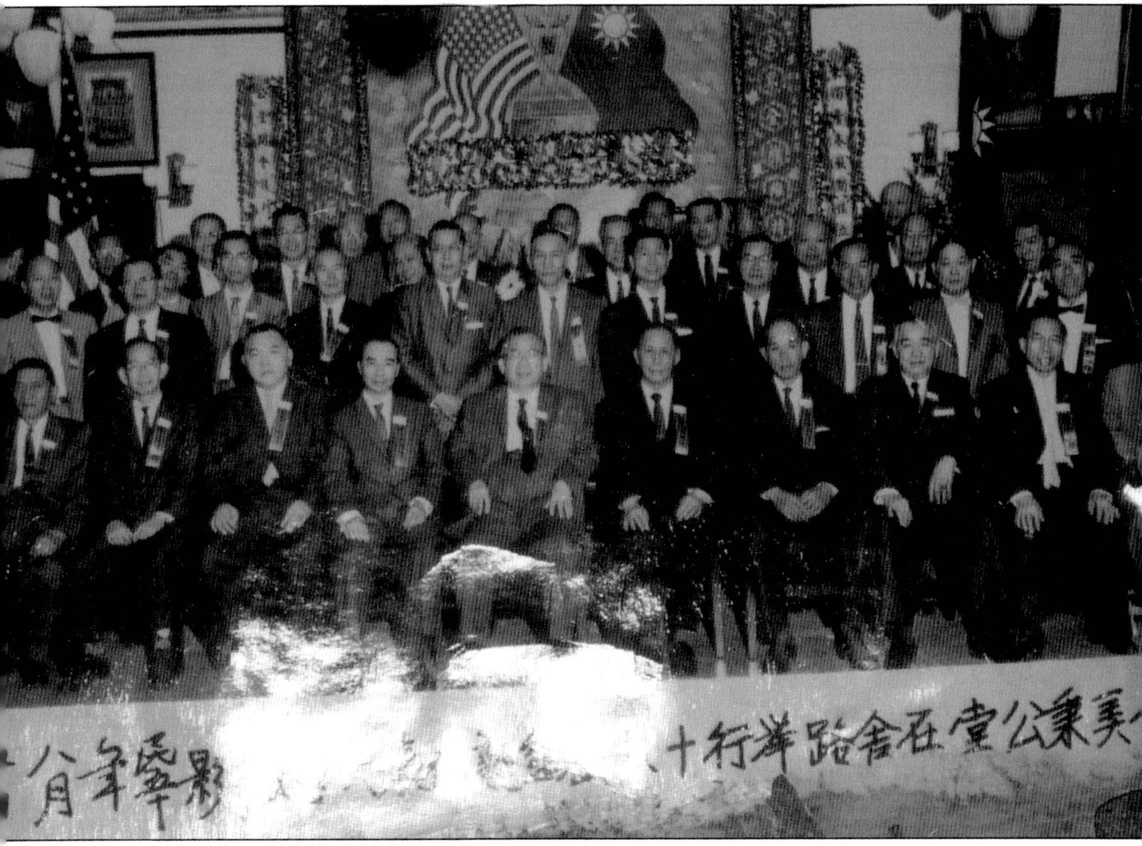

TONG 1950. This meeting of the Tong Association in the 1950s did not take place in Isleton. It is apparent that the association still had a large membership dedicated to the preservation of culture.

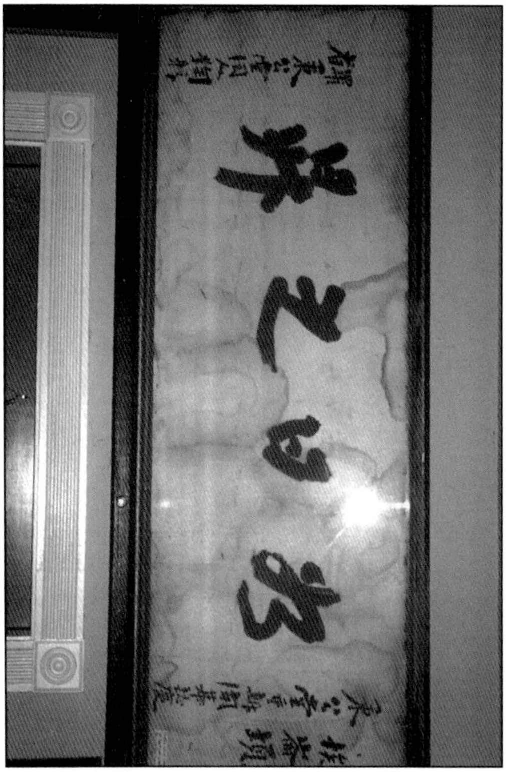

SIGN IN THE TONG, LOS ANGELES. This sign, currently over the front door of the Isleton Museum, was a gift from the Los Angeles Bing Kong Tong at the grand opening of the Isleton Tong. It reads, "The sun rises in the morning," meaning, we should be ready to greet each day.

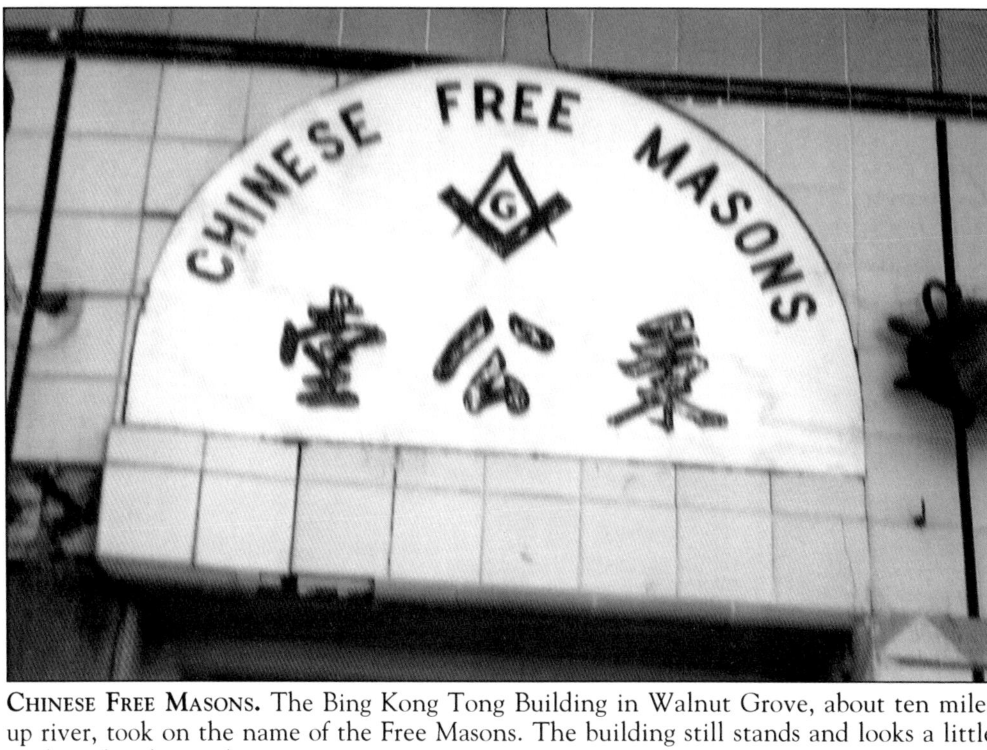

CHINESE FREE MASONS. The Bing Kong Tong Building in Walnut Grove, about ten miles up river, took on the name of the Free Masons. The building still stands and looks a little neglected without a buyer.

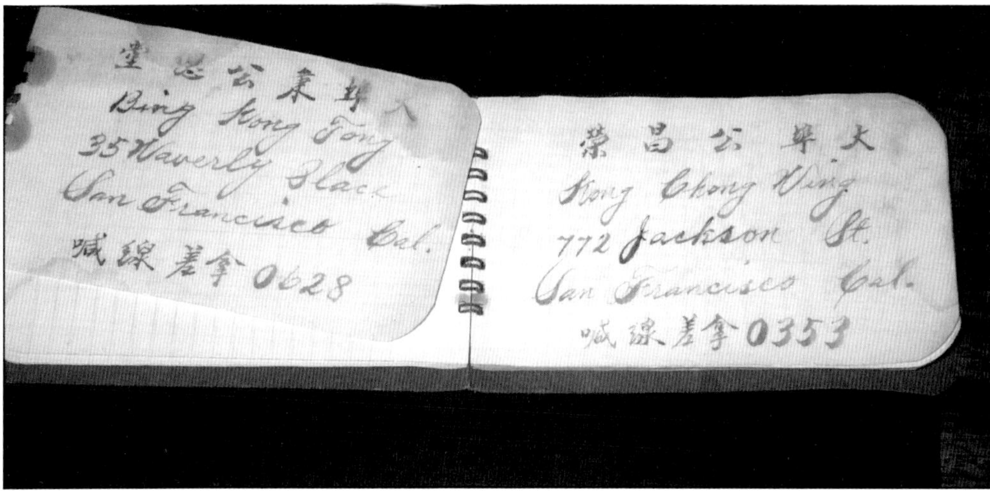

ADDRESS BOOK. This address book of other Tongs was kept in the office. There are 27 different Tong groups listed here.

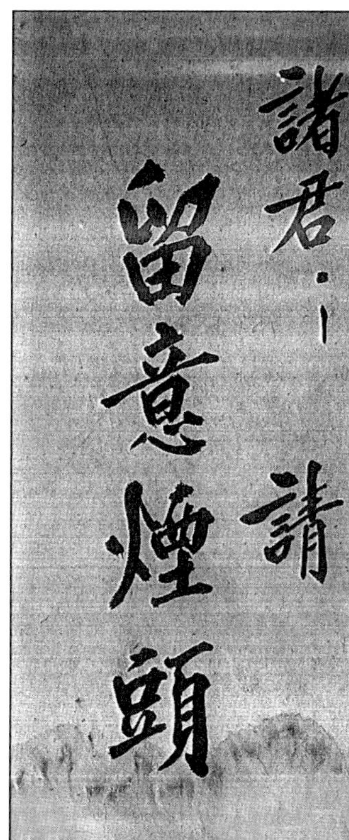

CIGARETTE BUTTS. This small sign was placed in appropriate places. It is translated to read, "Gentlemen, please take proper care of your cigarette butts."

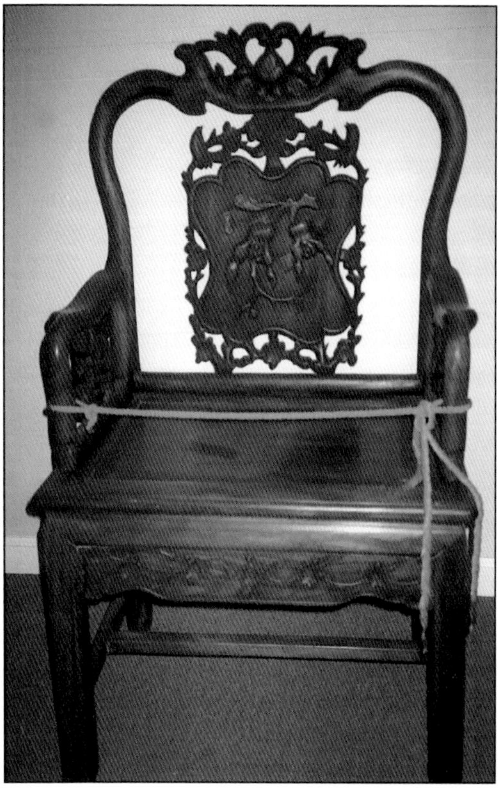

Tong Chair. The elaborate, carved chair is just one of many that were located in the Tong Building. Saved for special guests and dignitaries, it is a statement of the respect for elders. This particular chair is currently in the Isleton Historical Museum.

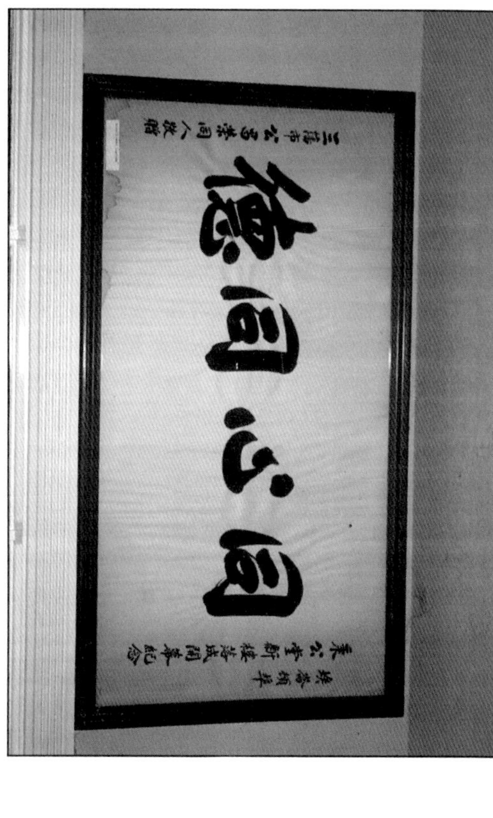

Over Window Gift. This grand opening gift, presented by the Los Angeles Tong, reads, "Always work together."

Embroidery Bird and Tree. This embroidery, a gift to the Tong, depicts the Land of Extreme Felicity in the West. The flowering of lotuses, floor of gold sand, and beautifully colored singing bird represent the Chinese ultimate paradise. The tree may be the Peach Tree of Immortality.

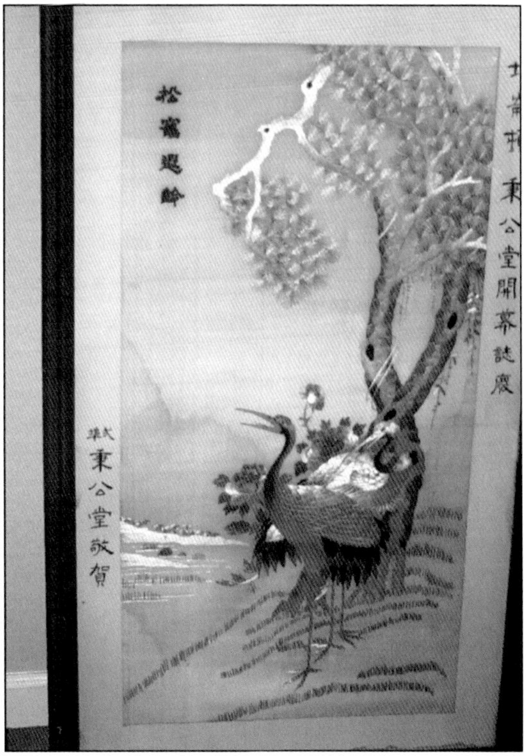

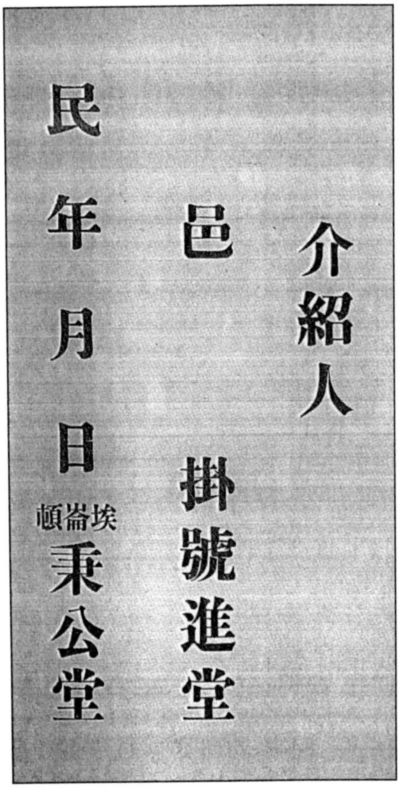

介紹人

邑　掛號進堂

民　年　月　日

埃崙頓
秉公堂

Application for Admission. To become a member of the Isleton Bing Kong Tong a person had to apply for membership. This is the application form.

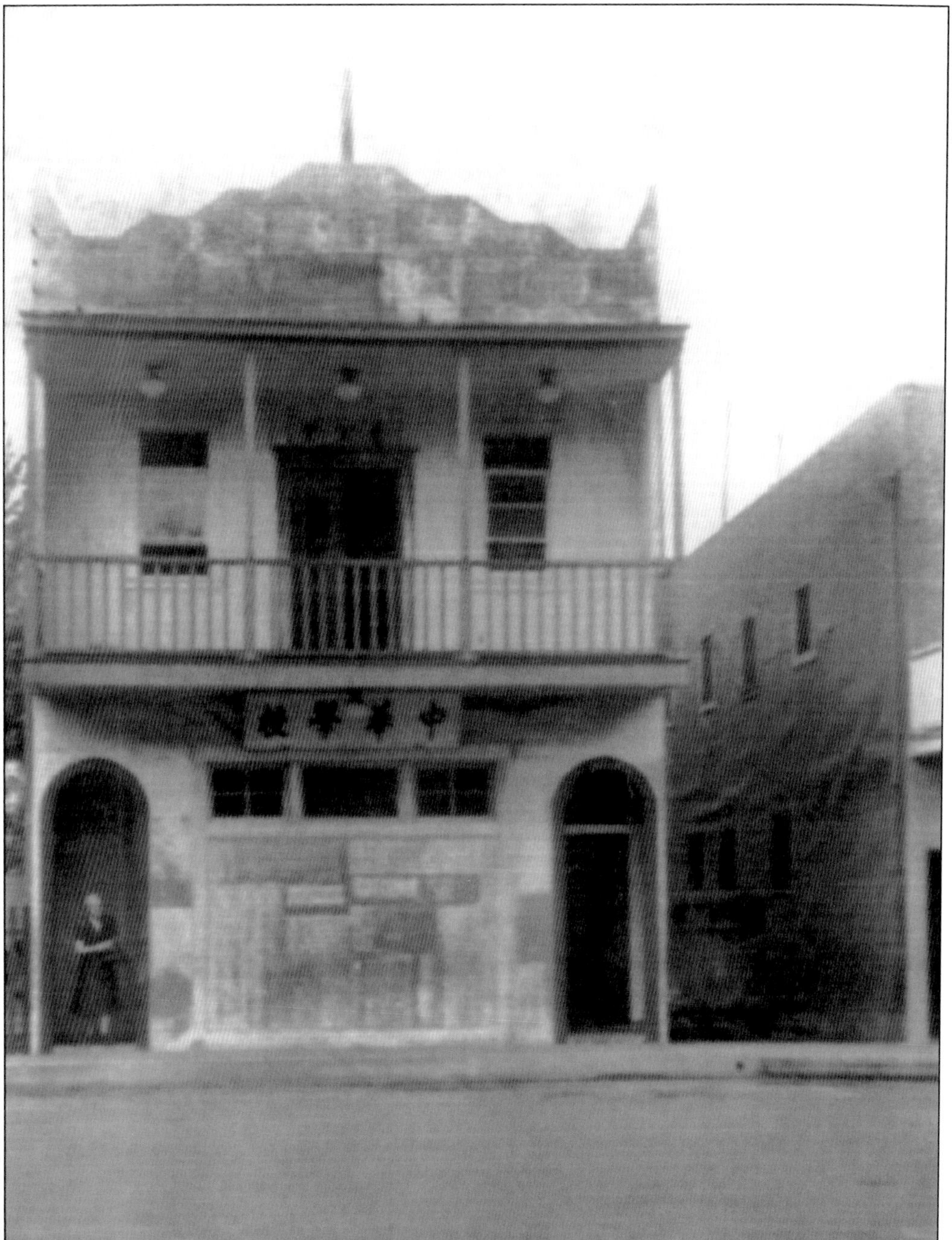

Tong Façade. The front of the Tong Building was designed with culture, form, and function all combined. The second-floor balcony was traditional. The signs, lights, double doors, and windows are carefully placed to draw attention to the center and quality of the building. The doors were painted red and opened in. The parapet and flagpole make this the most elaborate building on Main Street. It is also slightly higher and bigger. The arched lower doors, windows, and recessed middle give the building balance. This is the only building on Main Street with dual-front arched entries.

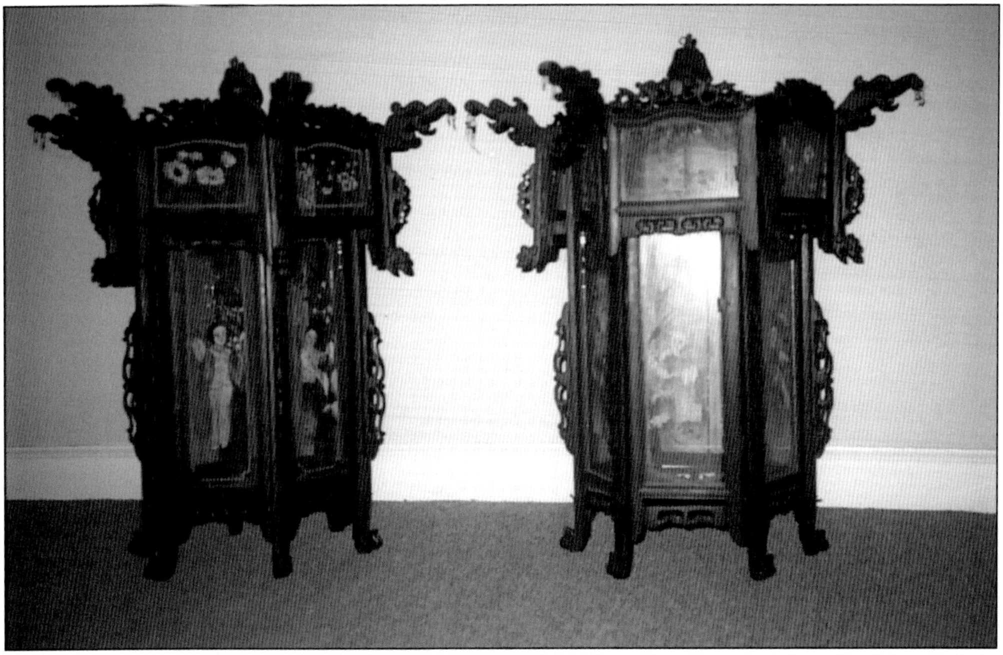

LAMPS. These special lamps from China were part of the furnishings in the Tong Building. Made of wood and glass and painted with natural setting scenes, they were for special occasions.

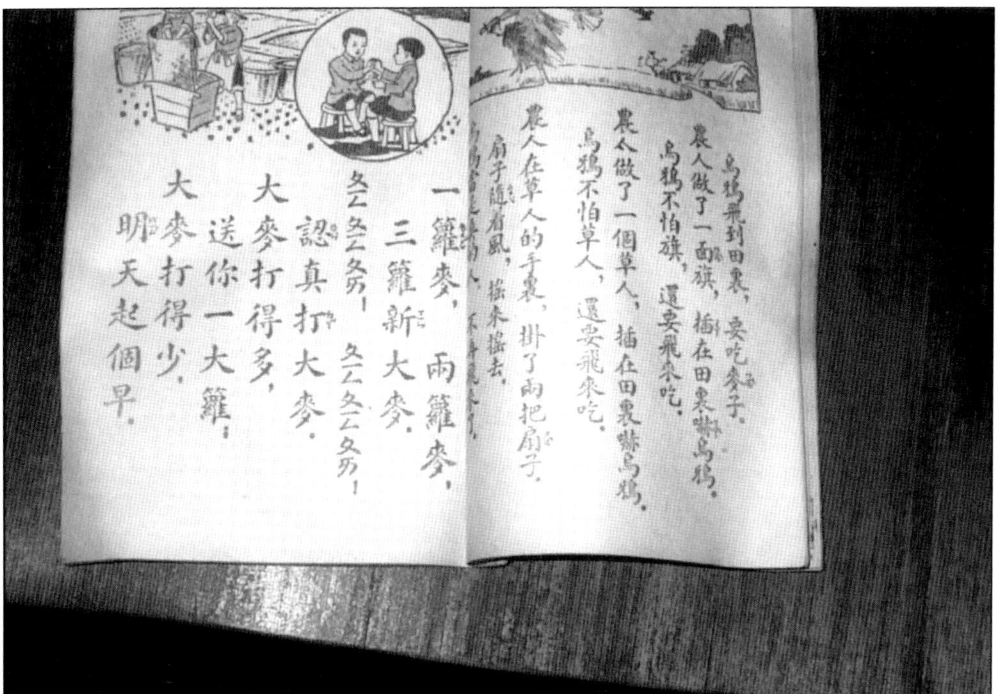

SCHOOL BOOK. Chinese culture was maintained in many ways. Children were expected to attend Chinese Language School every day after regular school. Language school was held in the Tong Building. This is one of the readers used to teach Chinese reading and writing.

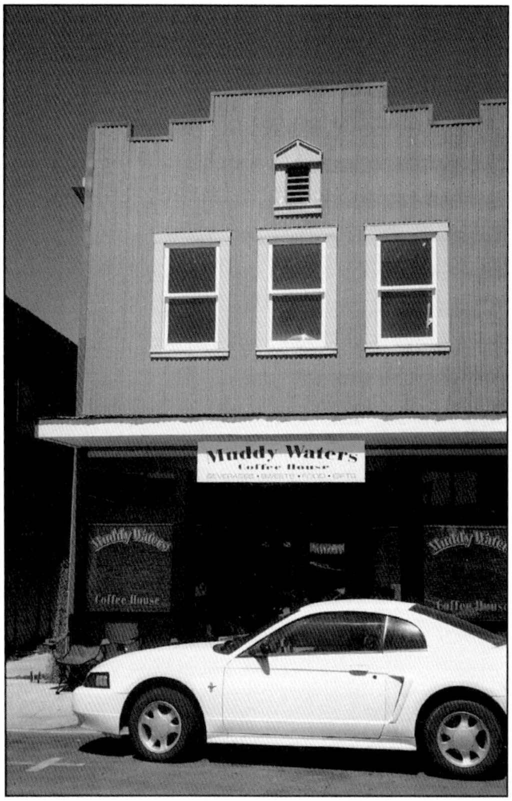

JEAN'S BUILDING. This is one of the few restored Chinese buildings on Main Street. Located just two doors down-river from the Tong, it was artfully restored with the same type of corrugated metal siding, windows, parapet, and vents. The interior is the original tongue-and-groove beaded fir.

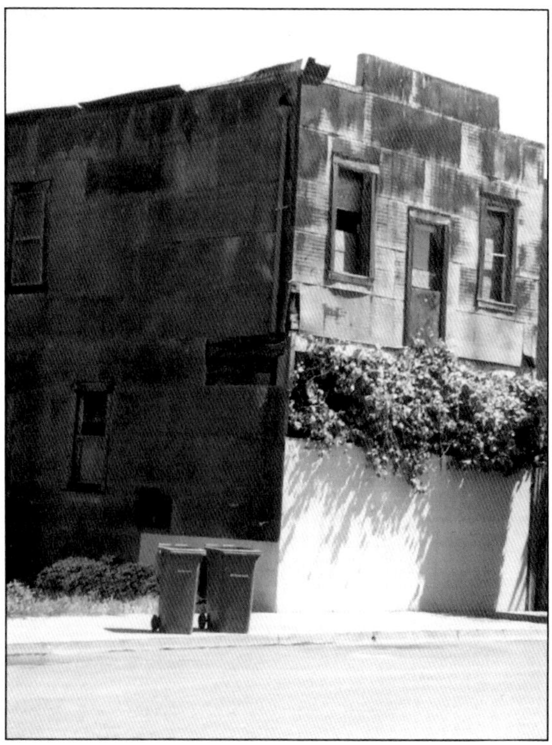

33 MAIN STREET. This once proud and useful structure awaits renovation in Isleton. The grapevines and pigeons have found a temporary home here. This building was one of those built by and belonging to the Chinn trust. It is two doors up river from the Tong Building. Similar in construction to the Tong, it has two large rooms, one upstairs and one down. Upstairs is divided into small rooms useful as bedrooms or storage. The bottom floor has a large open game room with locked cashier's cages at the back side.

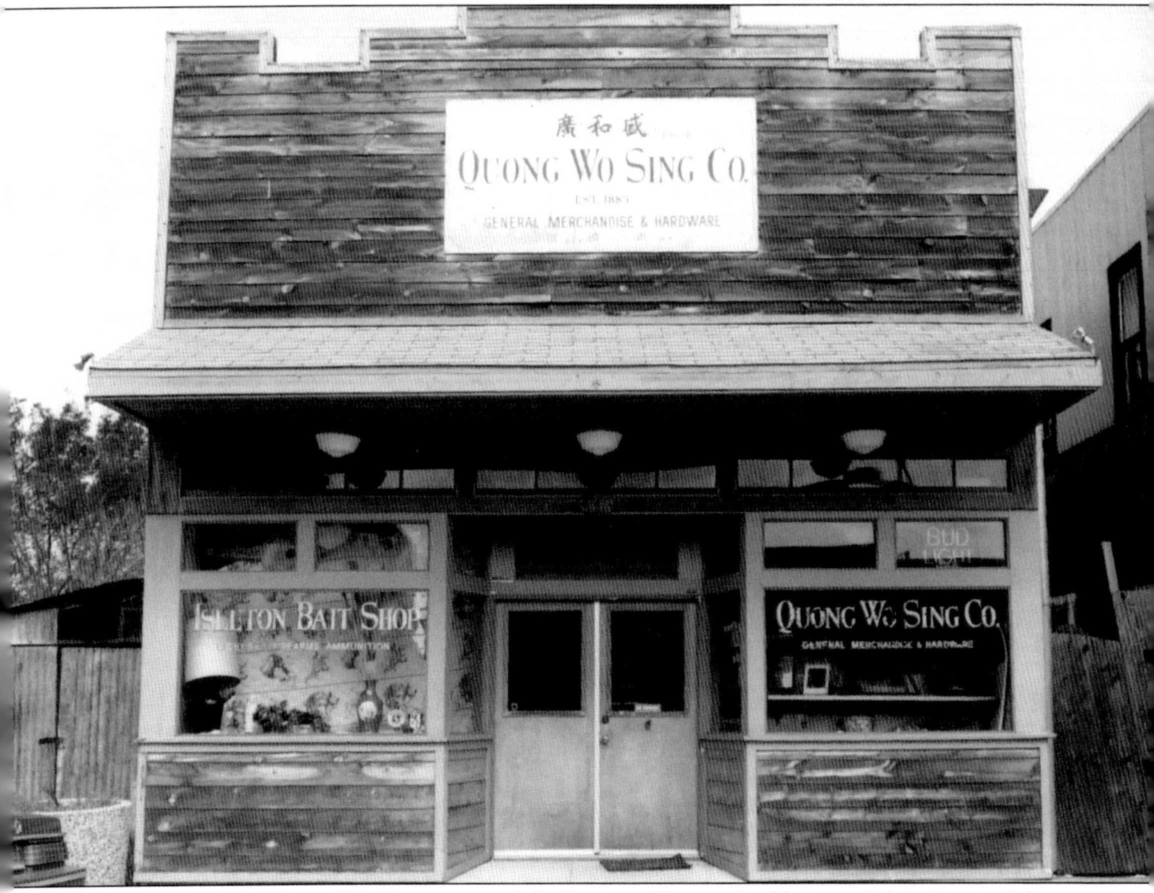

QUONG WO SING. Quong Wo Sing is one of the historic Chinese buildings on Main Street. It has served as herb shop, bait shop, and hardware store. It is still owned and lived in by the same family.

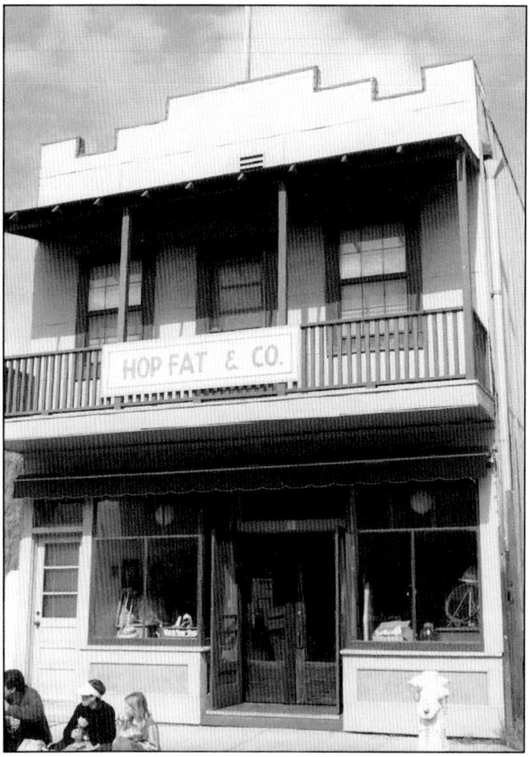

Hop Fat. This is one of the truly original buildings on Main Street in Chinatown. Hop Fat and Company has a beautiful façade, recessed double-front doors, a side entry to the upstairs, and large display windows. For a time it served as the Tong's building while the present one was under construction. The flag pole flew the colors for a few years. It was a general store with Chinese merchandise, including canned goods and fresh produce used by Chinese restaurants and homes. It is still owned by the original family.

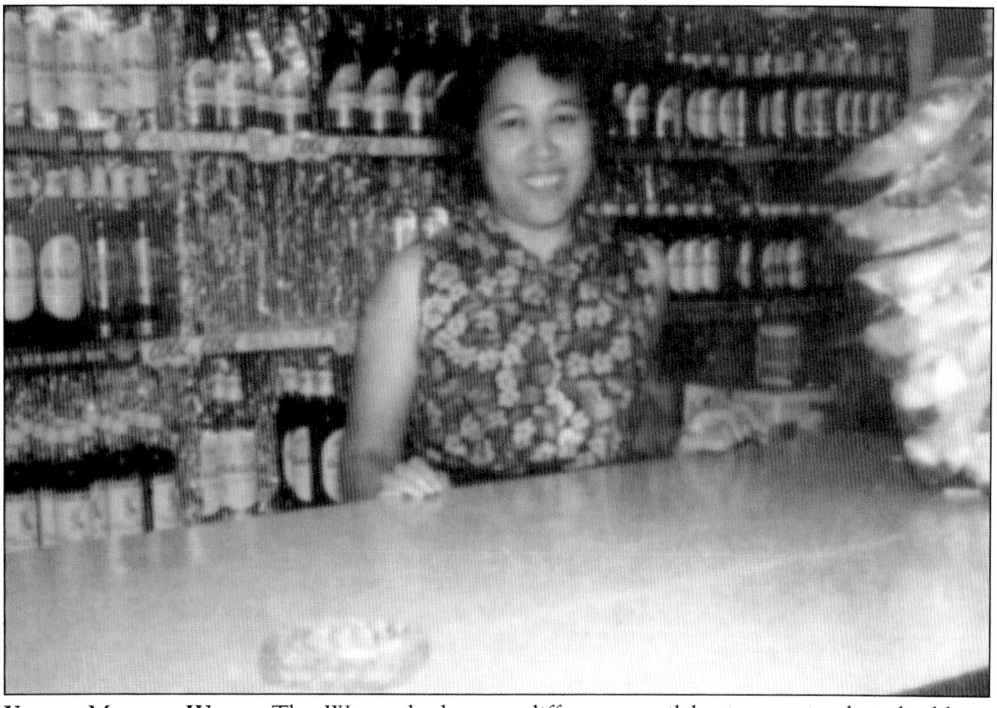

Young Marion Wong. The Wongs had many different retail businesses in their building. At one time it was a bar. Here Marian Wong waits for customers. Main Street business has frequently changed to meet the needs of the evolving downtown.

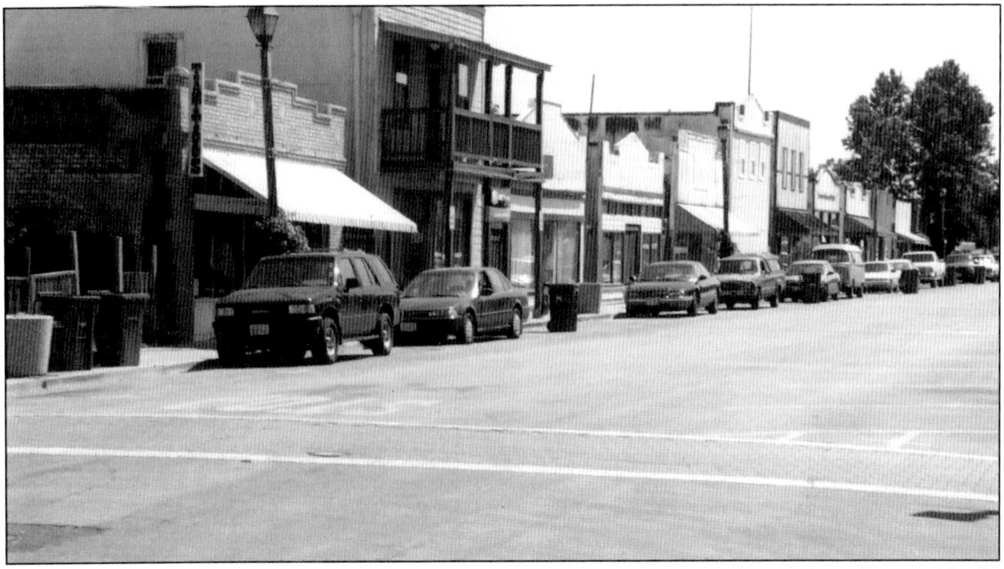

Japanese Main Street. The Japanese section of Main Street is similar to the Chinese block. There are fewer two-story buildings and fewer balconies. There was a bath house, a market, a barber shop, a bait shop, and a casino.

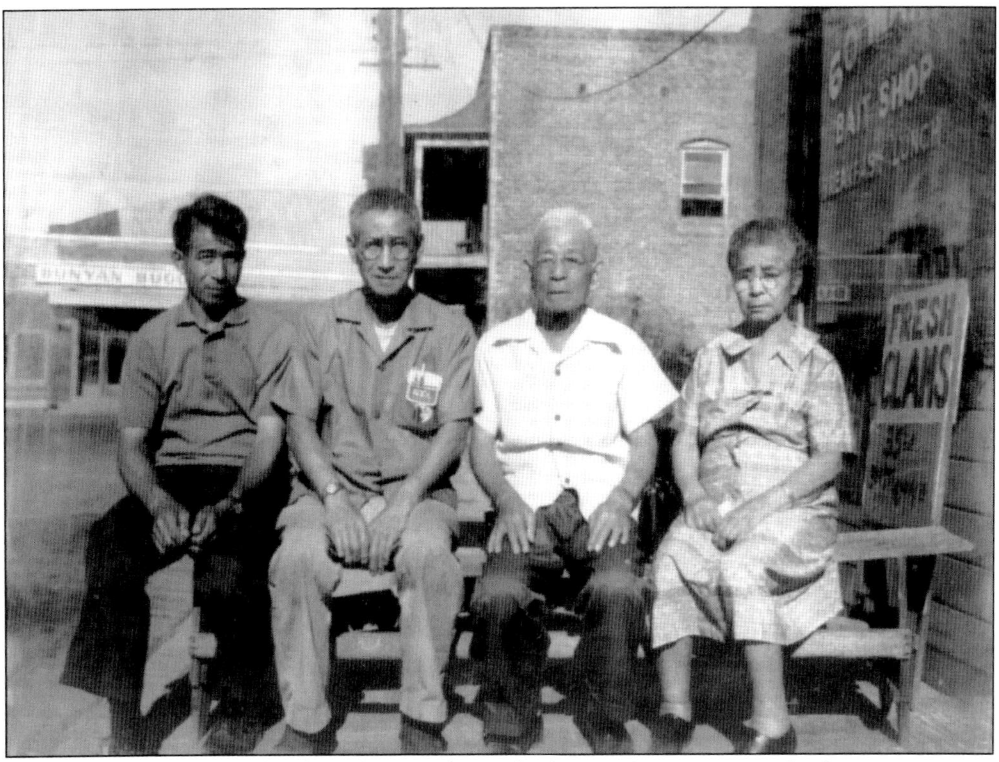

Japanese Bait Shop. This bait shop at the end of Main Street was in the Japanese section and was owned by Ben Shintaku and his wife. Behind them is the National Cannery. Besides bait, the shop offered lunch and dinner. Today the shop is the temporary home of the Isleton Historical Society and is owned by Sandy Longhoffer.

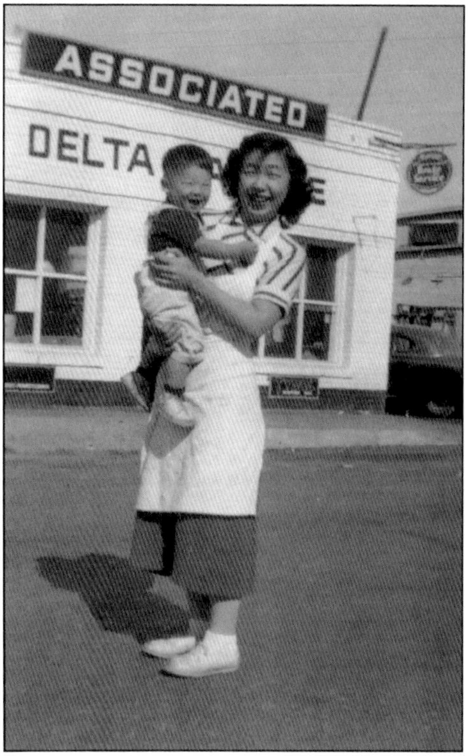

Josi Kamoto. Josi Kamoto and her son pose on Main Street in front of the Delta Garage. This garage was also known as Truman's. The building in the rear is the National Cannery. Not too long after this picture was taken Executive Order 9066 was signed and all of the Japanese left Isleton to go to internment camps.

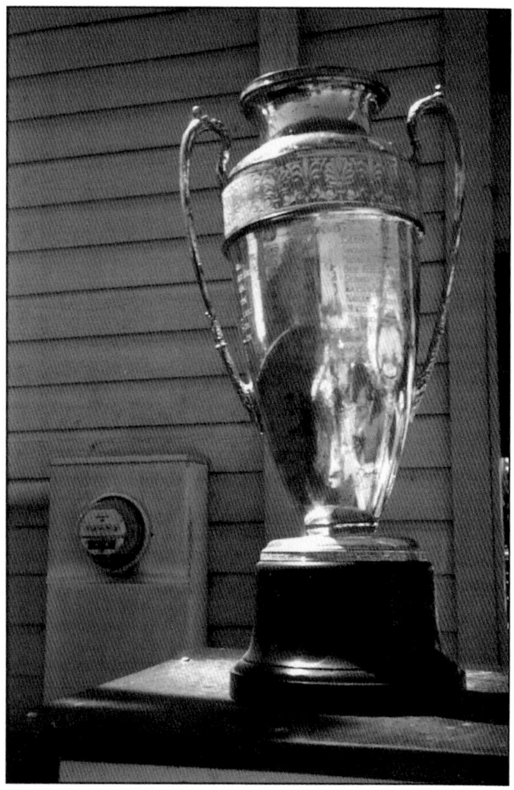

Japanese Sumo Trophy. The Japanese in Isleton competed with other Japanese community schools and clubs in contests. One of these was sumo wrestling. The Isleton team was well known and won many of the competitions. This trophy in the Isleton Historical Museum was awarded to the Isleton team many times. They competed as far away as San Jose.

Five

Festivals and Canneries

Harvest festivals are as old as farming. If the levees held and the hot sun dried the marshy fields, the wheat, asparagus, and other crops brought joy to Isleton. With transport to the cities, good prices, and a large supply of workers from throughout the world, Isleton prospered. The demand for white asparagus from Isleton spread overseas, and it wasn't long before railroads, canneries, ice houses, labor housing, and pickle factories came to Isleton. With a good place to live, a full stomach, good friends, and a good job at the cannery it seemed that a celebration was in order. In 1922 Isleton held a whisker growing contest, and in 1924 the first Asparagus Festival was held. Since then, Isleton has hardly missed a year. The Asparagus Festival became the May Festival, and now it is the Crawdad Festival. The canneries, railroads, and asparagus have all gone, but the spirit is alive. This photo of the Asparagus Festival is of the wagon with the queen and her attendants in 1925.

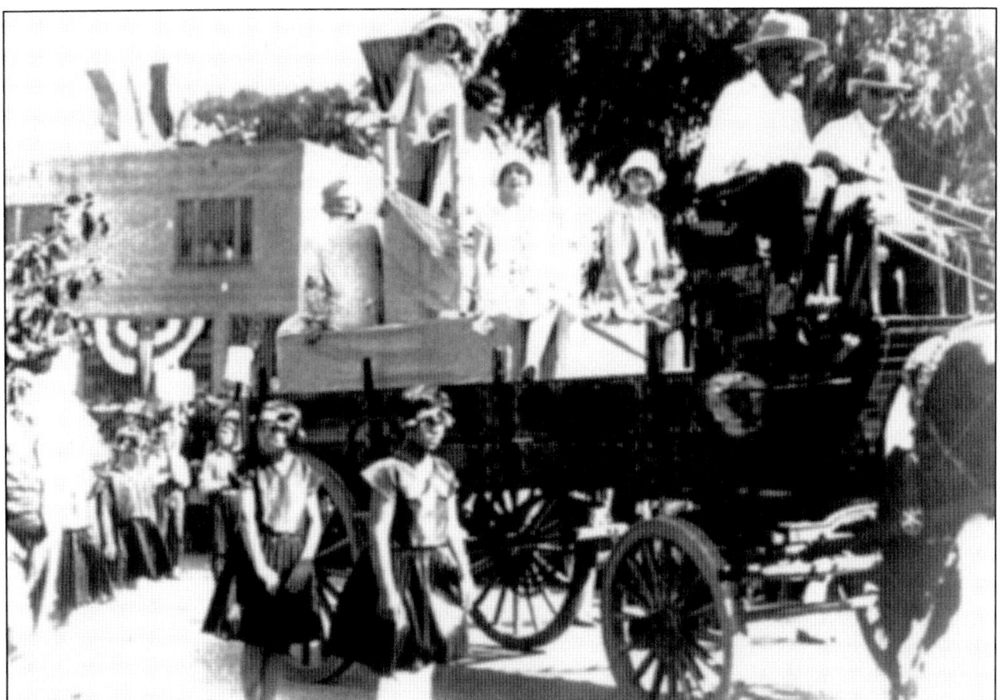

Asparagus Parade with Buggy. This view of the first Asparagus Festival Parade was captured from the Gardiner Improvement Building. There was a lot of preparation, from transportation to clothing. The community felt strongly about their festival, even then. People came from miles around to the Isleton Asparagus Festival.

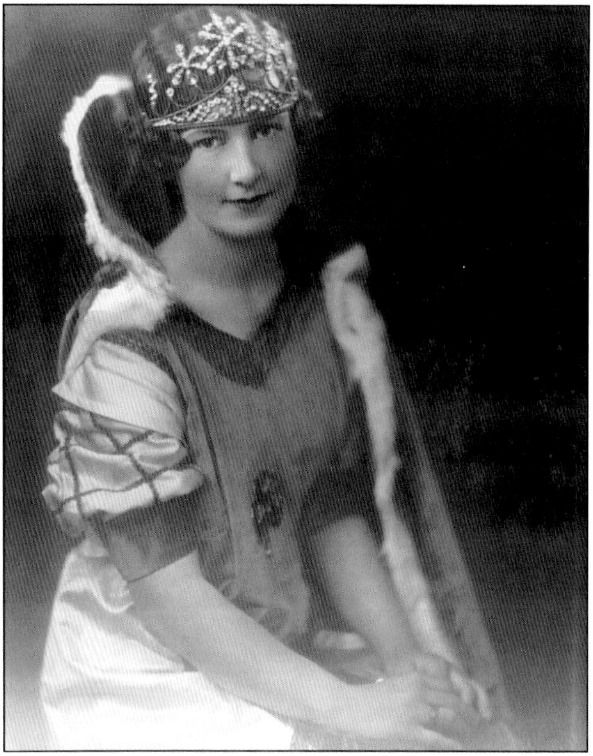

Queen Heimbaugh. The queen of the 1925 Asparagus Festival was Alice Perkins Heimbaugh. Alice was the daughter of Lena and Charles Perkins and married Fred Heimbaugh. She was born in Isleton. Her parents built their home here in 1906.

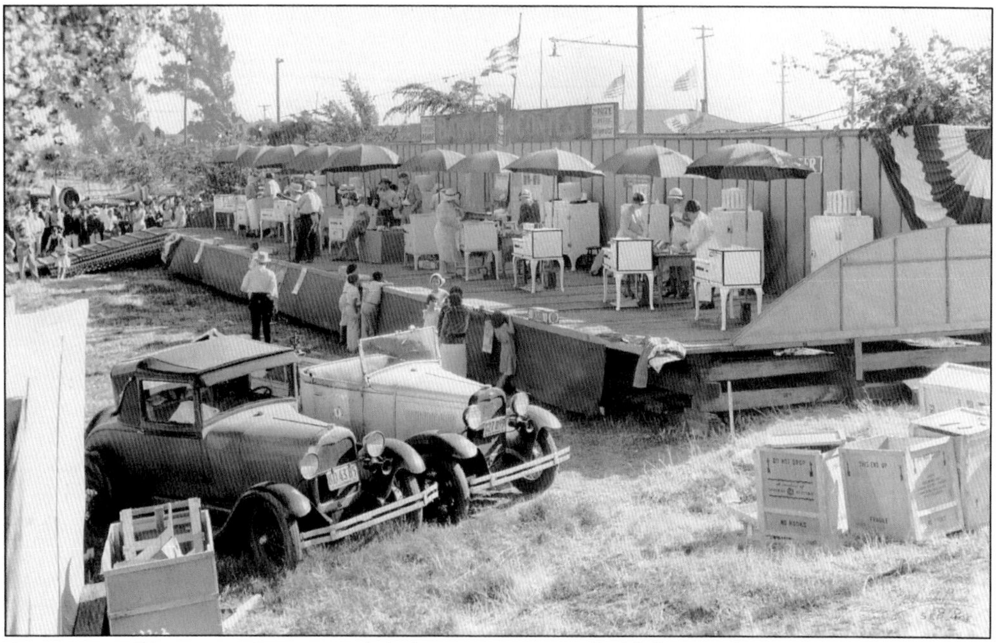

Asparagus Hotpoint Contest. A baking contest was held during the Asparagus Festival. It was held near Wilson Park and was hosted by Hotpoint. The winner won a free kitchen range. By the looks of the new Fords in the foreground the contest was managed by successful people. Note the umbrellas; temperatures in Isleton can exceed 100 degrees in July. With all those ovens going it must have been nice and "toasty."

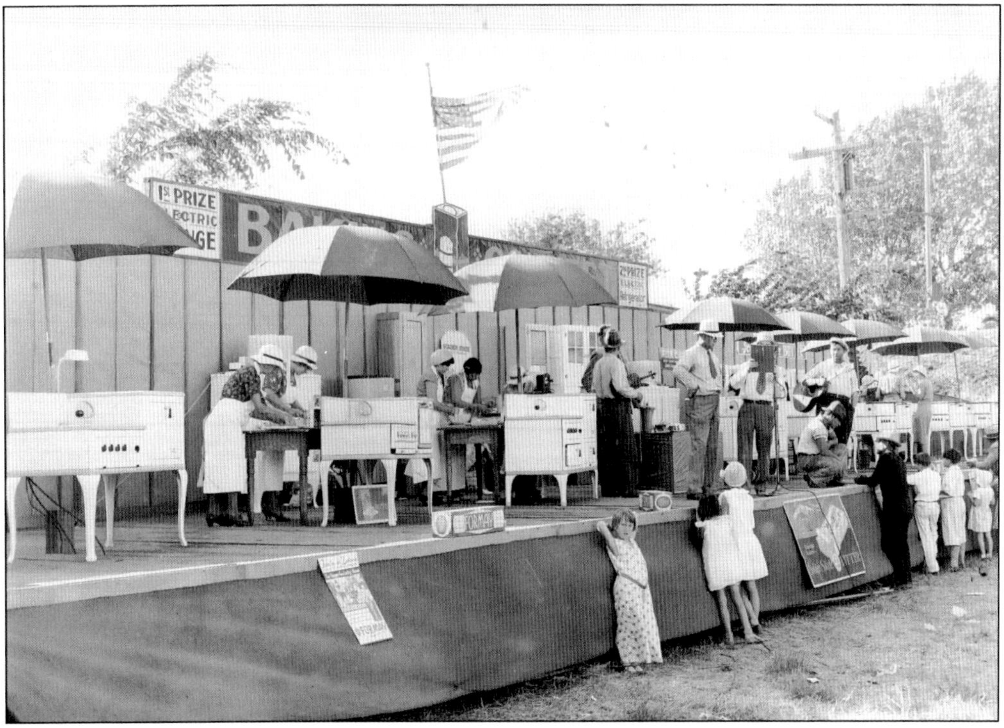

Asparagus Baking Contest. Shown here at the festival are aprons, hats, and rolling pins, all in concert with fiddles, guitars, and stage managers. The crowd is beginning to gather to encourage their mothers and grandmothers to victory.

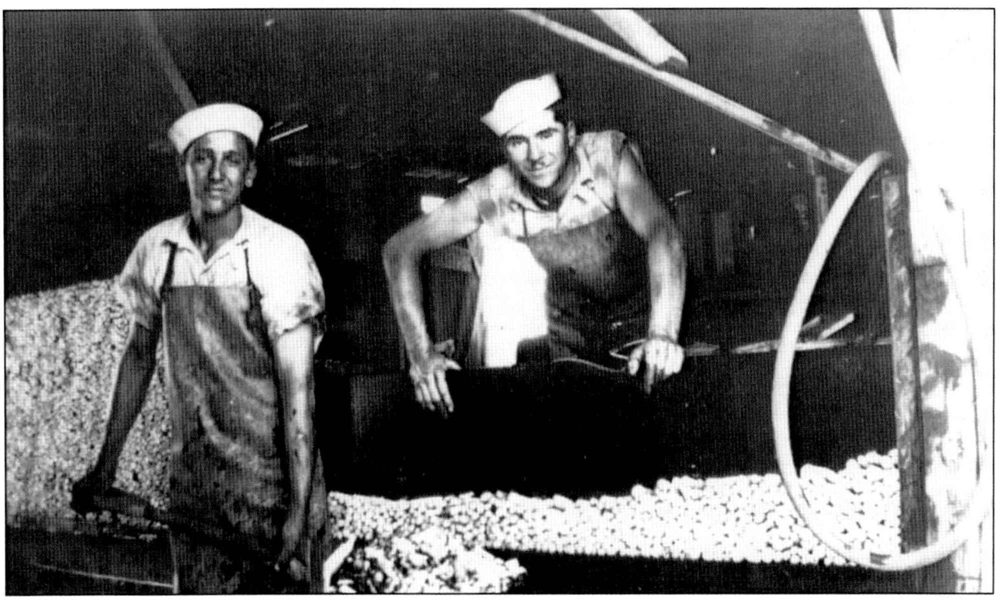

Cannery Workers. During harvest season, from June through September, the canneries work day and night. It wasn't uncommon to work a double shift. If the fruit ripened it had to be harvested and processed. It was hard, hot, and dirty work. Women worked the line while men worked in the warehouse or packing cases.

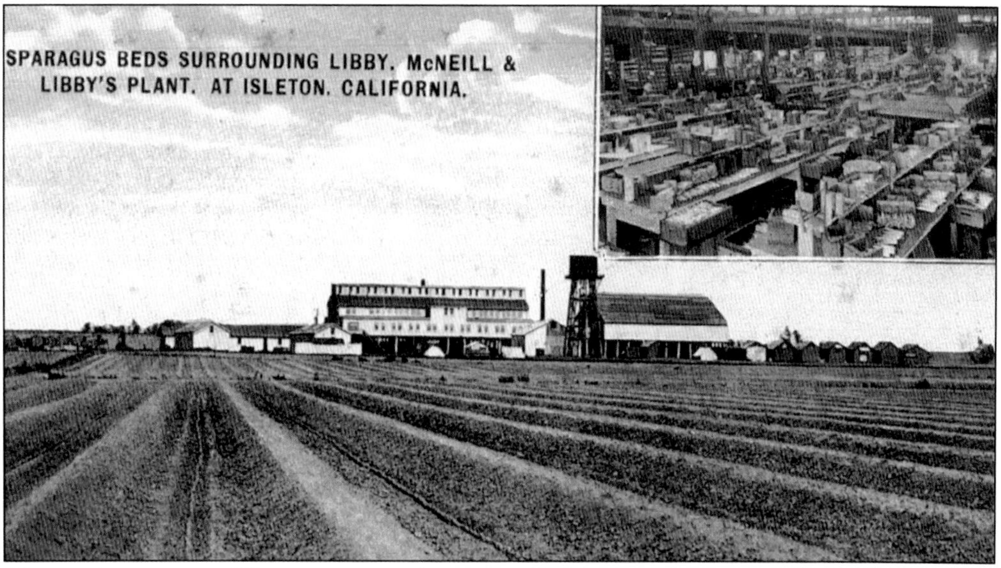

WHITE ASPARAGUS. White asparagus became a Delta specialty, especially around Isleton. A labor-intensive crop, it is seldom grown today. To keep the stalks from turning green the asparagus must be cut underground just as the tops break the surface. Farmers had to create mounds five feet wide over the asparagus plants to keep the stalks underground. Special cutting tools and ridging implements were used. Workers had to bend way over and dig under the soil to cut the white stalk.

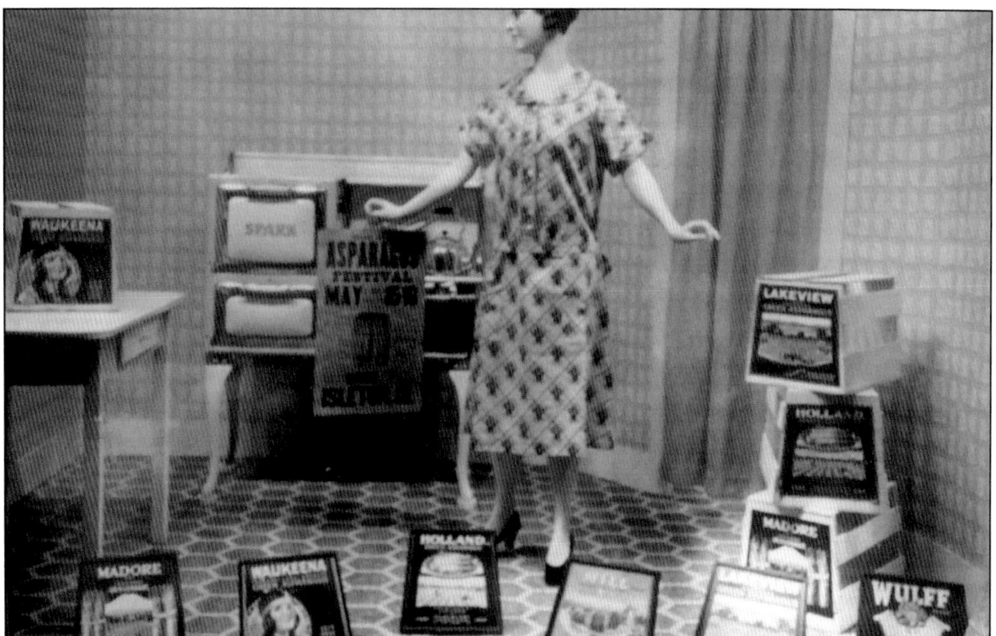

ASPARAGUS FESTIVAL POSTER. This is a poster for the second annual Asparagus Festival in 1925. World War I was over, the League of Nations had formed, and the flappers were having their hair bobbed. Spark ranges, linoleum floors, and Lakeview Green Asparagus were hits at the Isleton Asparagus Festival that year.

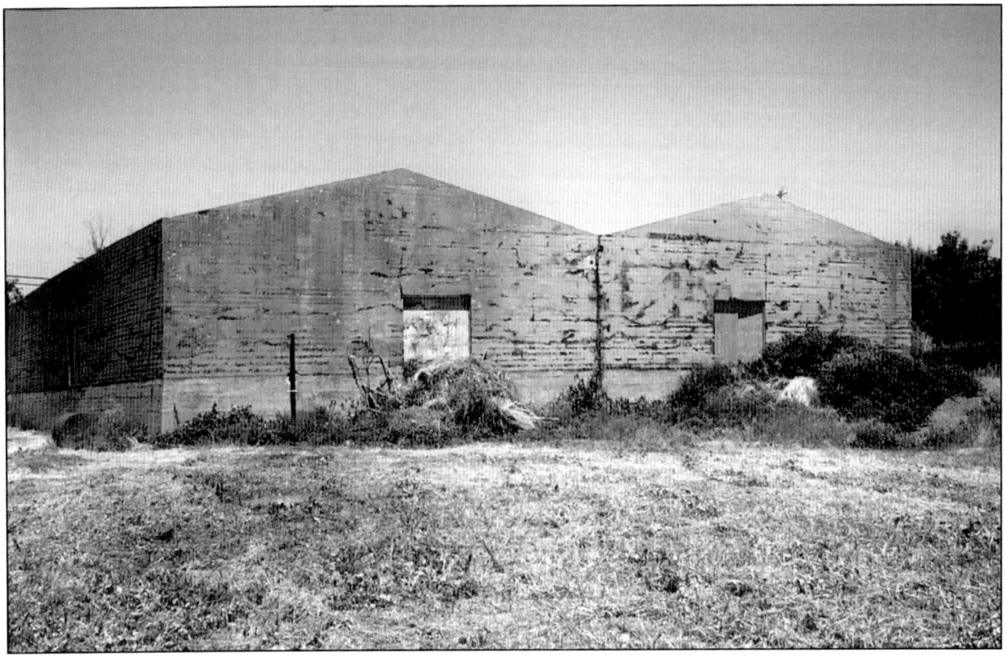

Barsoon Cannery. These large cement reinforced buildings are all that remains of the Barsoon Cannery. The buildings were used to warehouse canned fruits and vegetables. Hundreds of people worked here during the growing and canning season.

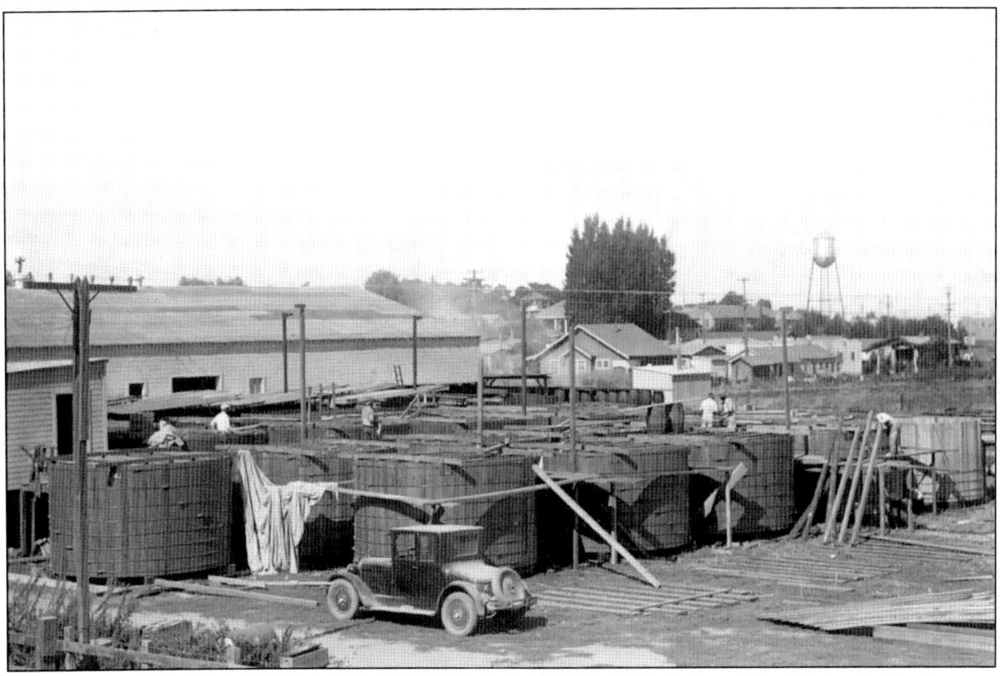

Pickling Works. The Delta was good for many different crops, not the least of which were cucumbers. Del Monte built a pickling factory just outside town. The vats were all constructed of Sitka spruce and the strong solution was unmistakable. When the plant closed down the vats were sold to interested buyers who made them into decks and hot tubs.

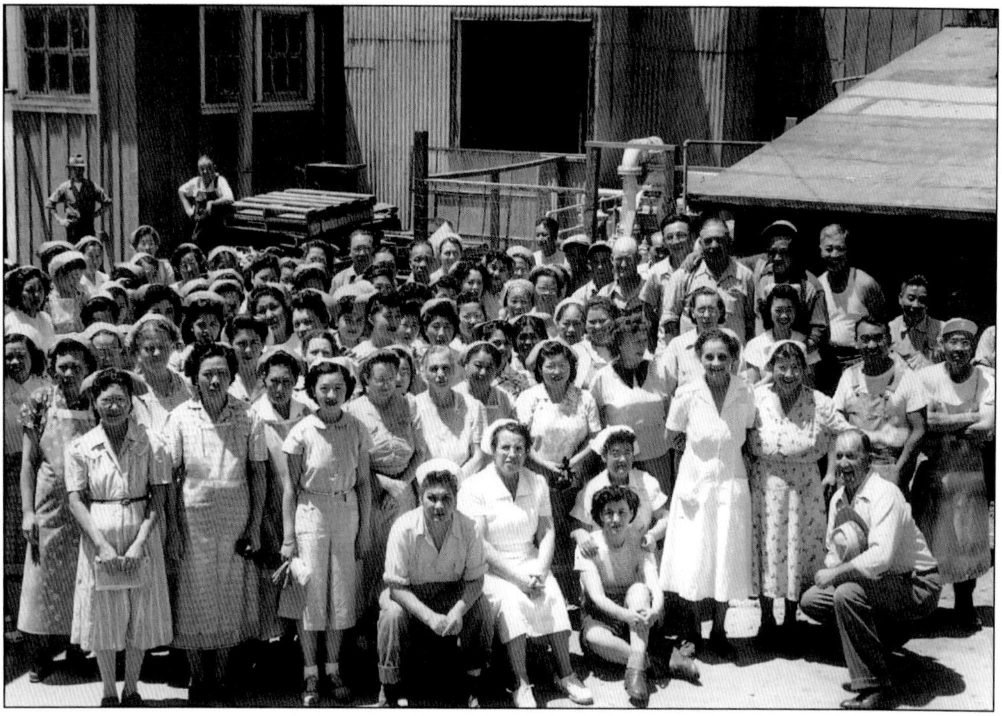

NATIONAL CANNERY. In its heyday, the National Cannery was a major part of Isleton. Located at the very end of Main Street, it was owned by Chinese businessmen and investors. During the summer months it kept the fruit and asparagus lines going night and day. From unloading trucks, to working in the warehouse, the National Cannery was hard and tiring work.

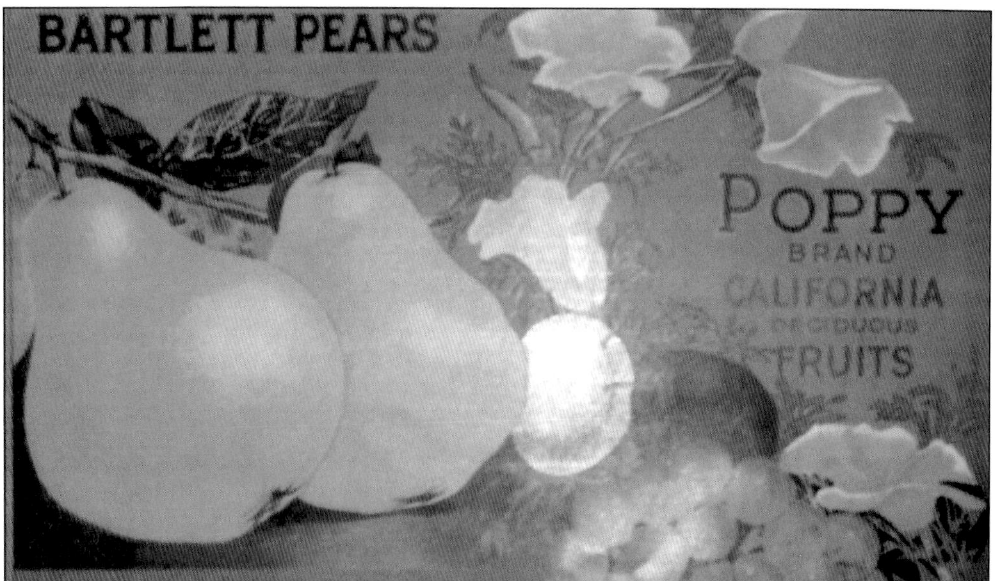

POPPY BARTLETTS. Pears have been a major part of the agrarian economy around Isleton. Bartlett pears sell well as fresh fruit and are used in canning for fruit cocktail and halves.

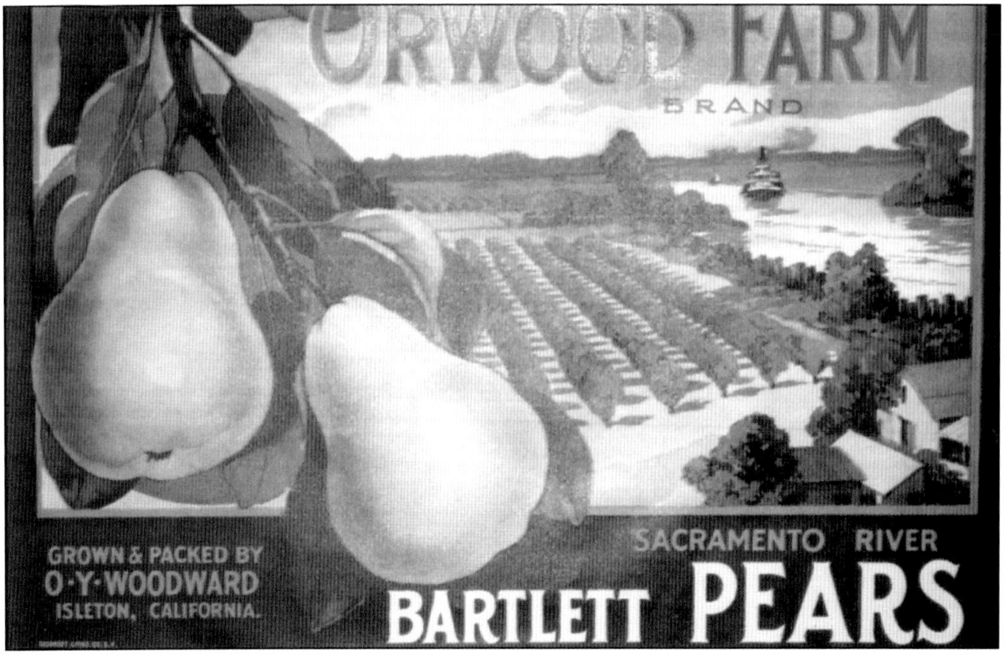

ORWOOD LABEL. Pears are a natural for the Delta. Many of the trees are below river level, but their root system does well in the soggy soil. They are high producers, fairly easy to harvest, and maintenance is limited to spraying and pruning.

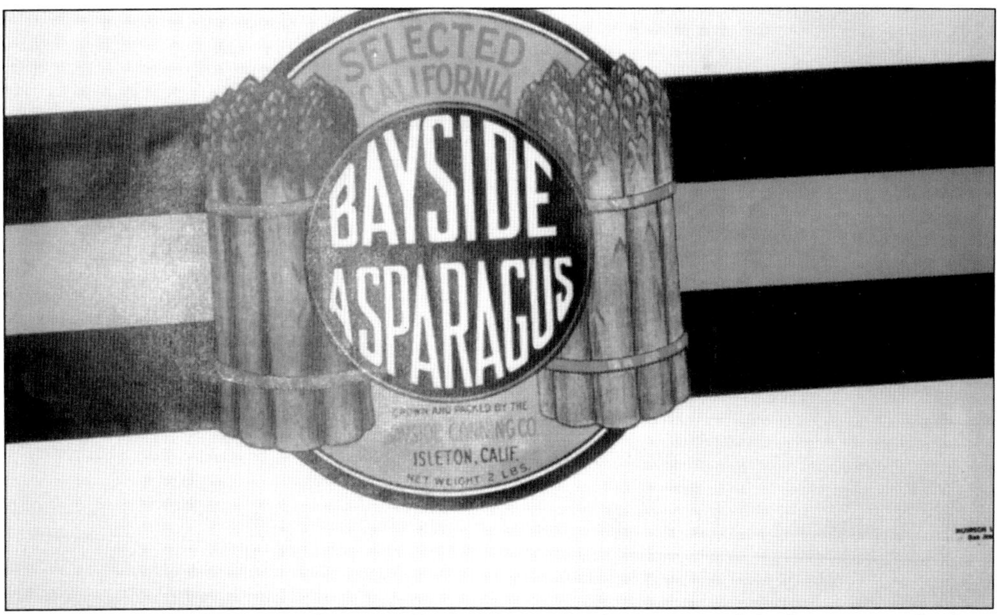

BAYSIDE CANNERY LABEL. The Bayside Cannery in Isleton canned both green and white asparagus. Bayside was a popular place to work, but the labor was demanding and very tedious.

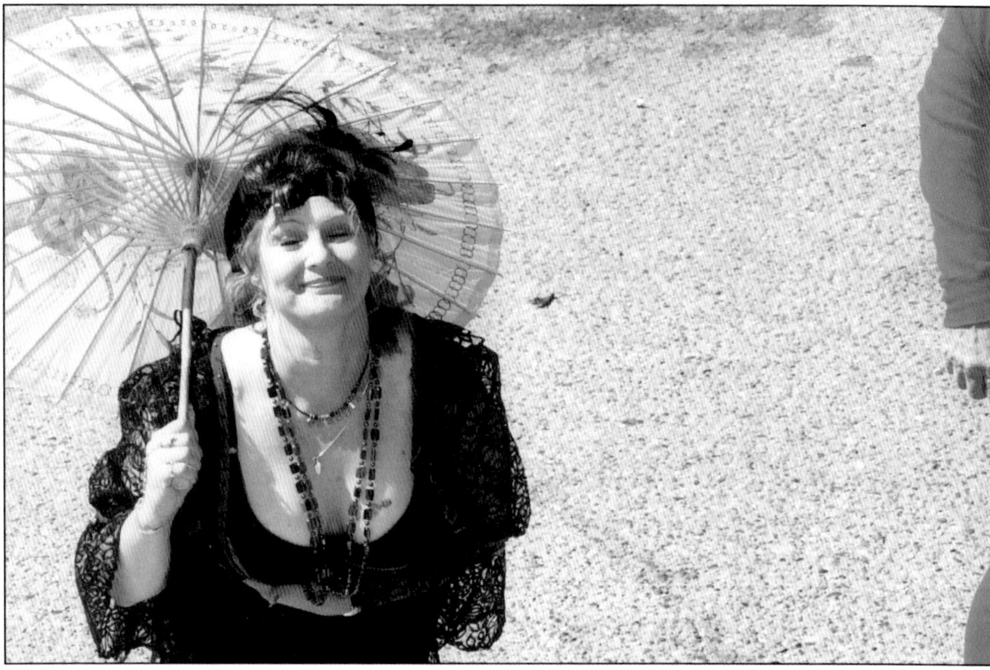

CRAWDAD LADY. The Crawdad Celebration celebrates a Southern delight that is close to the heart in Louisiana. Music, Creole food, alligators, and bales of hay add a bit of Mardi Gras to Isleton.

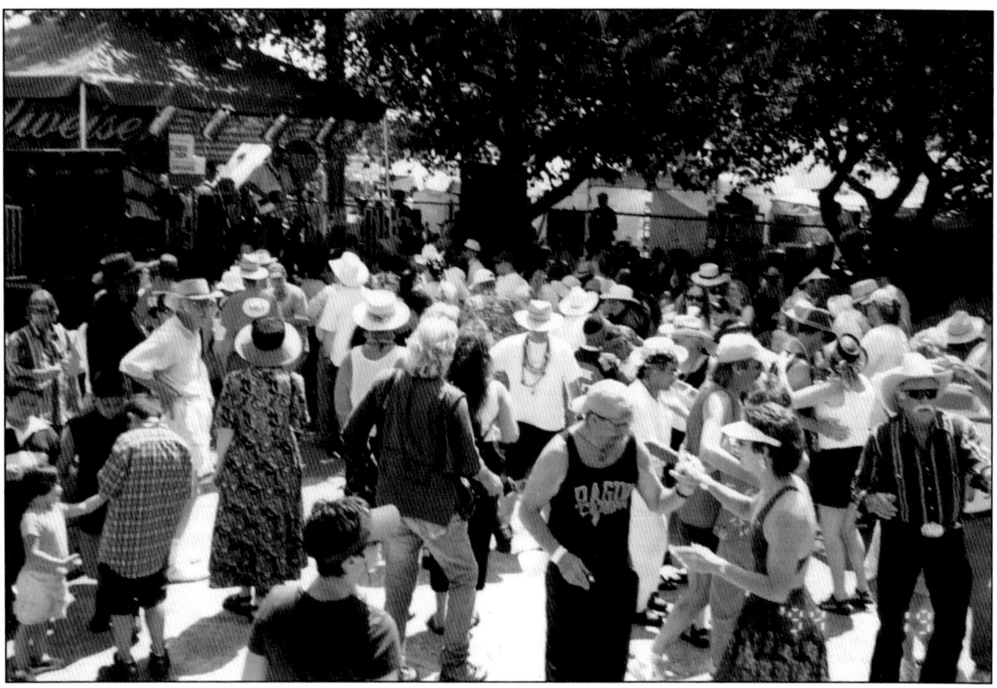

CRAWDAD DANCING. All ages learn to dance to Cajun music at one of the three music venues. Many of the bands come from Louisiana for the festival. Dappled in sunlight and shade, festooned in hats, sunglasses, belt buckles, and shorts, visitors tap their feet to the infectious rhythm.

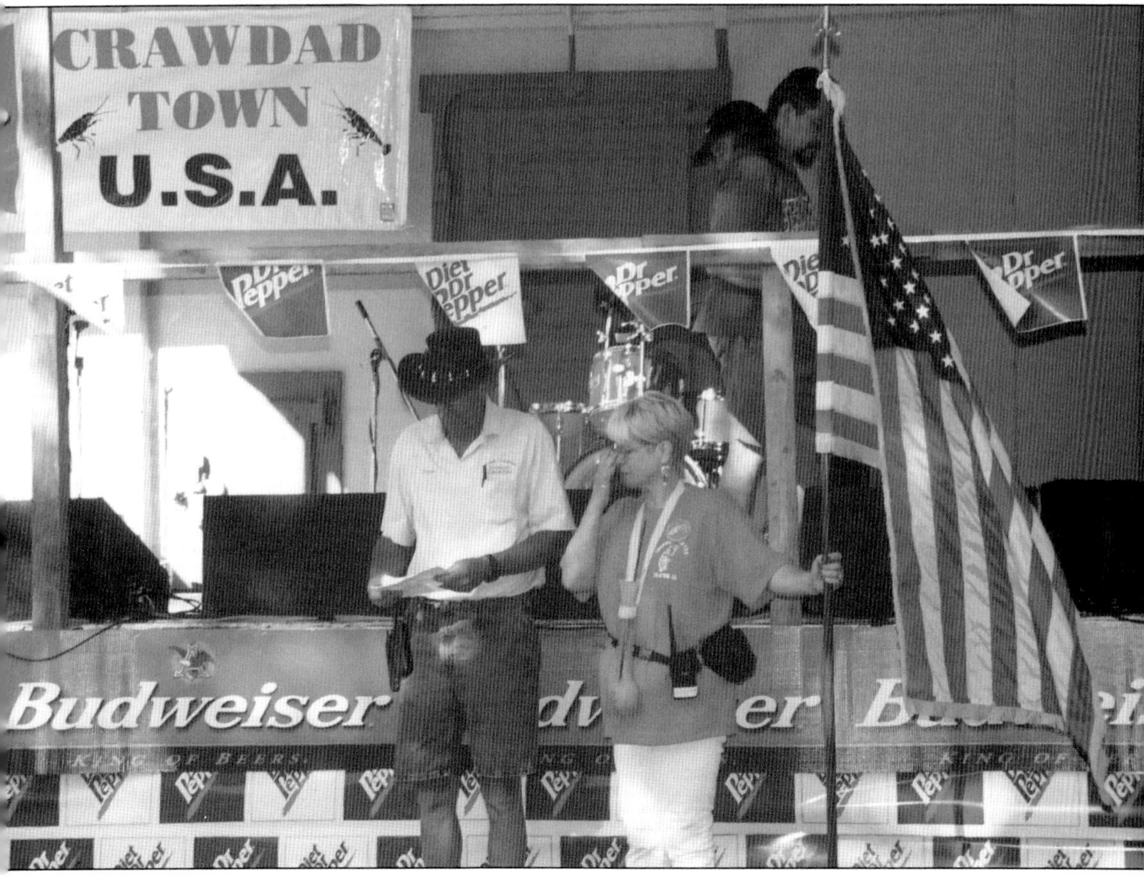

Hand and Morris. Charlie Hand (right) and Dennis Morris got everything organized for the Crawdad Festival a few years ago. With the help of "Babe" Glavin at the Chamber of Commerce, everything fell into place. One of the keys to the success of this giant festival is the organization and help of volunteers.

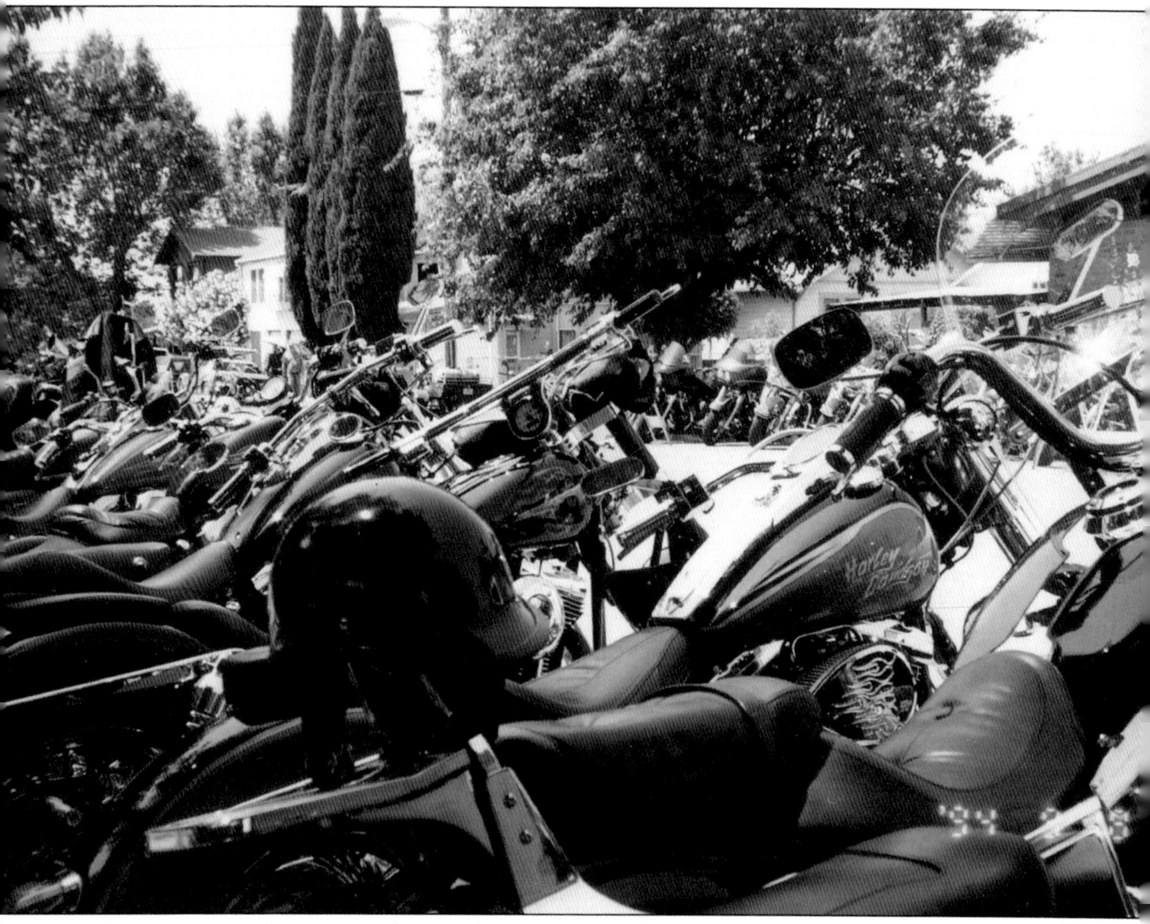

BIKERS AT THE CRAWDAD. Thousands of bikers invade Isleton for the Crawdad Festival. Special parking is provided, and it's worth the time to just stroll along the bike parking area and marvel at the polished chrome, paint, and the excellent condition of these machines. Be warned: when they start up and leave, it might get a bit noisy.

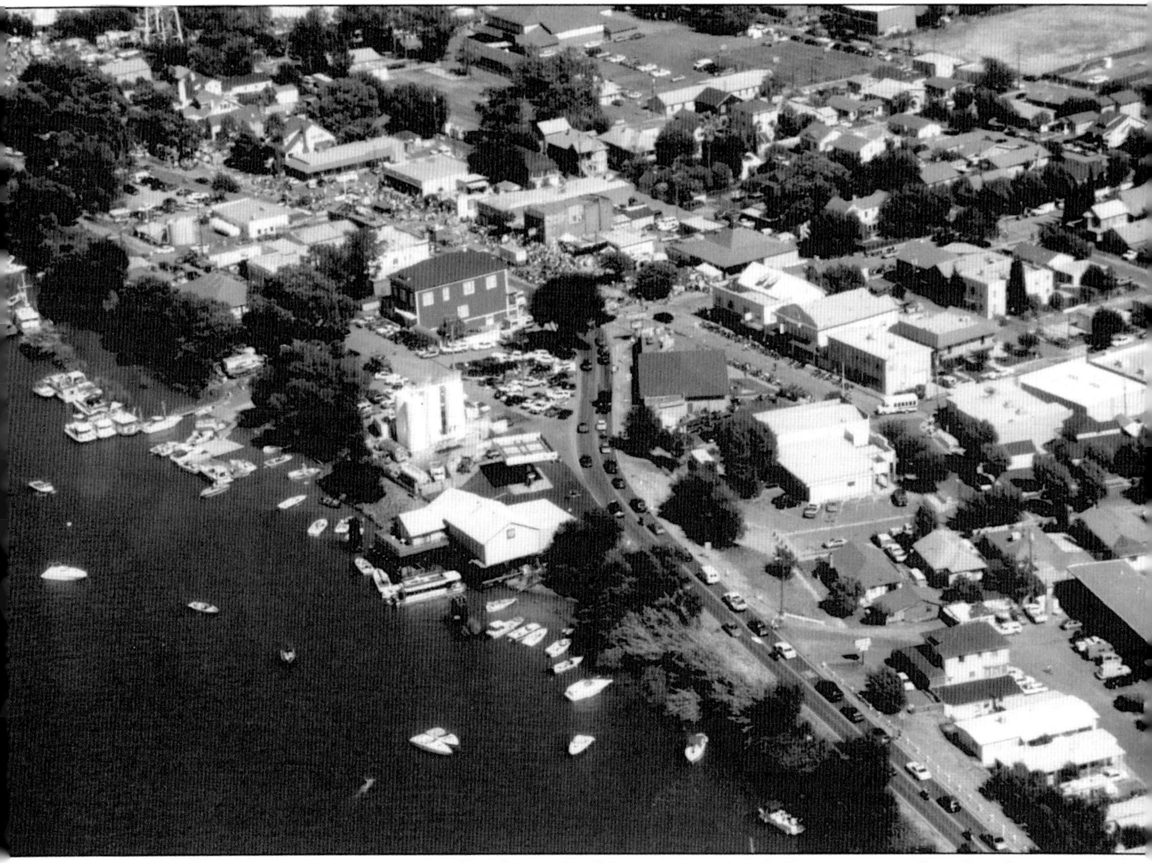

Aerial View of Second Street. The large building near the left center is the Gardiner Building. The supports for the water tower are in the upper left corner. The crowded street is Second Street. The line of cars on Highway 160 coming into town indicates that it must be early Saturday, and the festival is just getting started.

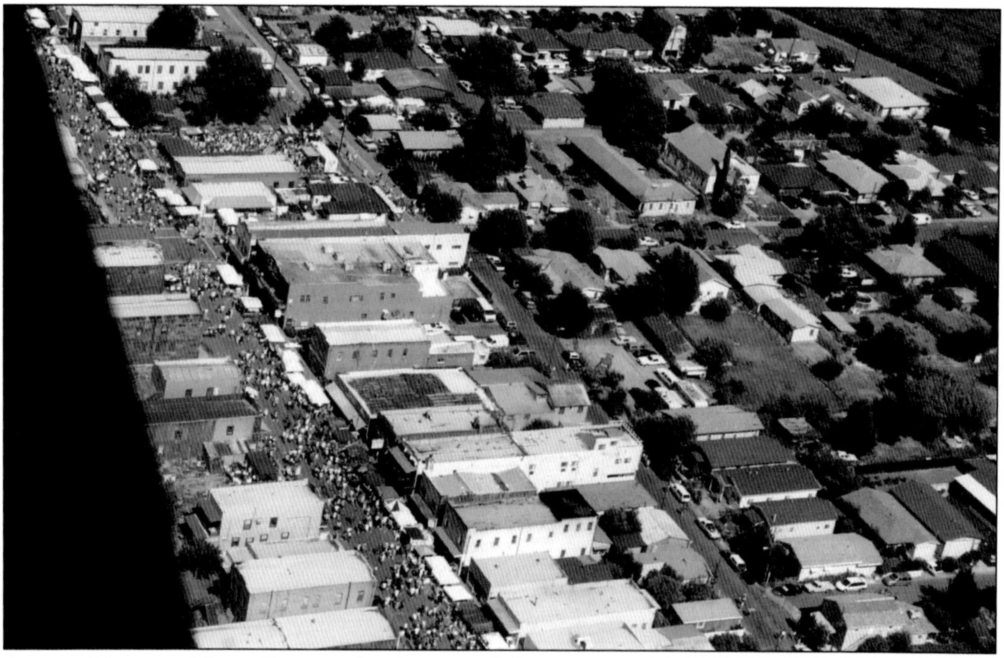

Aerial View of Main Street. At the top of the picture is one of the parking areas of the Crawdad Festival put on by the Chamber of Commerce. The entire historic Main Street is closed off, and booths line the right side of the street. The residences behind the business buildings are old homes with plenty of space for very nice gardens. The crowd is growing, so it must be early Saturday.

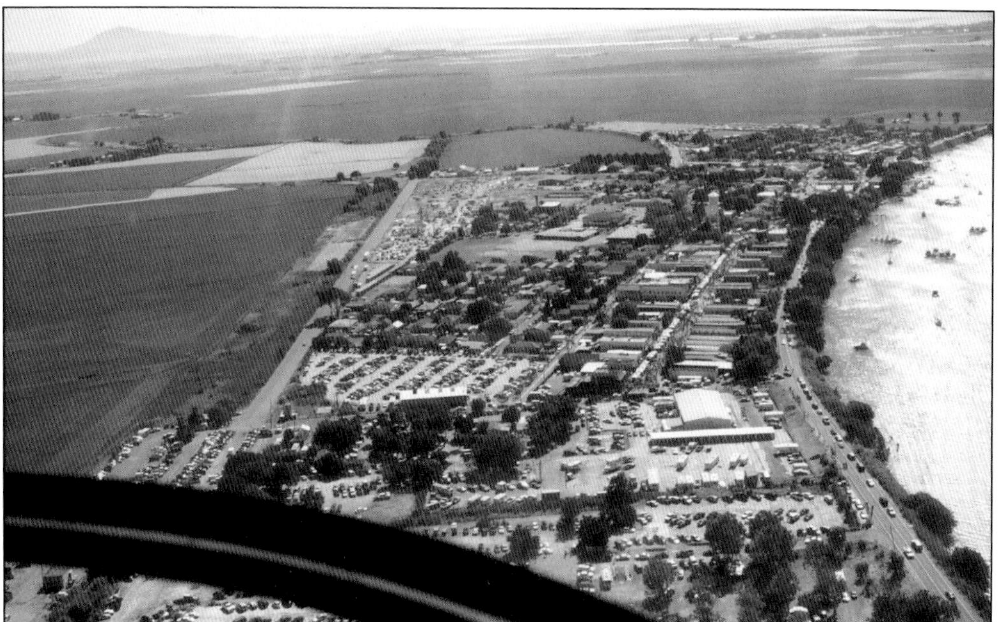

Aerial View of Fields. Isleton sits between the Sacramento River and productive farmland for as far as the eye can see. Mount Diablo rises in the background while cars turn off Highway 160 to park for the festival.

Libby Cannery Pilings. One of the largest and most successful asparagus canneries in Isleton was Libby McNeil. Located just north of town, it was a big business until the asparagus ran out. Asparagus has a limited soil life because it depletes the nutrients so quickly. Once the asparagus went elsewhere the canneries closed down and Isleton was left empty-handed. These dock pilings are all that is left of the Libby McNeil Cannery. The levee and trees shield them from view on Highway 160.

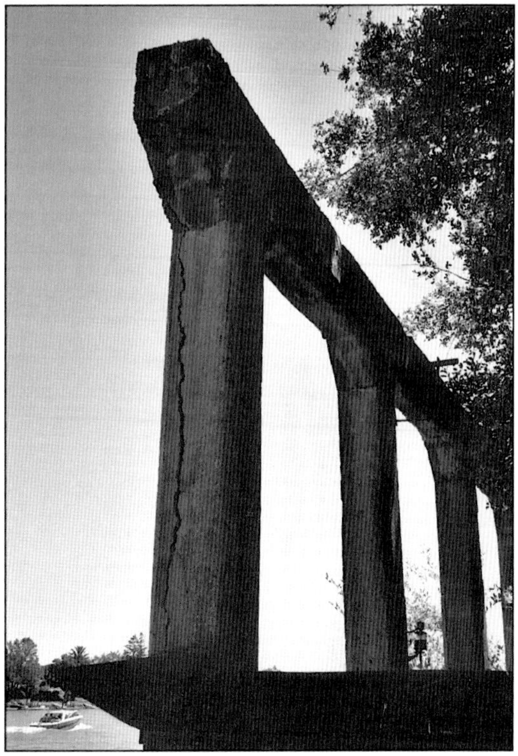

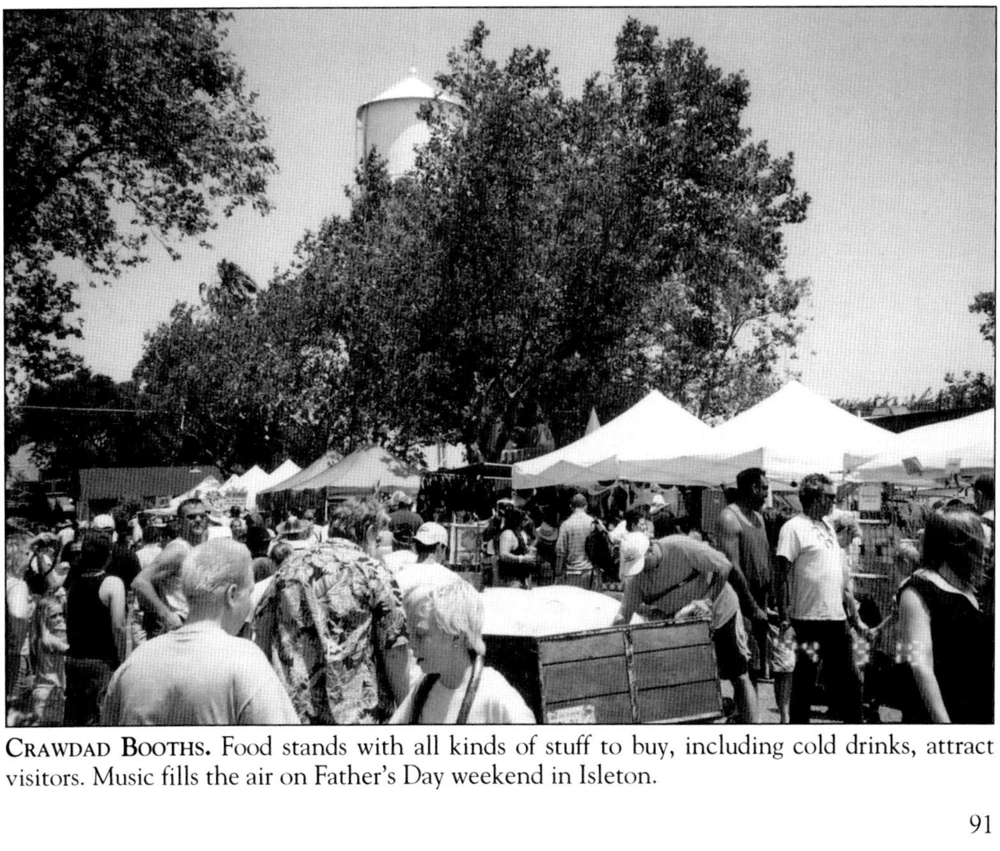

Crawdad Booths. Food stands with all kinds of stuff to buy, including cold drinks, attract visitors. Music fills the air on Father's Day weekend in Isleton.

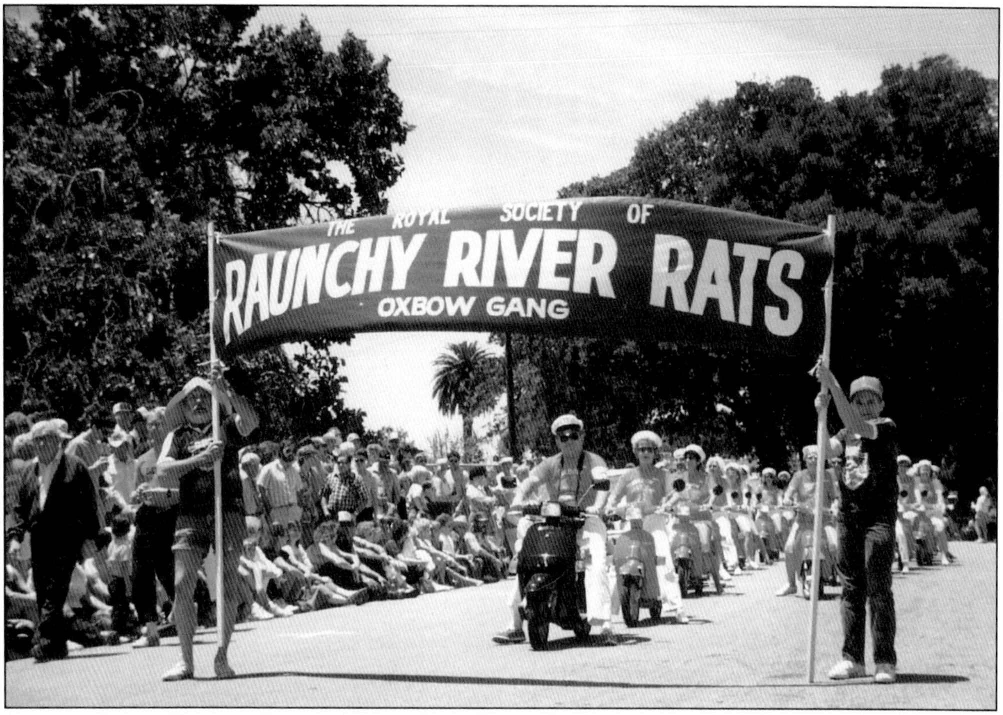

PARADE RIVER RATS. The residents of nearby Oxbow Marina joined the fun in 1988 with scooters. Their entry into this wonderful, fun party was appreciated by the large crowd.

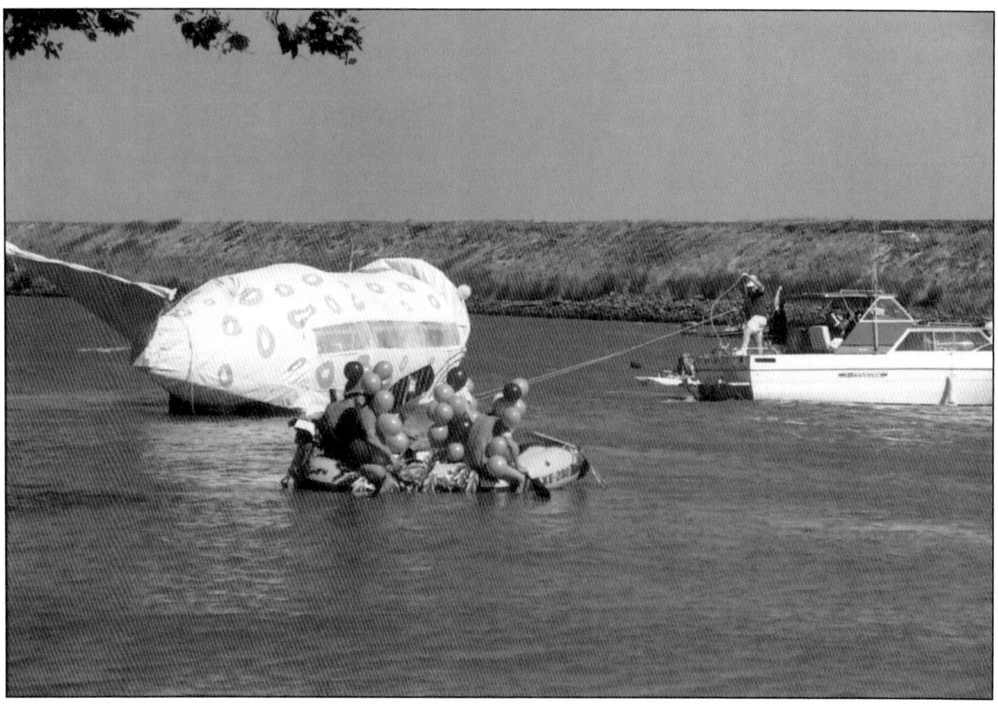

BALLOON BOAT PARADE. In the mid-1980s the Crawdad Festival featured crazy boat races and boat parades. Two of the more unusual are shown here from the 1988 festival.

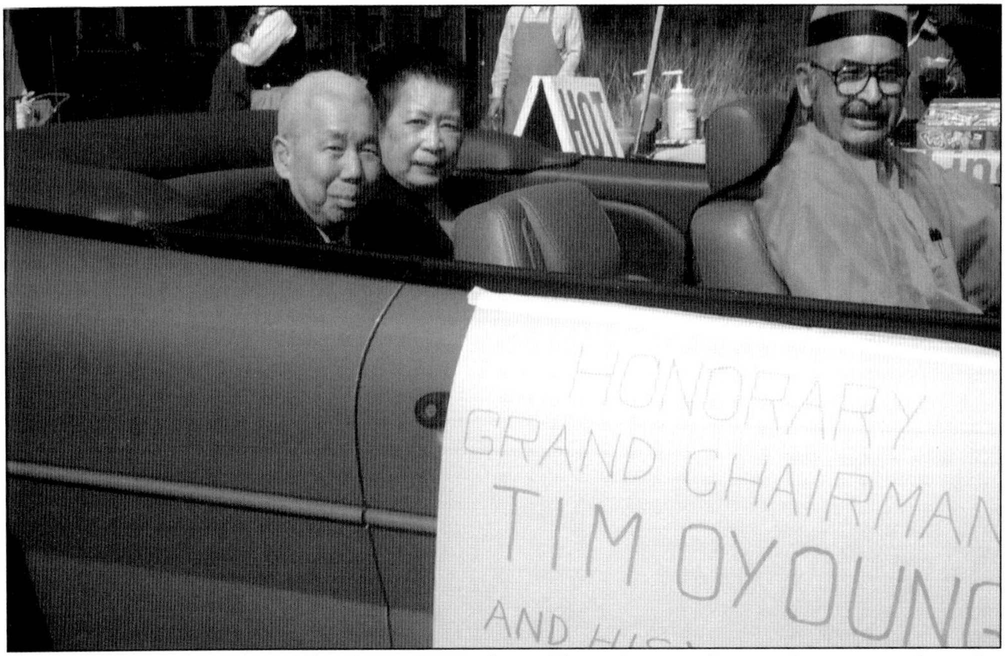

TIM OUYANG, CHAIRMAN. The Asian Festival would not be complete without a parade and a festival chairman. Here Mayor John Perez escorts Tim Oyoung and his wife June down Main Street to kick off the Asian New Year's Festival. Rickshaw rides, Asian dance groups, lion dancers, a dragon, firecrackers, and Taiko Drummers are all a part of the festival.

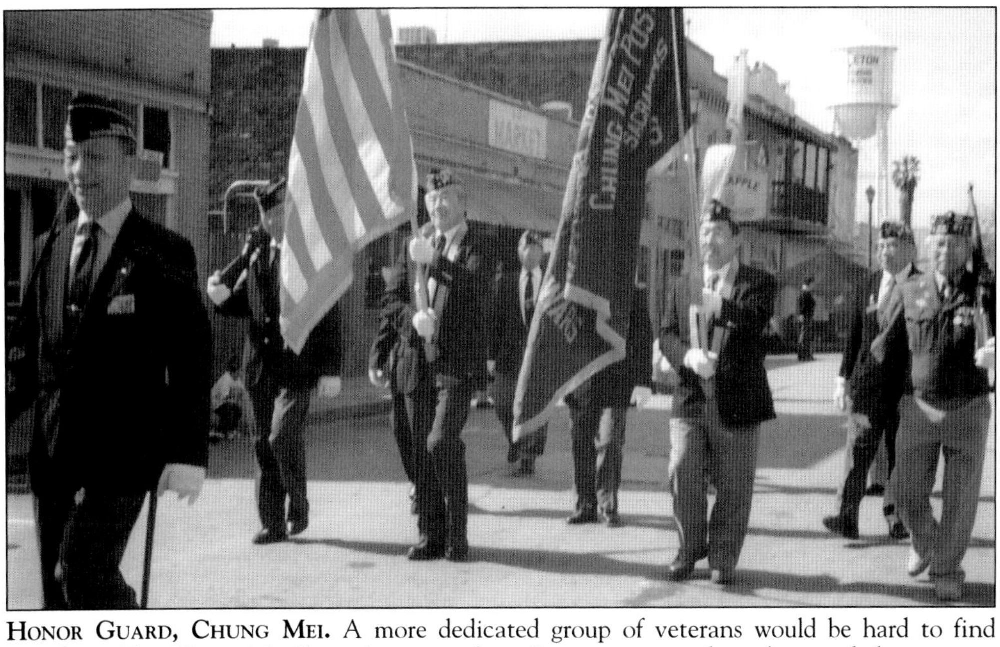

HONOR GUARD, CHUNG MEI. A more dedicated group of veterans would be hard to find anywhere. The Chung Mei Post of veterans from Sacramento are the color guard almost every year for the Asian festival. Many of these men fought in World War II. It is impossible not to notice the ribbons, old uniforms, antique rifles, and most of all, their pride. Some of these old warriors were born and raised in Isleton.

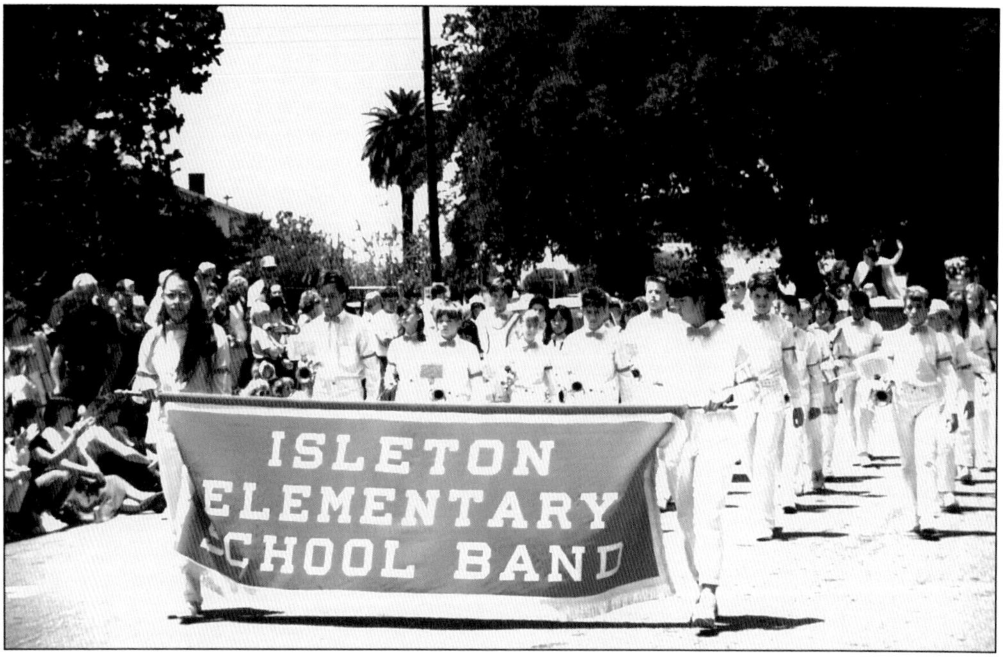

Isleton School Band. After the eighth grade, students from Isleton take the bus to nearby Rio Vista to attend high school. The citizens of Isleton are proud of their students. The band is dressed up and marching in the 1987 festival parade.

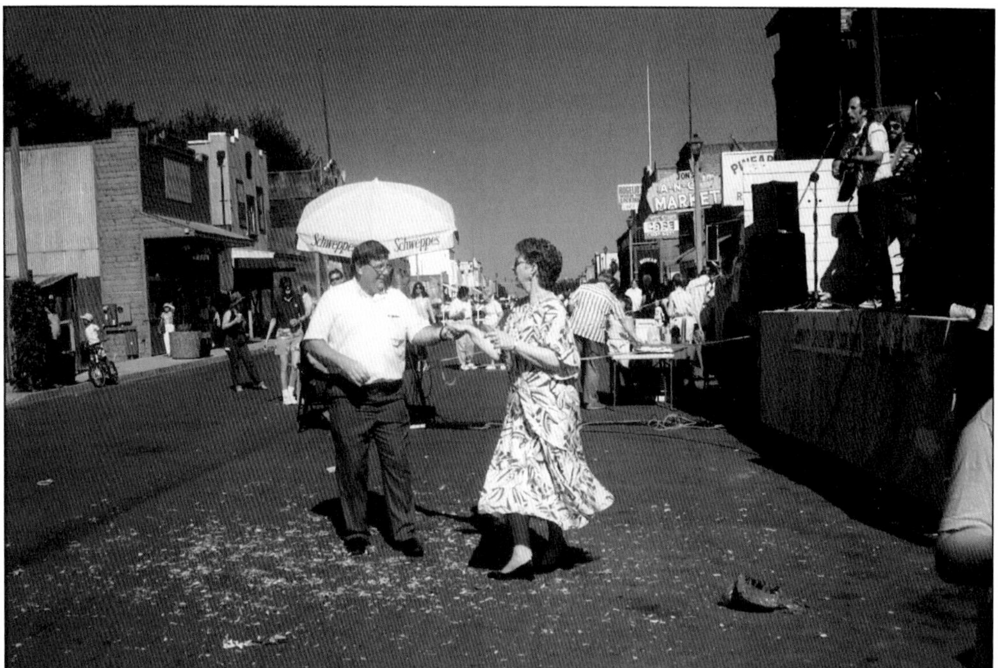

Apple Dance. Mayor George Apple and his wife Cheryl do the swing at the Asian Festival in 1988. The residue on the street under their feet must be firecracker paper left by the good luck dragon.

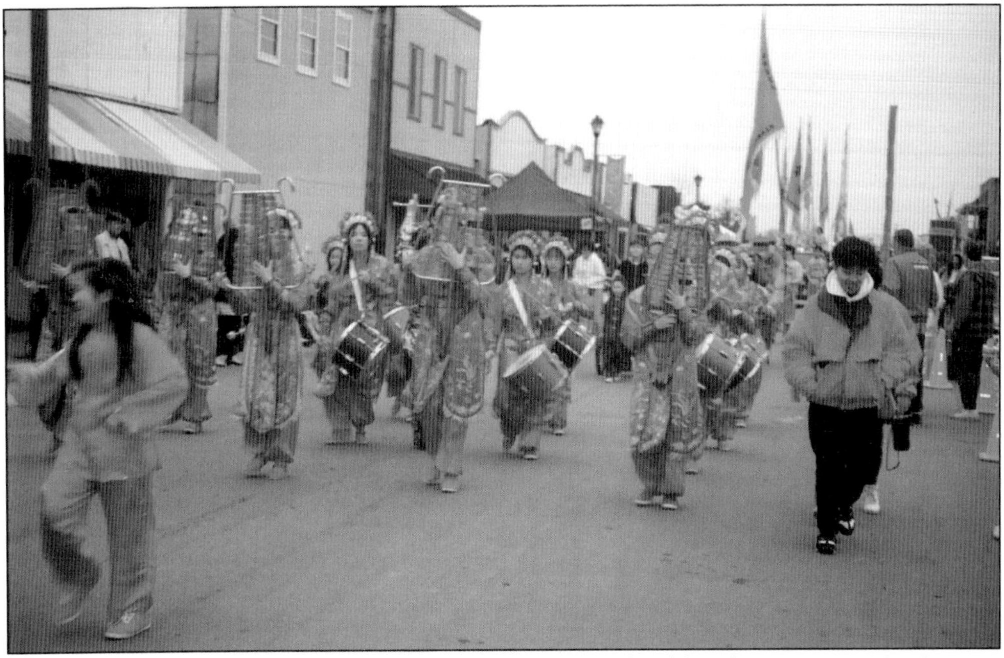

CHINESE GIRLS BAND. The St. Mary's Chinese Girls Bands adds color, music, and culture to the Asian Festival. This group is from San Francisco and helps to make the Asian New Year a festive occasion.

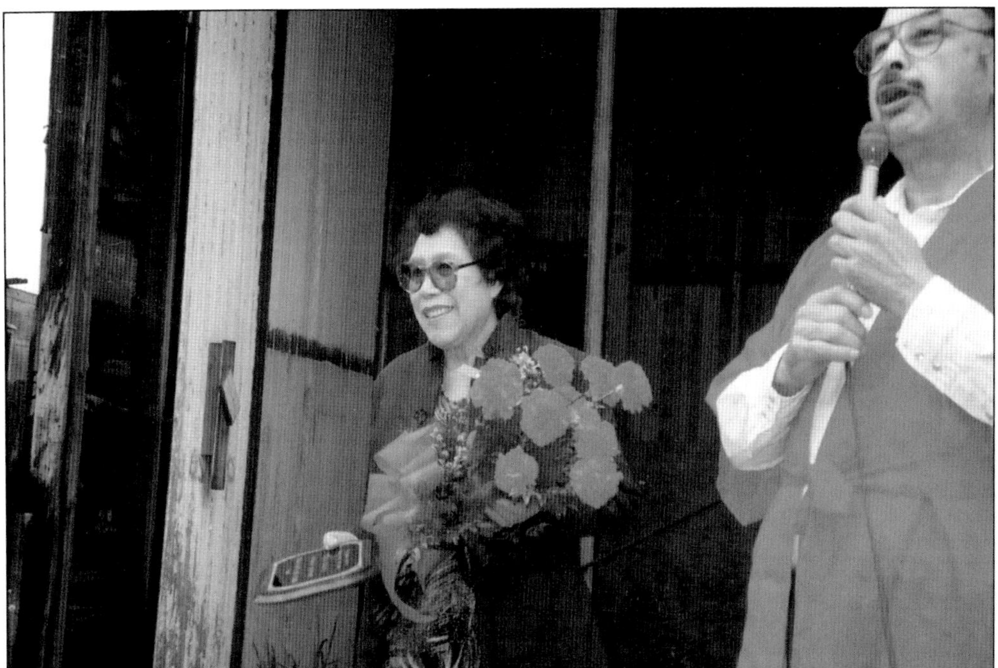

MARION WONG. Marian Wong, a longtime resident and avid community volunteer was honored as chair of the Asian New Year's Celebration in 1987. John Perez, president of the Main Street Merchants Association, is bestowing the honor.

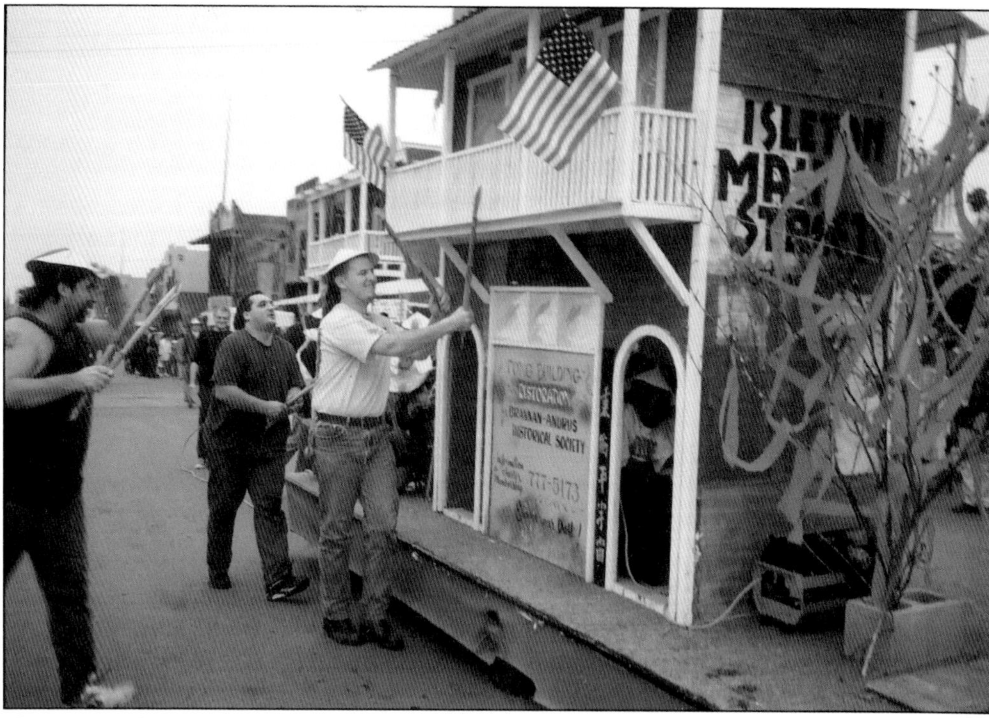

HISTORICAL SOCIETY FLOAT. A replica of the Tong Building is made into a float for the Asian New Year's parade.

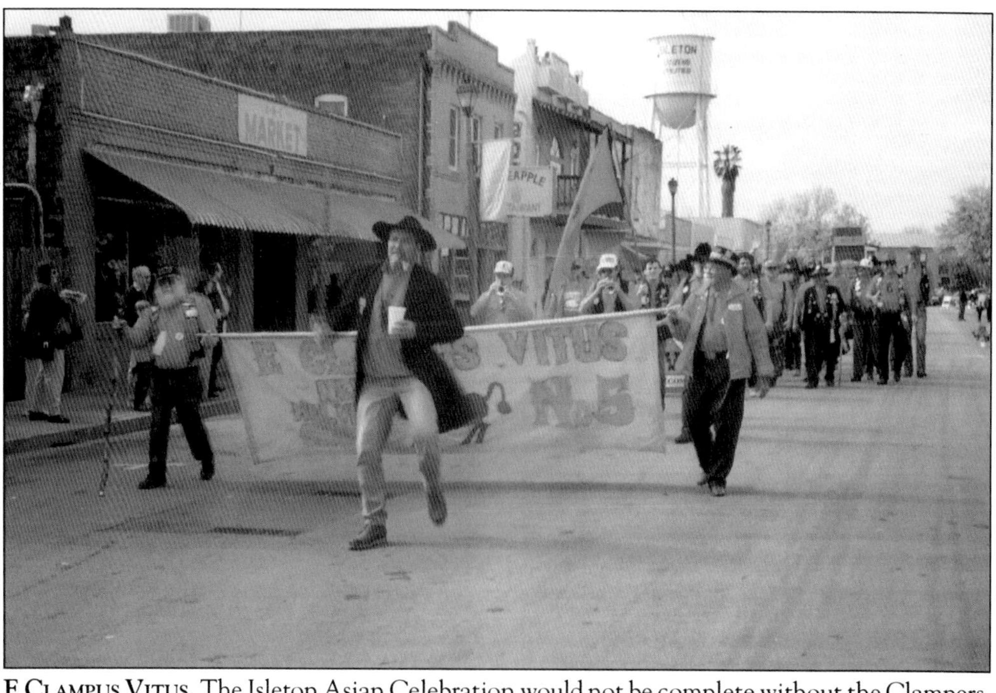

E CLAMPUS VITUS. The Isleton Asian Celebration would not be complete without the Clampers. History and celebration go together as these proud revelers initiate the proceedings and laugh their way to honor the Year of the Ram.

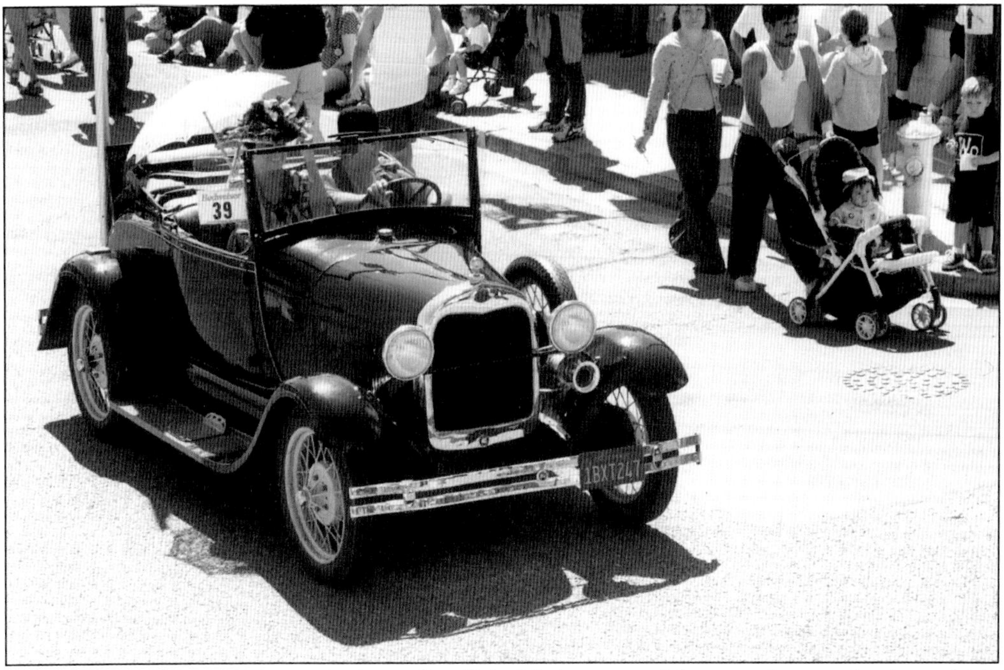

Old Car at Asian Parade. A classic Ford Model A convertible joins the parade. It wouldn't be a parade without one, and it wouldn't be a parade without a kid in a stroller to enjoy the celebration of the Year of the Tiger.

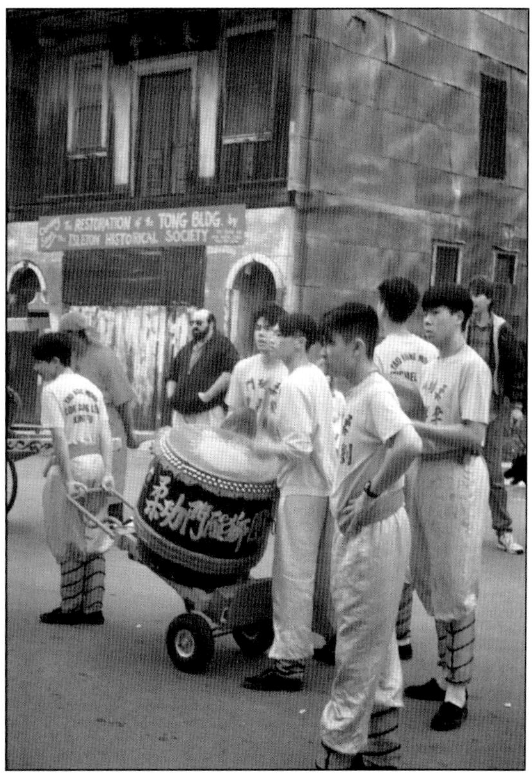

Taiko Drummers. The Taiko Drummers take a break during the Asian Festival. The building in the background is the Tong Building.

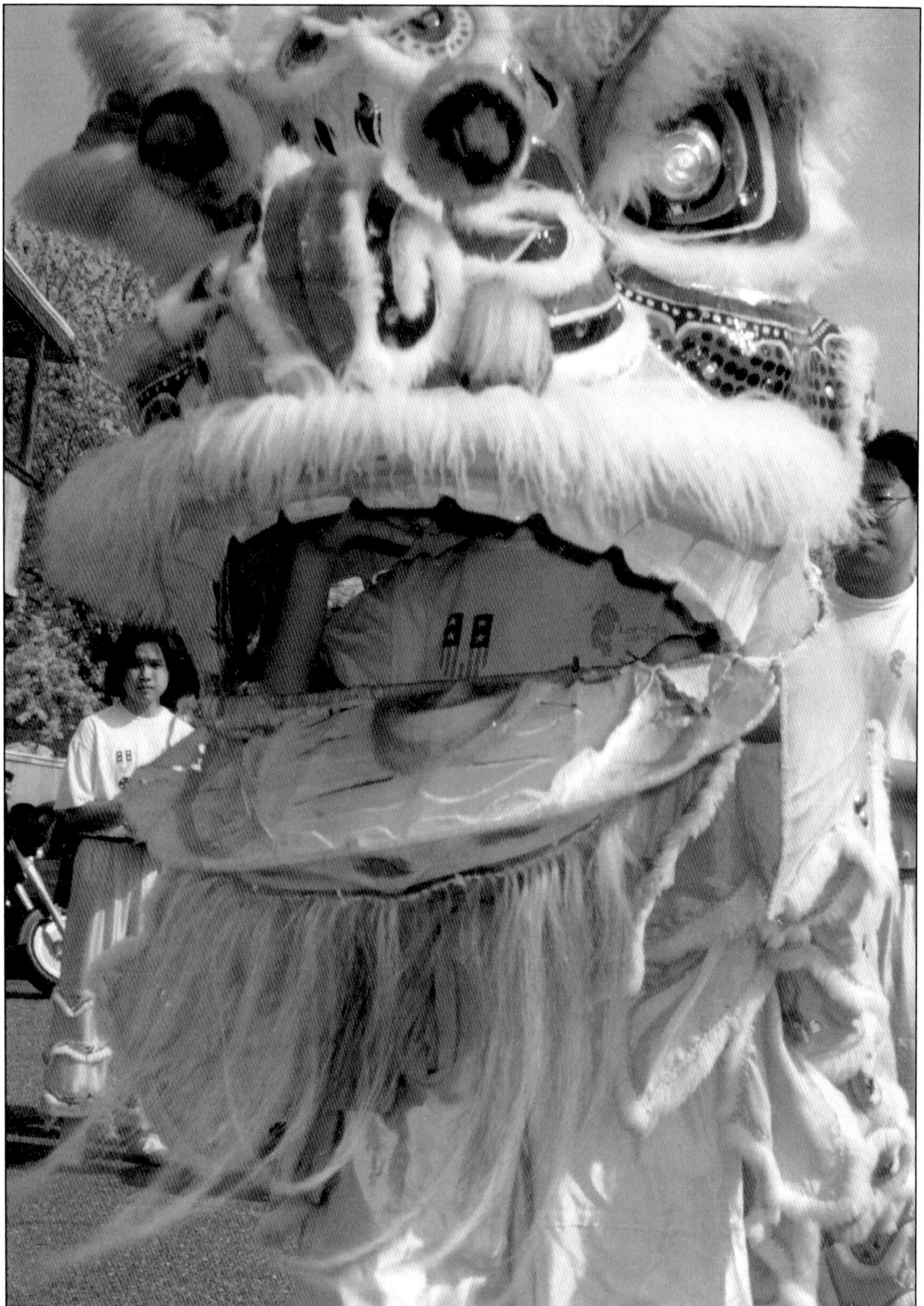

Lion Dancer. This dragon, seen here during the Chinese New Year parade, is looking for lettuce leaves. It is colorful, loud, and very busy.

Six

CRAWDADS AND TOURISTS

Since World War II, Isleton has been hit by some difficult times, but that might be a benefit. Most of the workers' children have gone to college and have settled elsewhere. Many of the businesses have closed leaving vacant buildings, and the rural setting is a reminder of a previous era. Movie companies come to Isleton often because it makes a perfect movie set for an "old town." Main Street doesn't have much activity anymore, and the city is in need of cash flow. Isleton is pretty quiet, except for the Crawdad Festival.

However, the values implanted 130 years ago still linger in the fabric of Isleton. Ideals of integrity, community, hard work, respect for nature and family, and perseverance were established here by Chinese immigrants and early pioneers. While the rapidly growing social order seems to have passed Isleton by, some urbanites are beginning to realize that these ideals are a prerequisite for developing a strong identity. Isleton might serve as a statement about where we should be.

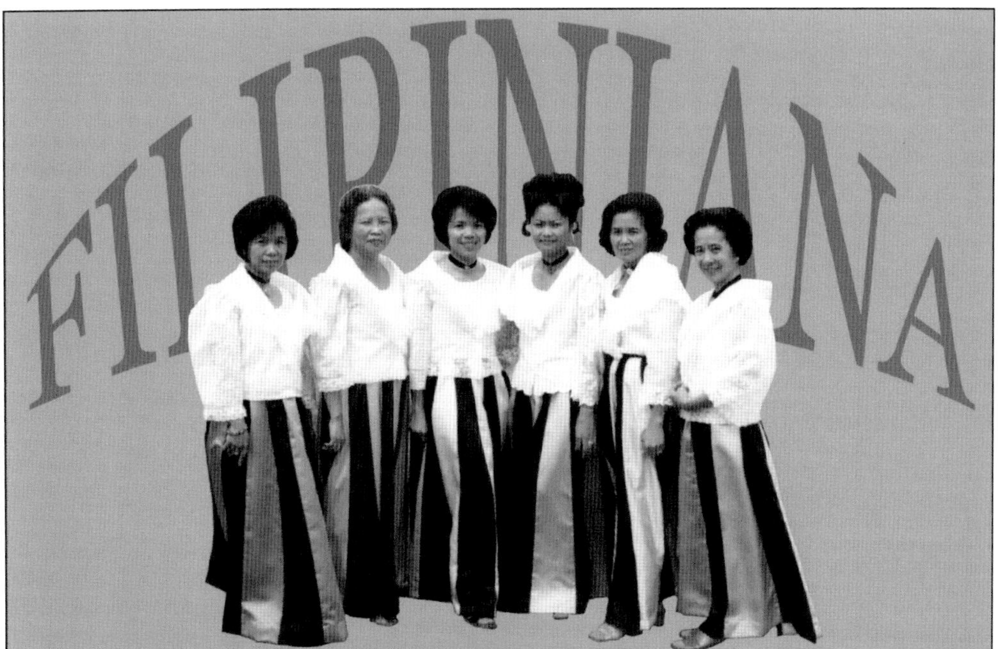

FILIPINO WOMEN POSTER. The Filipino community is a very strong and active part of Isleton. This culture has kept their own festivals and celebrations, and participates in the activities of the rest of the community. This group is posed to advertise a very important celebration.

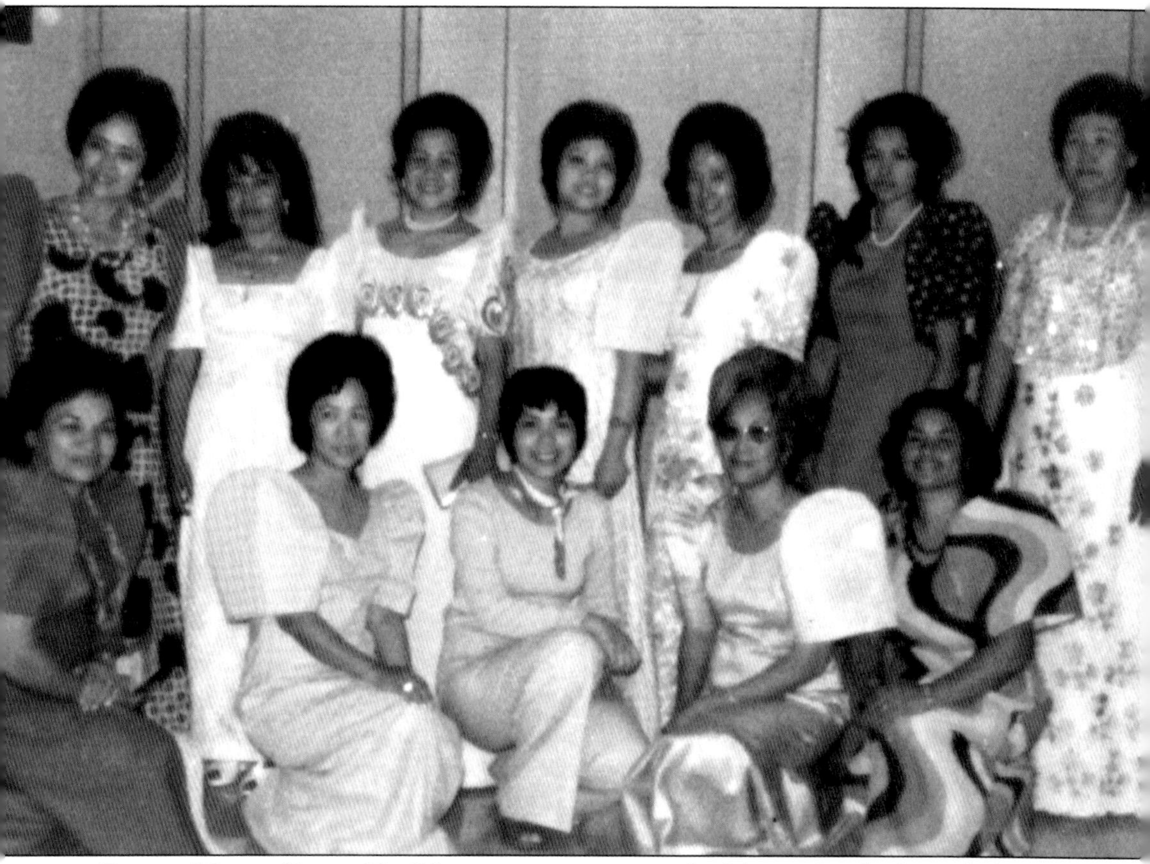

Filipino Women Group. The Filipino community started in Isleton after the Spanish-American War. By 1920 Filipinos were working in agriculture throughout California's Central Valley. In Stockton, Isleton, and Sacramento there are strong Filipino communities.

PINEAPPLE. Shown here is the chef known affectionately as Pineapple, who cooked for years at his Chinese restaurant on Main Street. His frenzy of cutting and whipping up his special dishes was admired throughout town. He was especially loved by children for his stories and friendship.

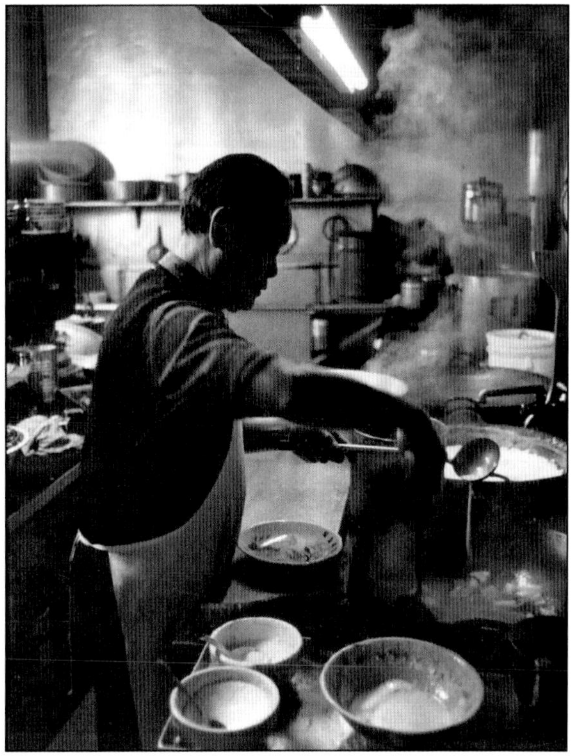

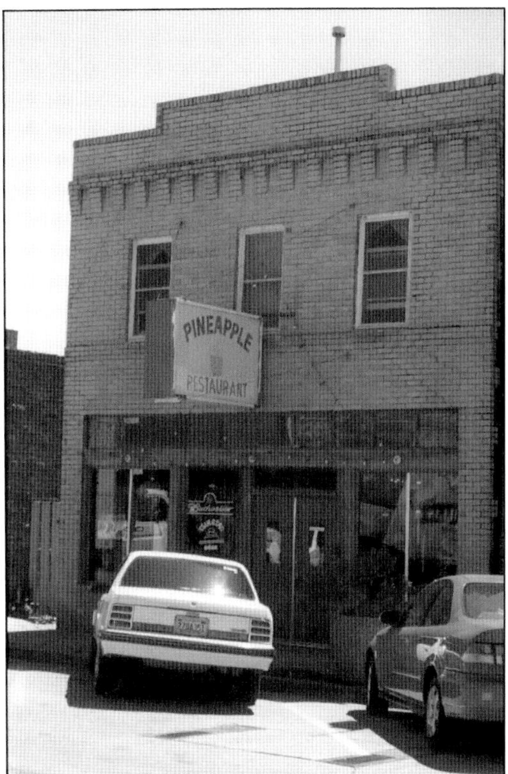

PINEAPPLE RESTAURANT. One of the attractions on Main Street is the Pineapple Restaurant. Still traditional food, it was originally operated by Kun Chang.

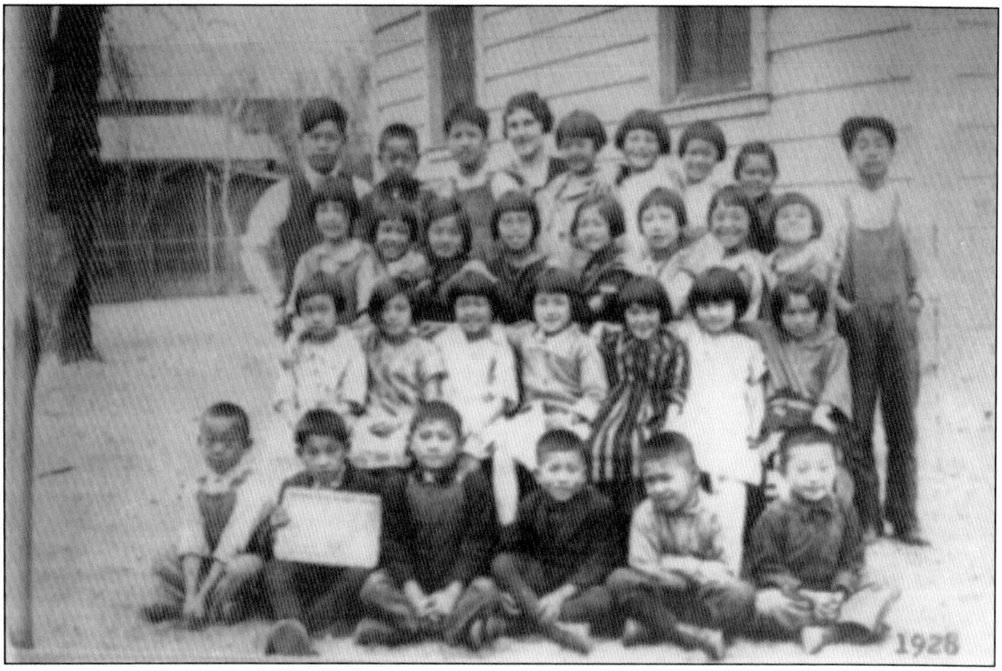

ASIAN SCHOOL, 1928. The students of the Asian school in 1928 were taught separately from the "white school." It was located on the same property but in a different building.

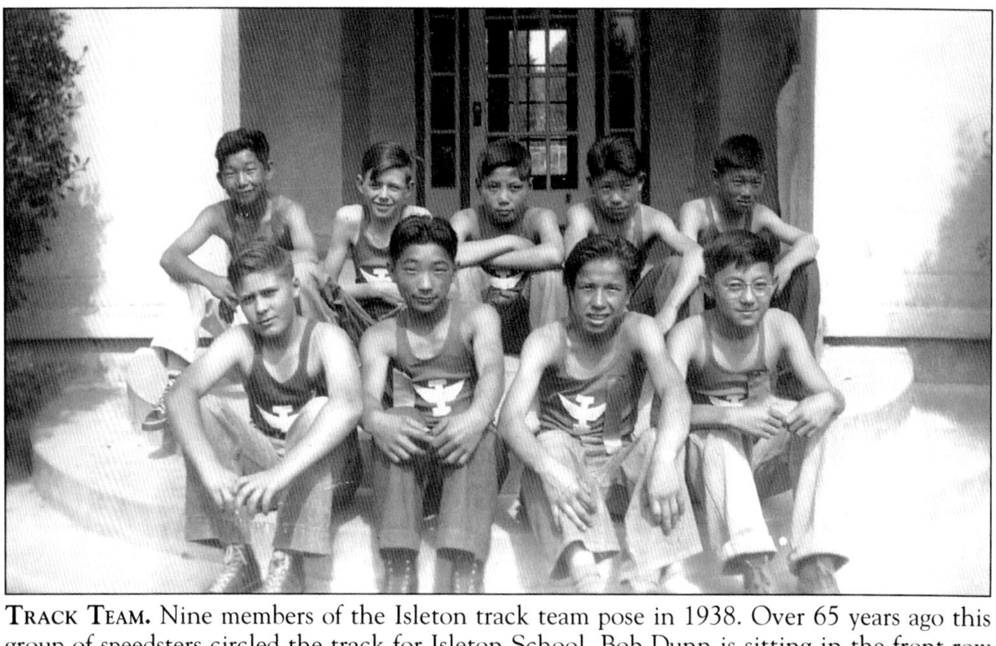

TRACK TEAM. Nine members of the Isleton track team pose in 1938. Over 65 years ago this group of speedsters circled the track for Isleton School. Bob Dunn is sitting in the front row on the far left.

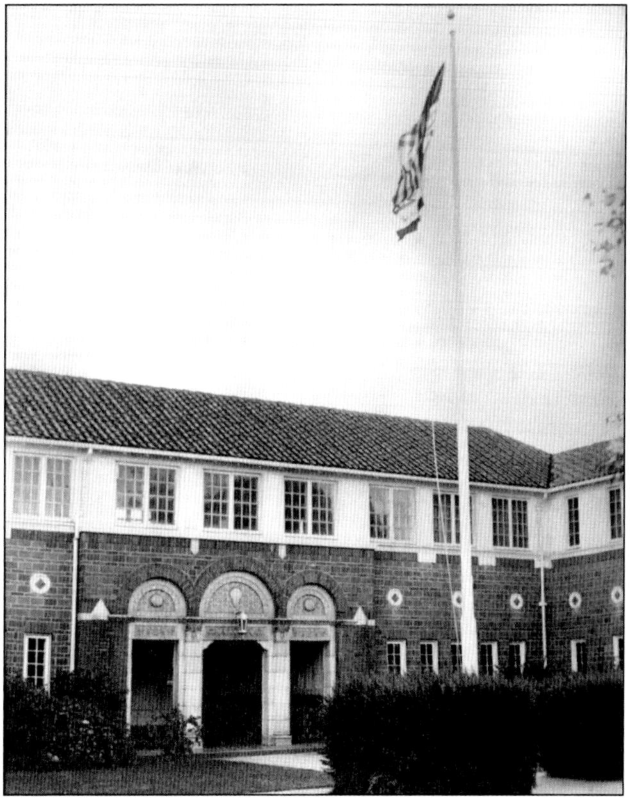

ISLETON SCHOOL. This beautiful school, Isleton Elementary, was a landmark and source of community pride. Unfortunately, it was not constructed to handle California earthquakes. The school was deemed to be seismically unfit and had to be demolished.

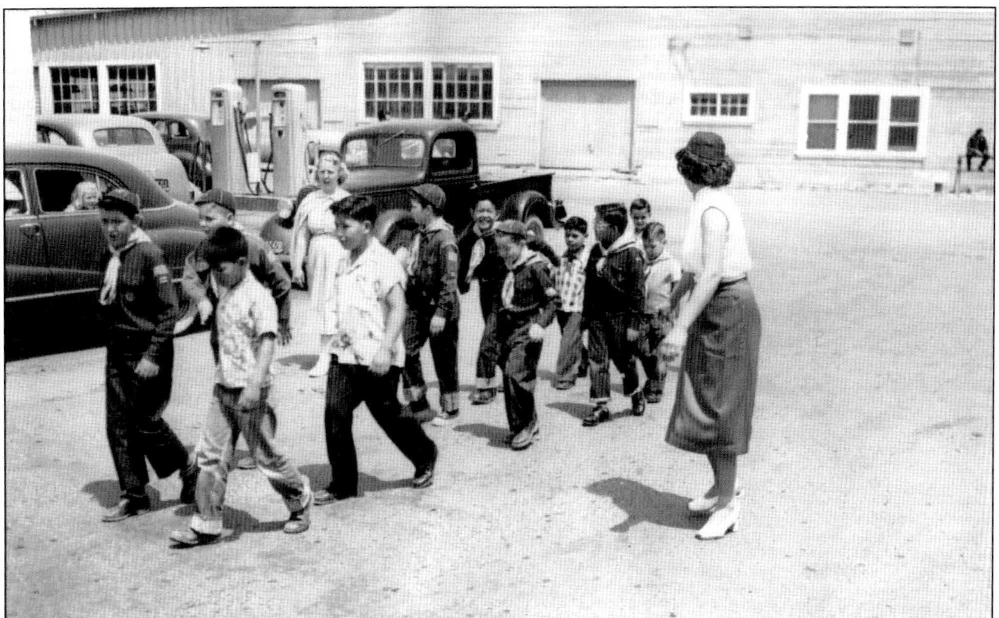

BOY SCOUTS, 1951. The Boy Scouts look like they are practicing for a parade, learning to march in step. Could they be rehearsing for the May Festival? This practice was held at the end of Main Street.

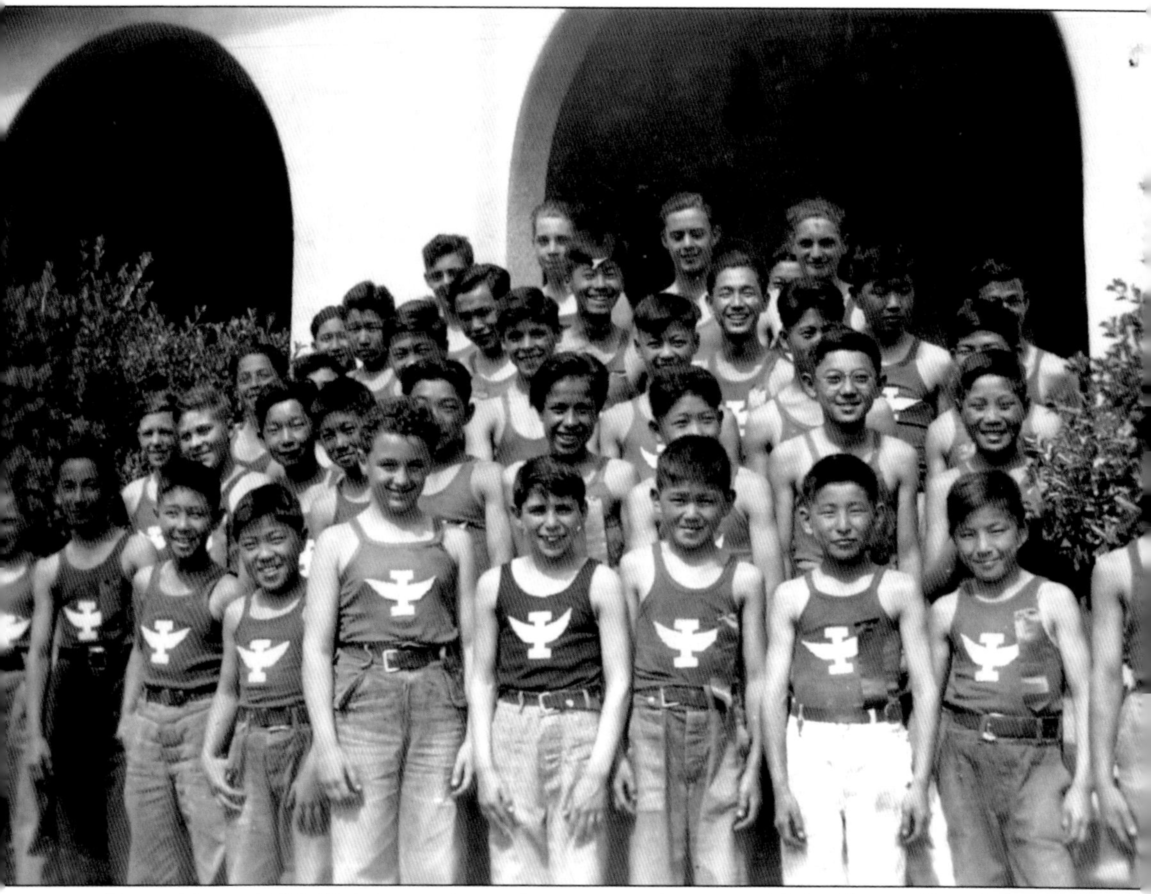

Track Team, 1938. This image shows the entire track team in 1938. Almost 40 students made the team that year. They got jerseys, but it looks like they had to wear jeans. Their meets were well attended and a source of community pride.

DELTA *KING* SMOKESTACK. The original *Delta King* smokestack sits on a levee in Isleton and is being used as a storage shed. When this famous ship was in physical and financial trouble parts of it were auctioned off. The smokestack came to Isleton where it still stands.

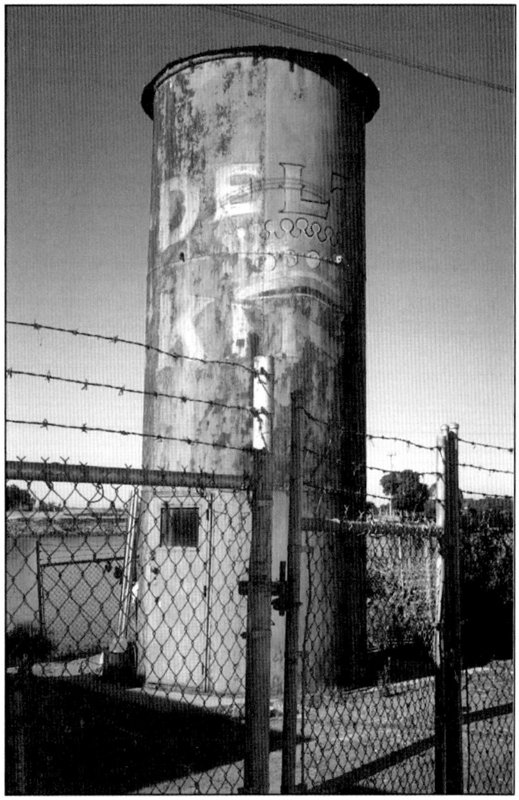

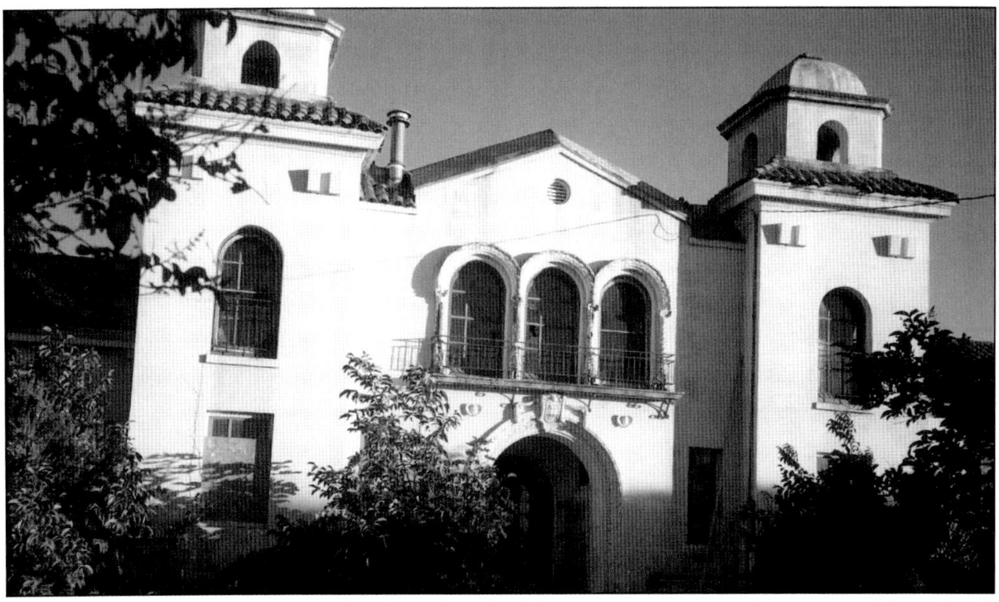

BEAVER UNION SCHOOL. Now abandoned and sold to private parties, this once public school, designed by William Weeks, was the pride of Grand Island. In the Spanish Colonial style it is a formidable statement about the depth of the culture that once existed here. Since the canneries have closed and small farms and farm labor have virtually disappeared, the few children on Grand Island go to school in the River Delta District.

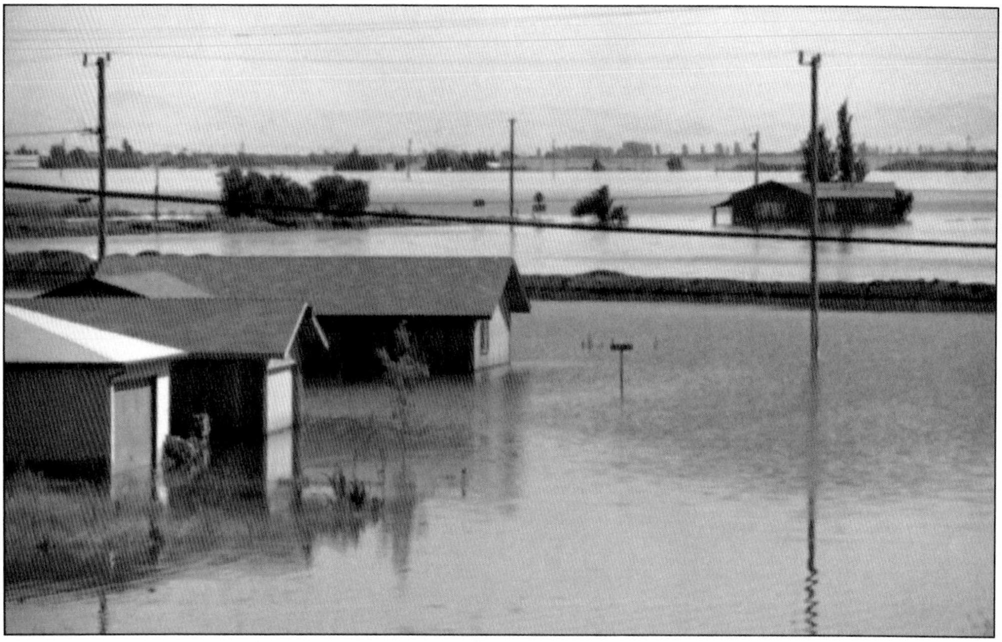

The Flood of 1972. On June 21, 1972, the levee broke on the southern end of Andrus Island, dumping 58 billion gallons of water onto Andrus and Brannan Islands. The flood closed 16 resorts. Although much of the City of Isleton is on high ground and was not heavily hit by the flood waters, the sewage and water systems were flooded and closed down. The people of Isleton proved how strong they were, and when the water was finally pumped out, some eight months later, they began rebuilding.

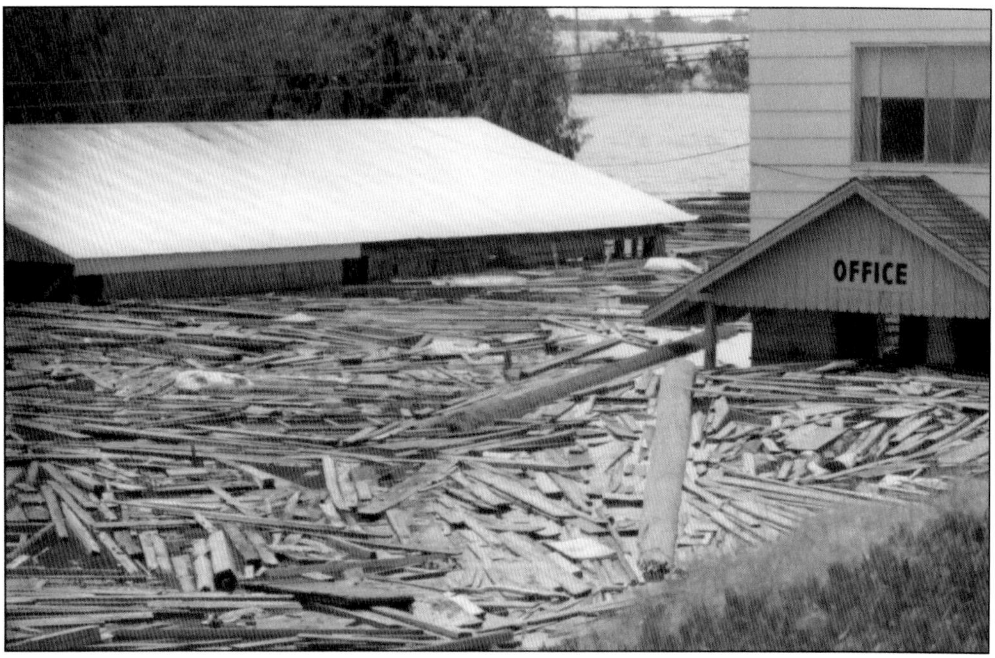

Flooded Loop. One of the hardest hit areas by the 1972 flood was the Marina Loop area. Many of them were damaged severely because of their elevation and proximity to the levee break.

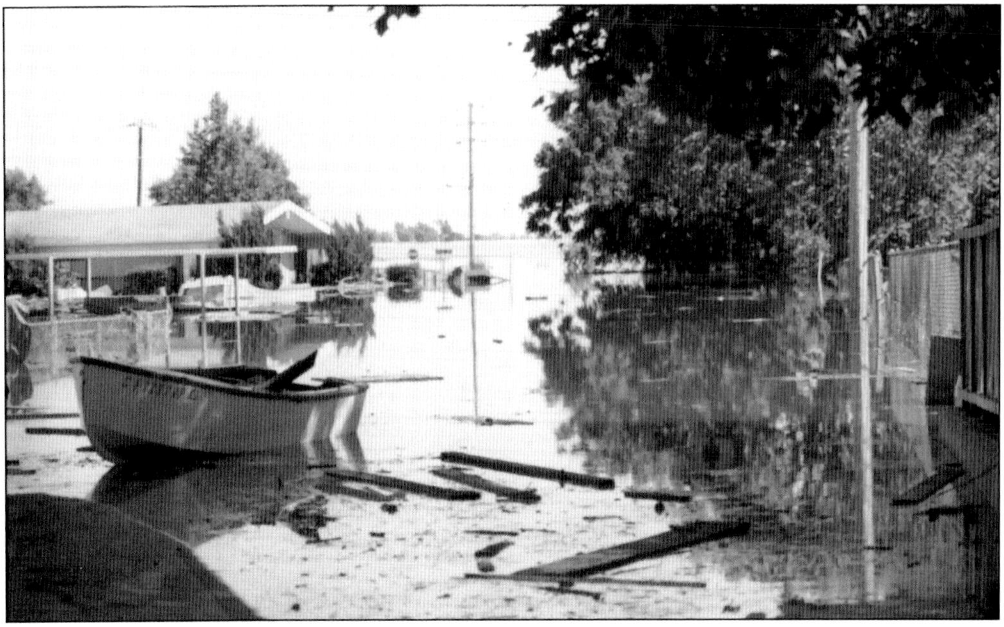

Flooded School. The Isleton Elementary School was hard hit by the 1972 flood. Some classrooms were badly damaged and teachers had to double up their classes. Urban Gasperi, a senior teacher, remembers coordinating his spelling bee with the teacher he was sharing the room with: first one teacher's word, then the other.

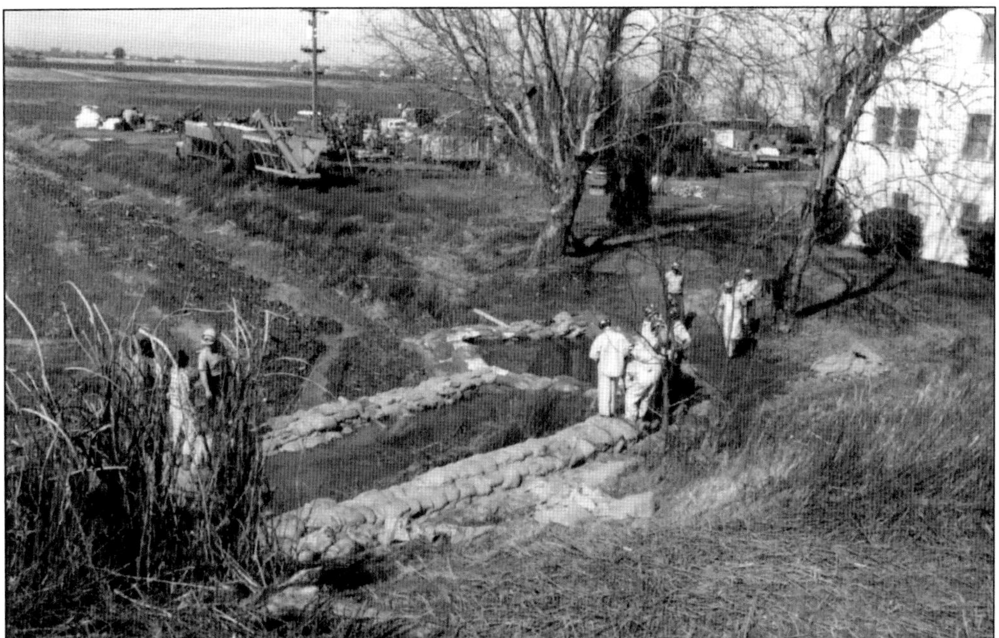

Boil in Field. When the river rises the volunteer firemen watch the levees for boils. These are areas where the strong hydraulic pressure of the river emerges onto the land on the other side of the levee. Here a boil is dealt with to keep it from spreading and doing more damage. Constant vigilance is necessary during these high river times.

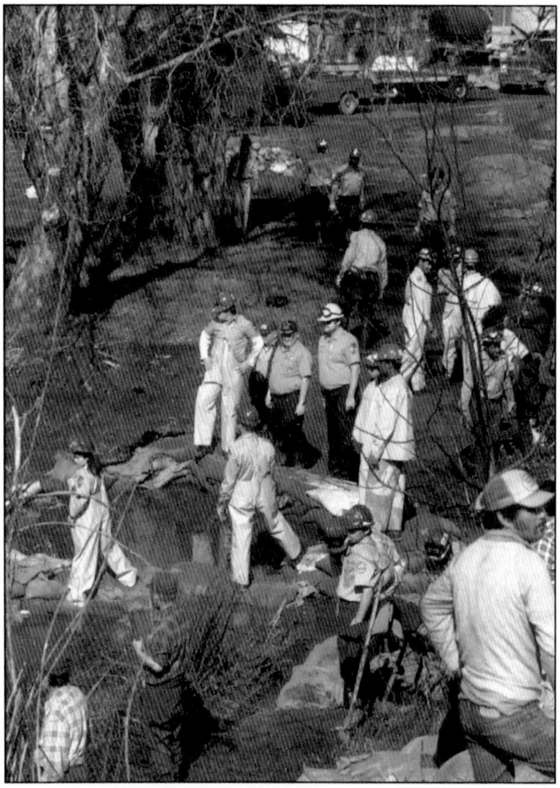

Boil with Workers. This boil has created quite a stir. Anxious volunteers carefully watch the surrounding area for more of these. A break in the levee would be disaster. Hard hats are required, and rain suits indicate a big storm.

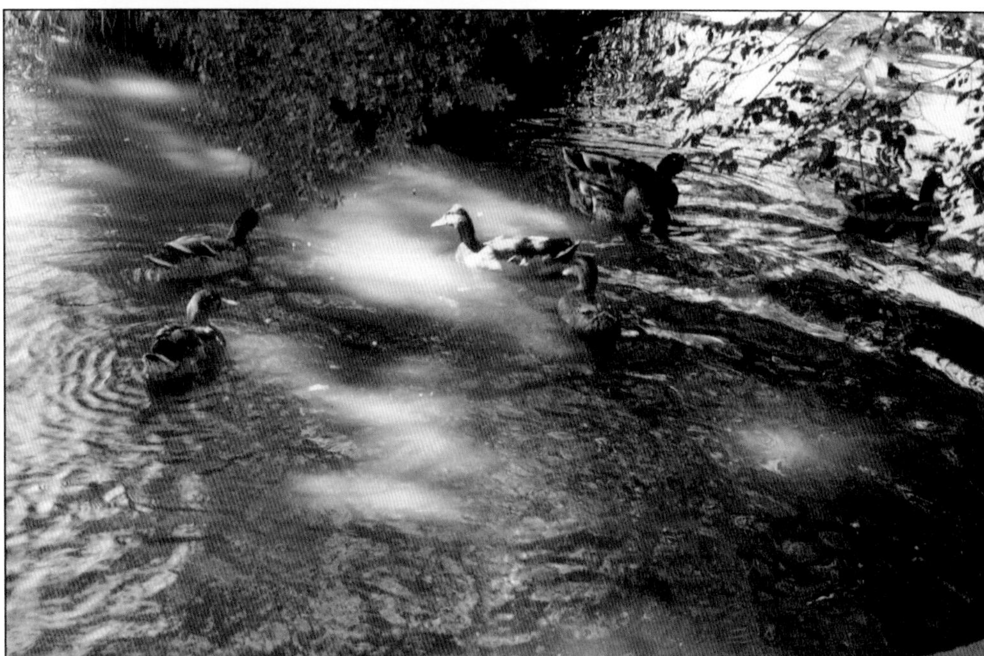

Ducks on the Water. Duck and fish are not all that is found in the river. Beaver, muskrat, and large amounts of shellfish attract those with a license. The environment and habitat have changed significantly with reclamation, trapping, and hunting.

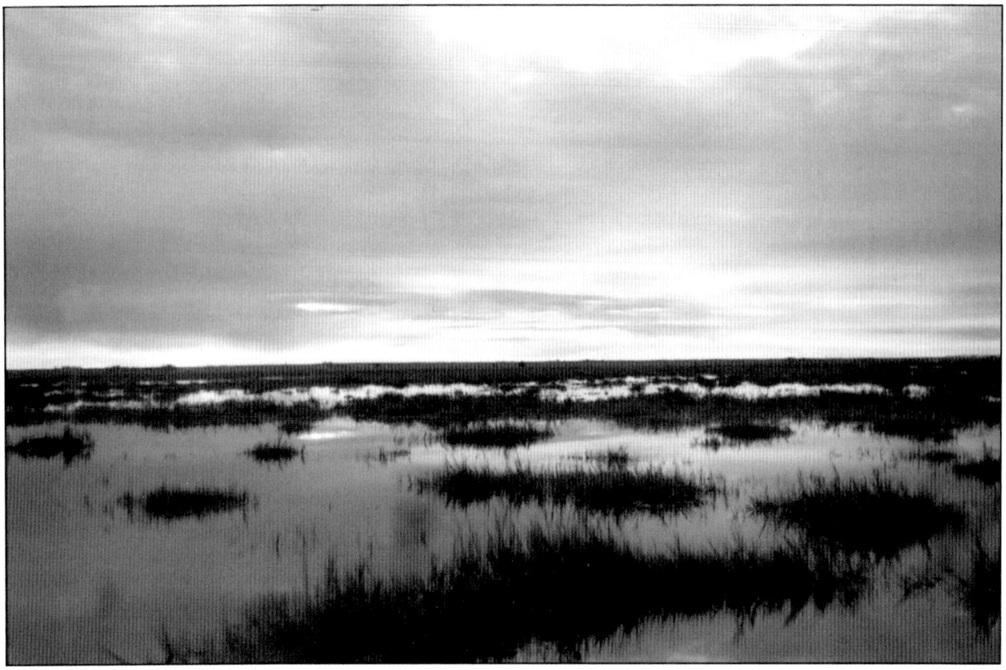

MARSHLAND HUNTING. In the fall the marshlands flood and ducks and geese interrupt their journey to enjoy the rich feeding lands of the Delta. Thousands of flying birds blacken the sky and feed in the fallow grain and corn fields. The morning sun gives a little light to hunters who wait for the birds to land.

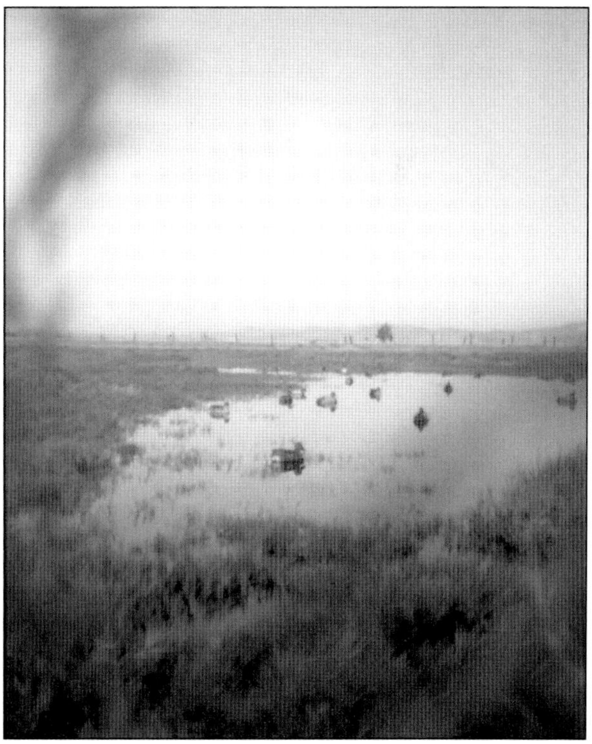

DUCKS IN SUNLIGHT. With the sun peering through the fog, the ducks have landed and the hunters enjoy a beautiful sight.

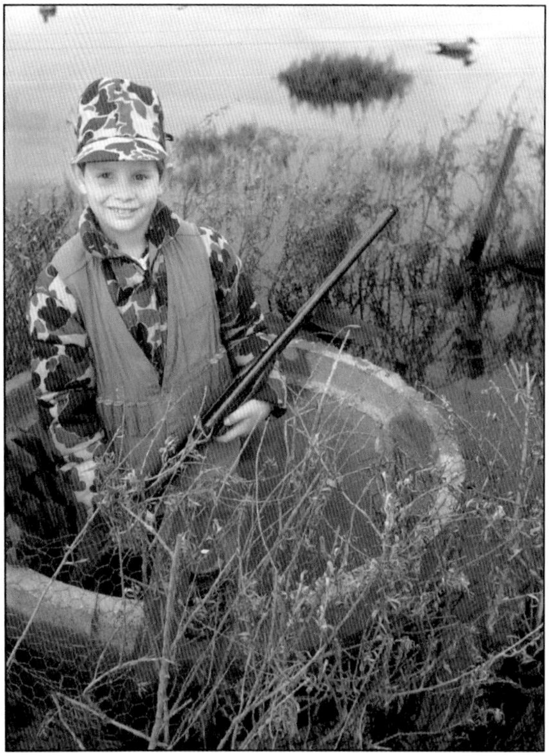

HUNTER HOOT. This young man, Hoot Apple, is getting a few lessons from his dad. The decoy behind him doesn't seem to be getting much action.

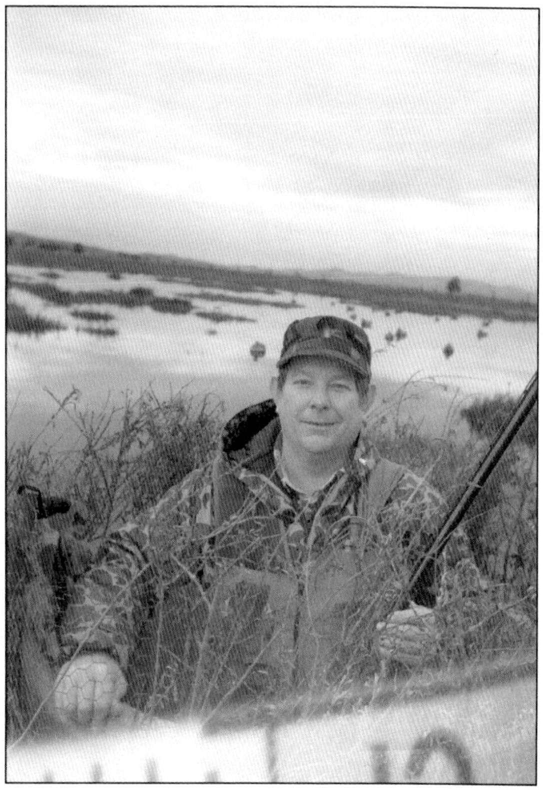

HUNTER GEORGE. Here is Hoot's father, George, with the hat, shotgun, decoys, and camouflage suit. He's looking forward to getting his limit of ducks and then a big dinner.

Max with Fish. This proud fisherman, Max David, caught these two on the river in 1941. He said it was a good day and that his family ate well.

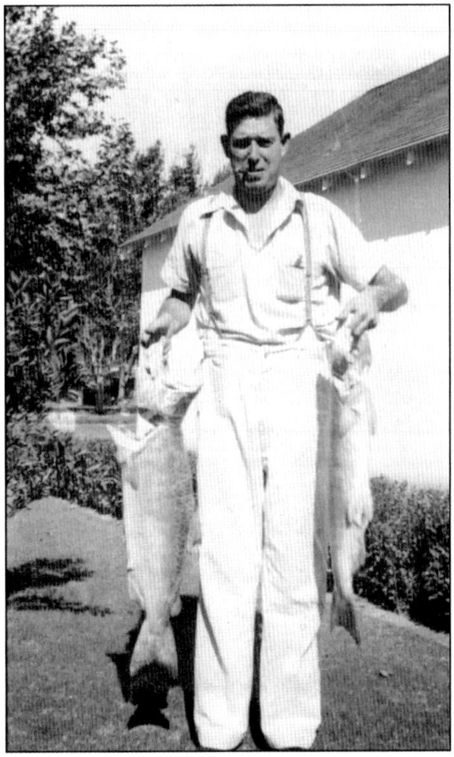

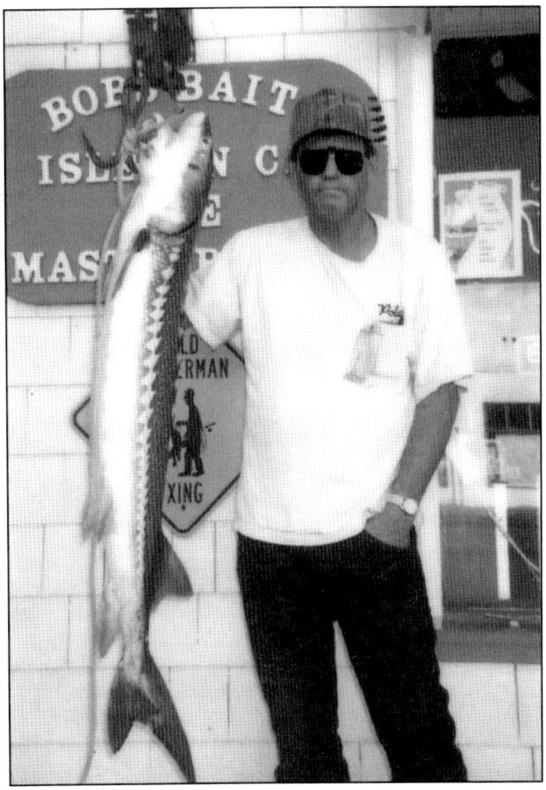

Larry with Sturgeon. A nice sturgeon was caught by Larry Tigert, a local fisherman, using grass shrimp in Cache Slough. The sturgeon weighed in at 35 pounds.

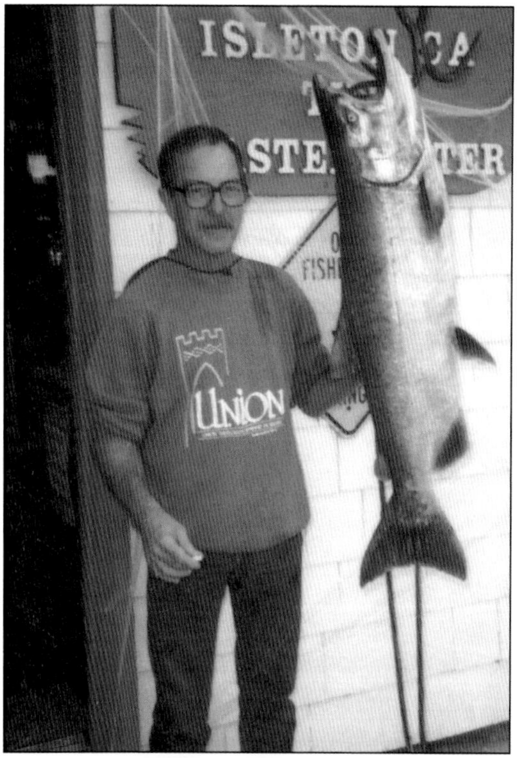

King Salmon. The chief recreation for locals in Isleton is fishing. Dave Blair caught this 30-pounder while trolling in October of 1999. This catch is representative of the pictures taken at Bobs Bait Shop in downtown Isleton.

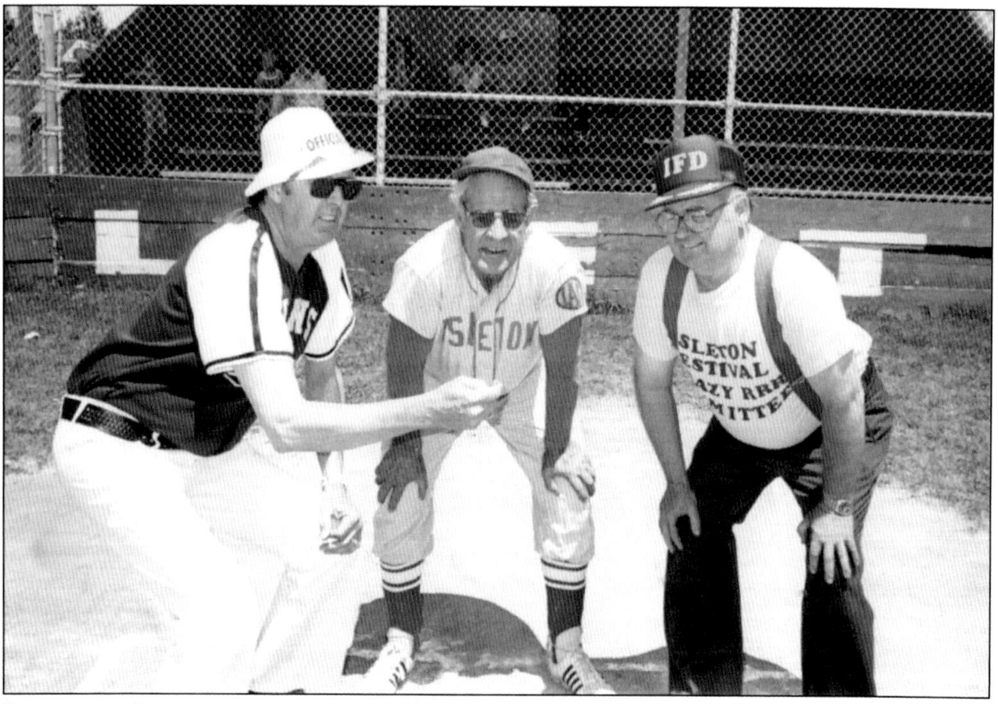

Bob Dunn Flips. Community spirit abounds at Wilson Park in Isleton. The firemen have challenged the policemen to a ball game, and Bob Dunn is flipping the coin. Cecil Tomlin, on the right, represents the fire department while Johnny Golden is the captain of the police team.

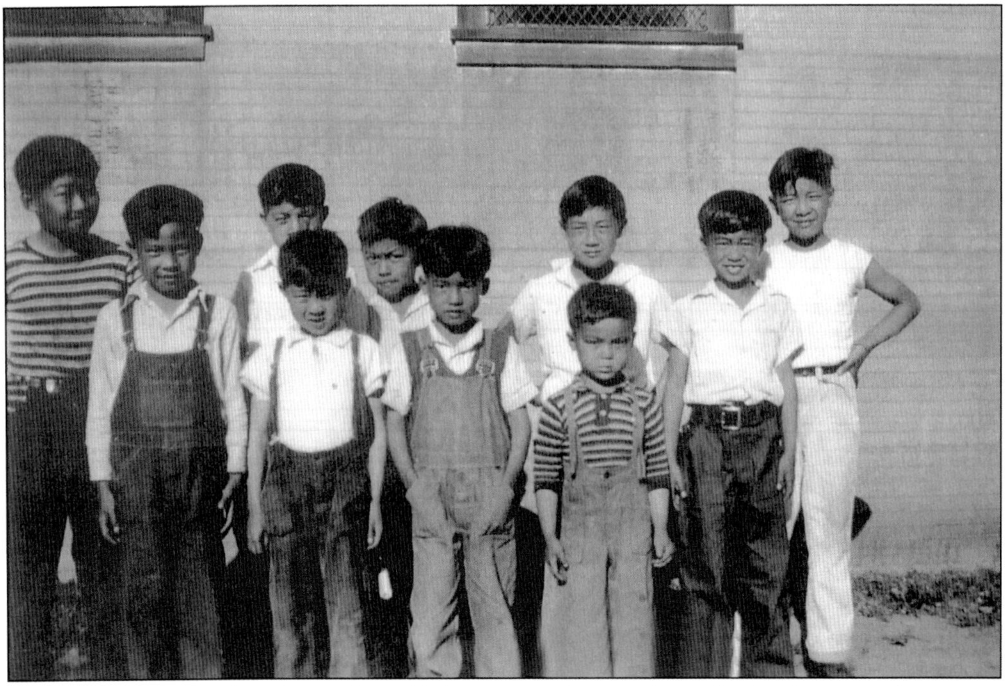

BOY'S CLUB, 1941. The Isleton Boy's Club was a good way to keep the local pre-teen boys busy. Aside from the regular activities, there were summer camps, basketball at the lot next to the Tong Building, fishing trips, and meetings with nearby community Boy's Clubs.

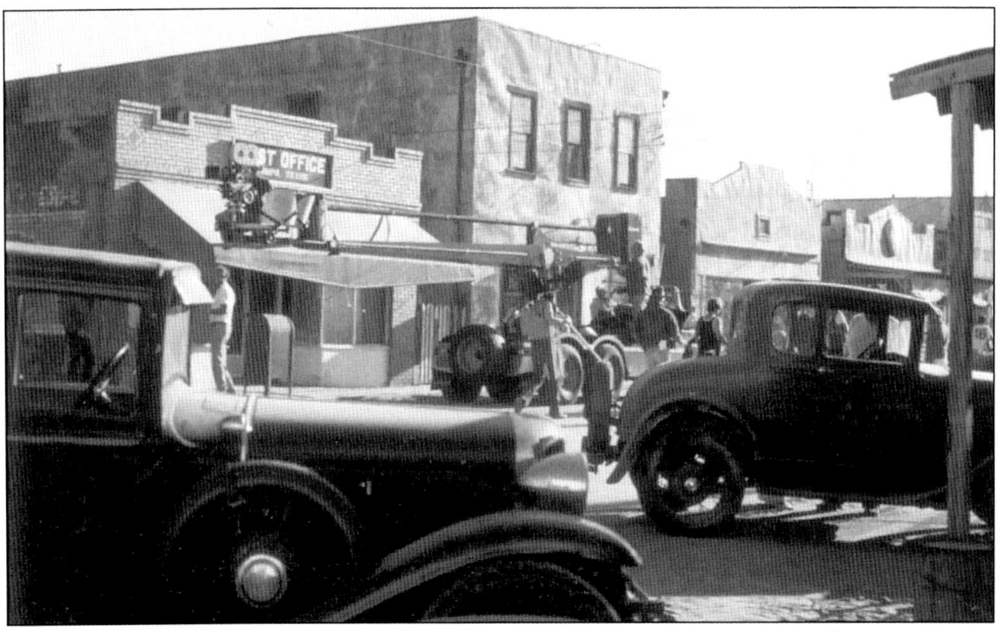

WOODY GUTHRIE. The movie, *Bound for Glory*, was made in Isleton. Main Street, with the old buildings and street covered with dirt, made a perfect set. The story of Woody Guthrie, and his move from the Dust Bowl to California, was filmed in Isleton with only a few changes in the old downtown.

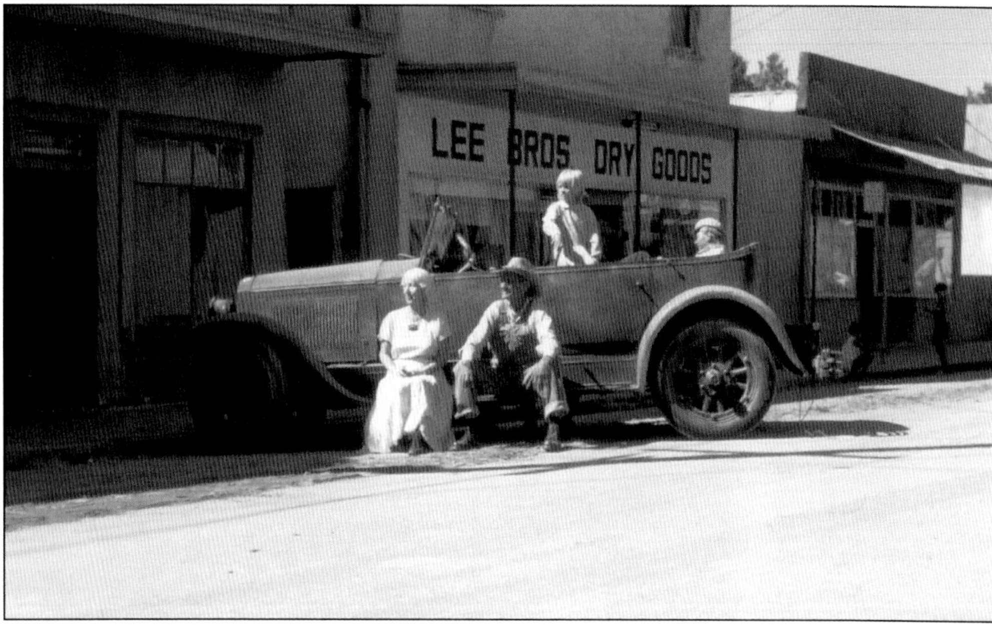

Bound for Glory Car. This car was one of the props in the movie. Main Street was filled with Hollywood stars, lights, and props for over a week.

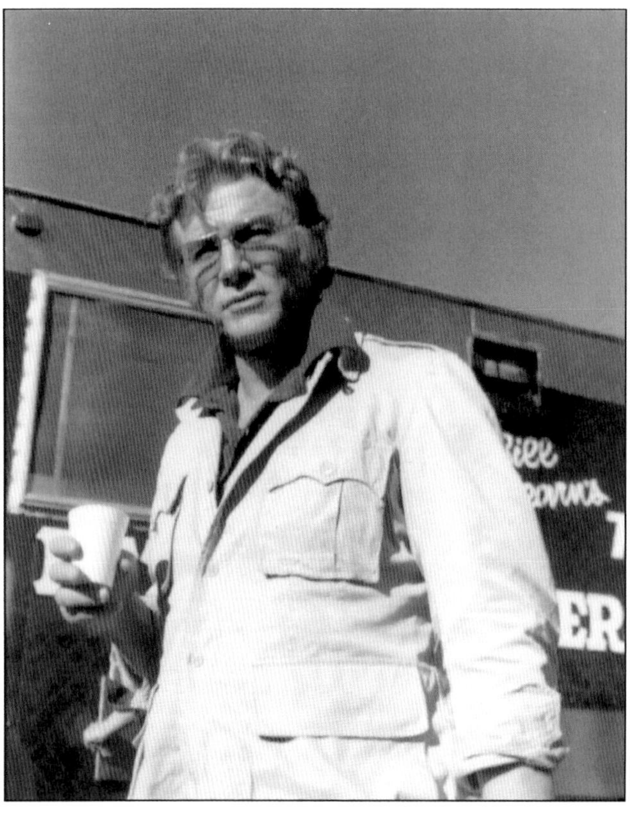

Movie, *Tiger Walk*. Steve Forrester played the title role in *Tiger Walk*. He is seen here taking a break from the action of his work on the movie set.

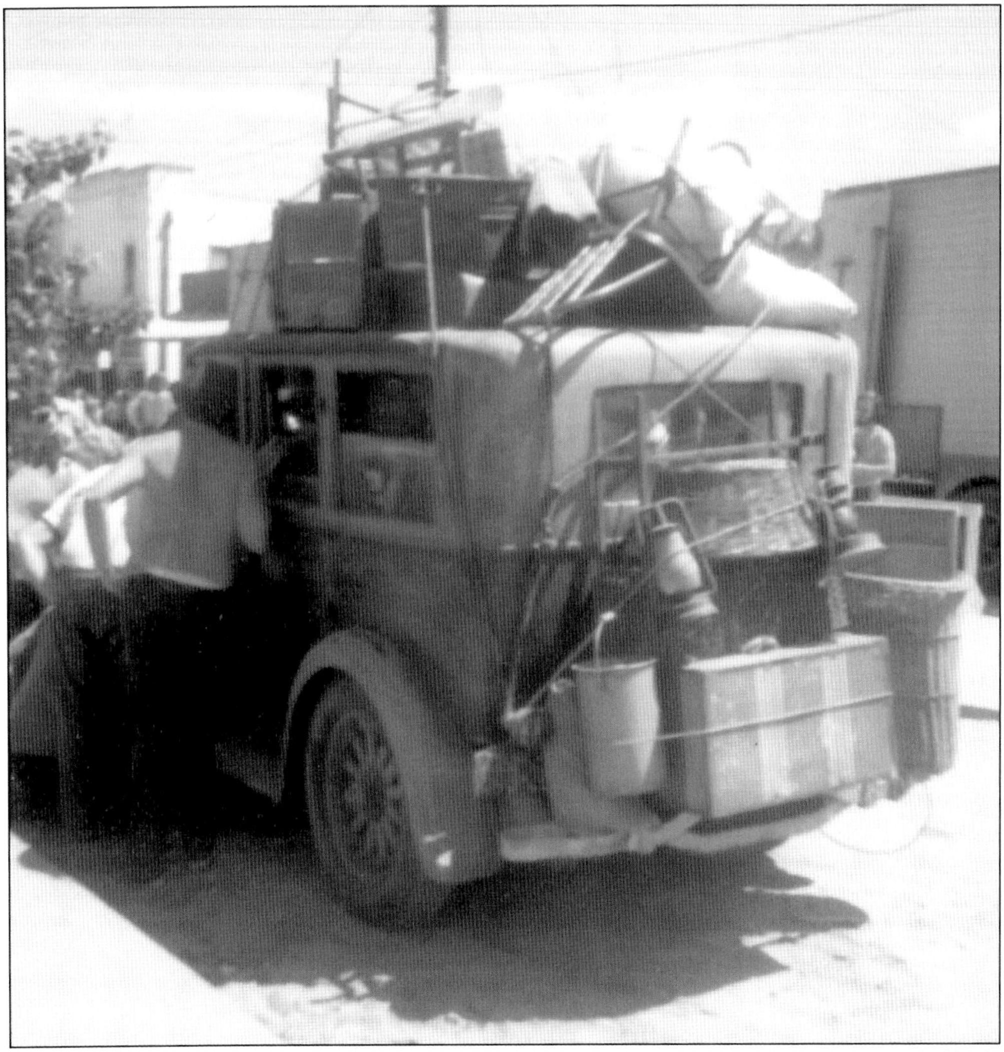

BOUND FOR GLORY CAR. Woody Guthrie (played by David Carradine) and his old car, piled high with all his family possessed, are on their way to escape the dust storms on the Great Plains.

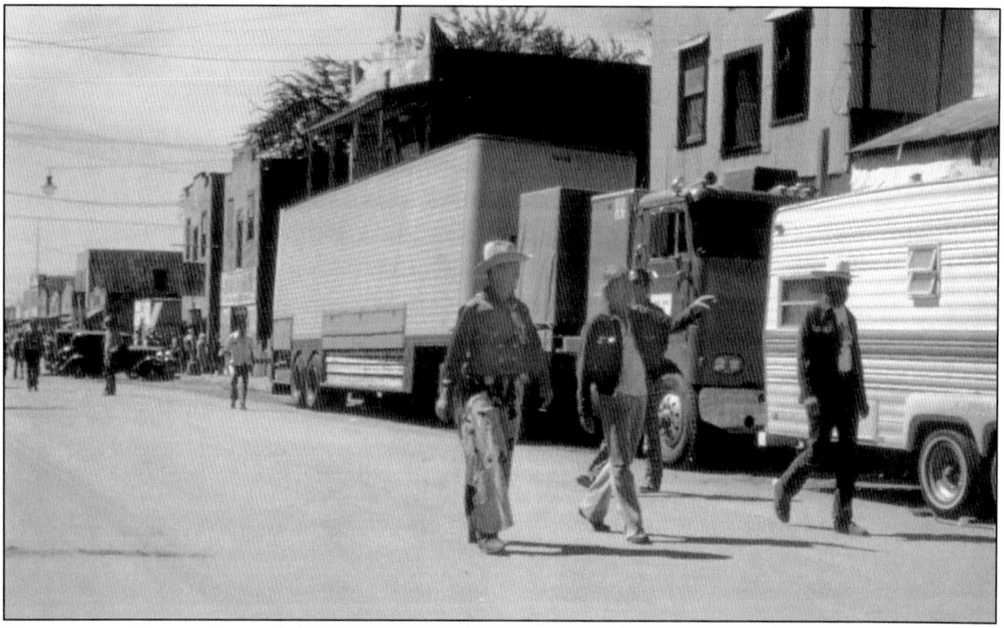

Bound for Glory. Several different movies have been made in Isleton. The river and old store fronts have been used in *Treasure Island* and *Bound for Glory*, the Woody Guthrie story. Mickey Rooney was a star here many years ago.

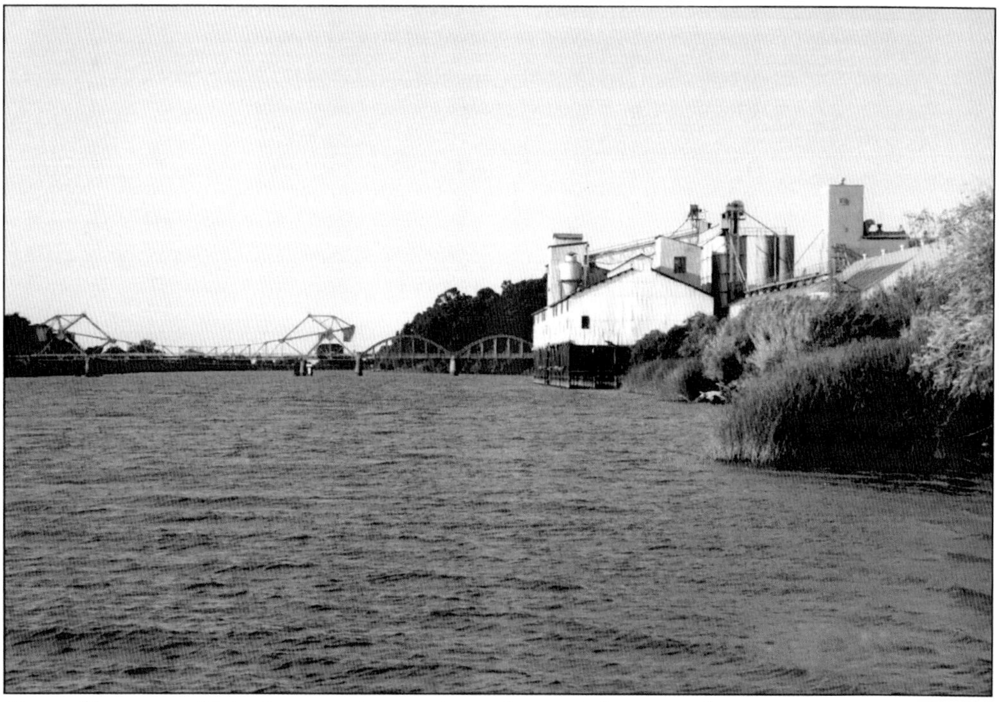

Grain Elevator. This giant warehouse, the scales, and the grain elevator were once a vibrant part of the local economy. Large ships filled their holds with grain directly from the large storage facility. Corn and wheat are still major crops, but trucks do most of the transport now. This plant is near the Isleton Bridge.

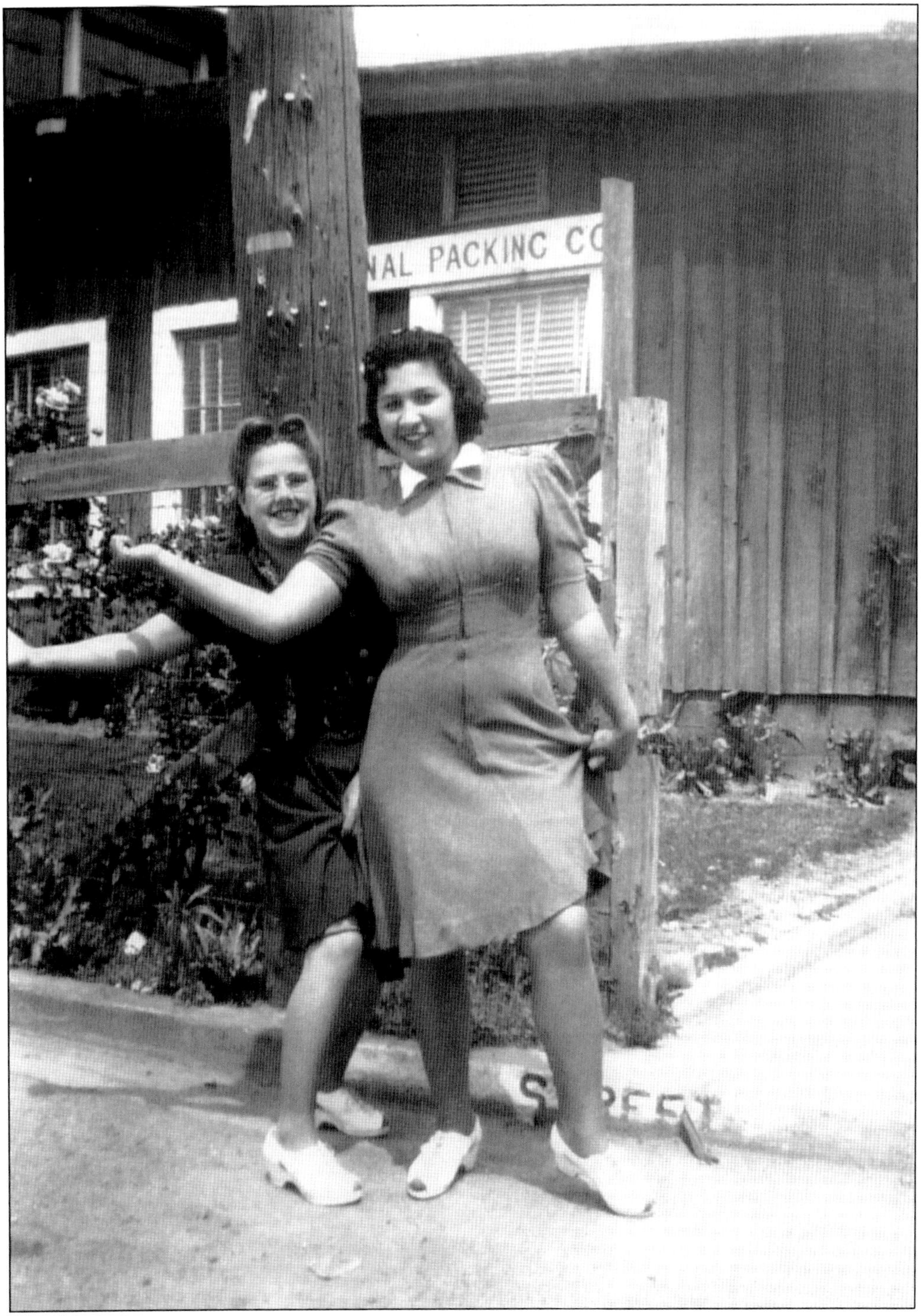

HITCHING A RIDE? These two beautiful ladies are posing in front of the National Cannery. Maybe a brand new Packard or LaSalle will stop and give them a ride up river.

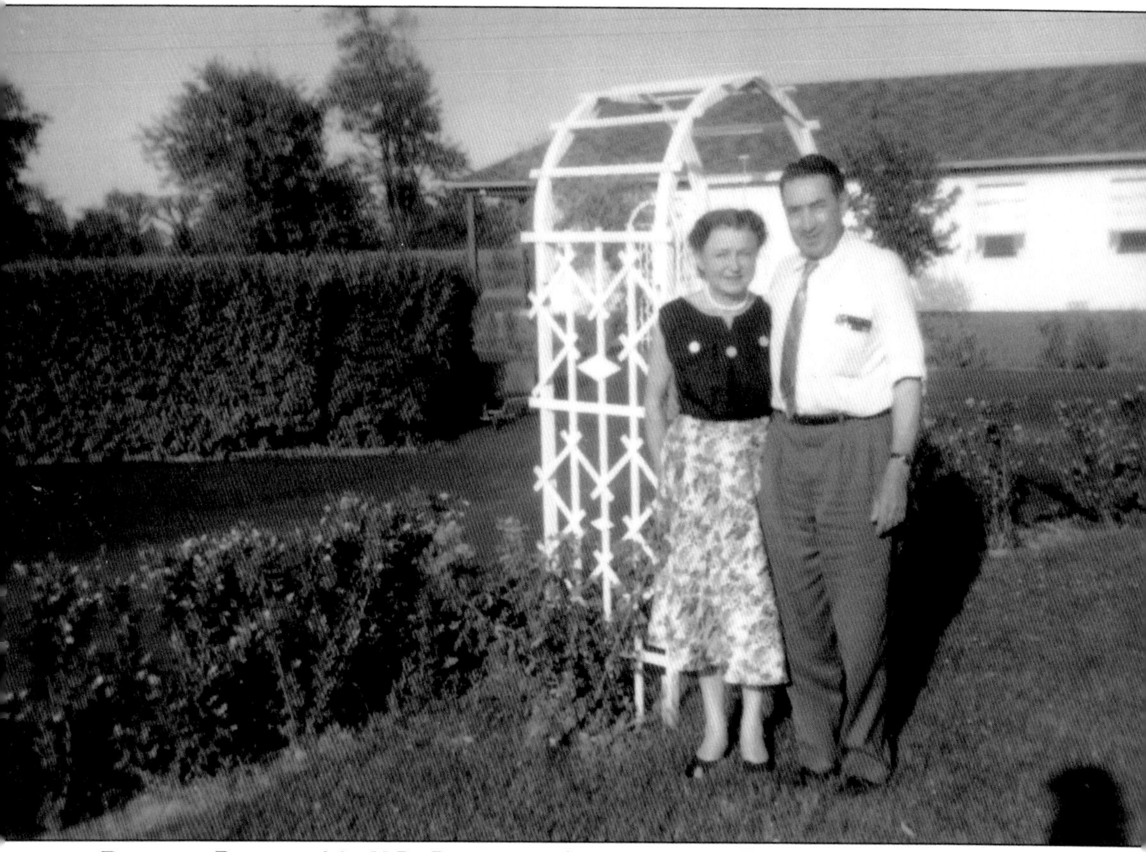

Dunn to Present. Mr. H.R. Dunn passed on in 1984 and Mrs. Dunn was postmaster for the 32 years leading up to 1966. Son Bob Dunn, a charter Lion, kept the business operating until 2003. Bob has been very active as a community leader, historian, writer, and president of the chamber of commerce.

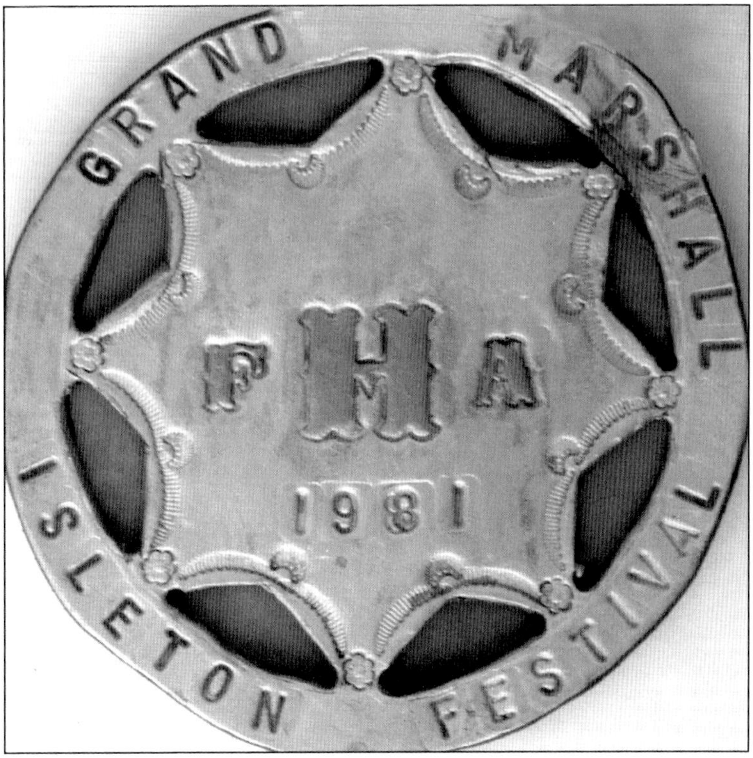

HEIMBAUGH CHAIR. The badge of the 1981 Isleton Festival Grand Marshall was worn by Fred Heimbolt. As a mayor, a member of the city council, a leader of the chamber of commerce, and a volunteer fireman, Fred was well liked in the community.

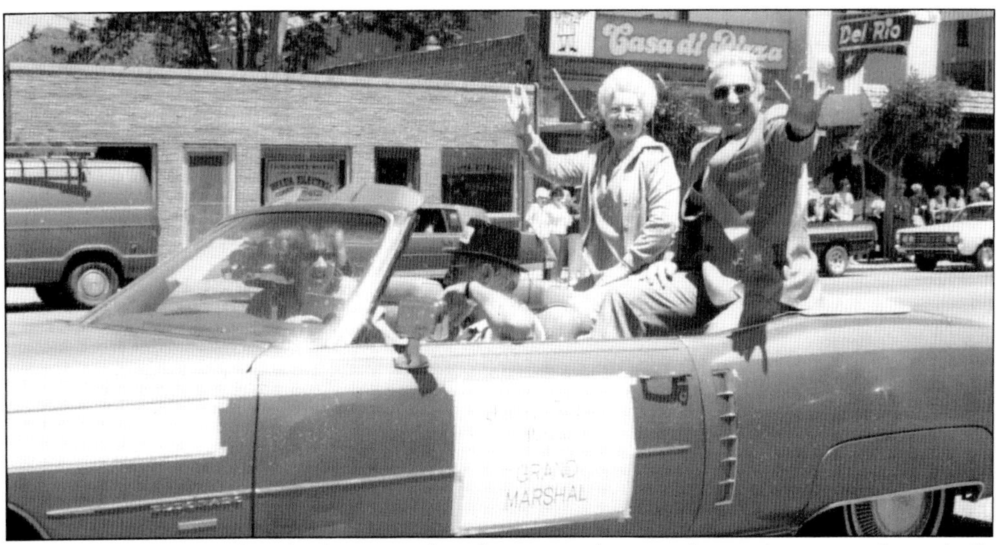

FRED AND ALICE. Fred and Alice Heimbaugh are seen here in their roles as grand marshalls in the 1981 festival parade. Alice was the daughter of Charles Perkins, was queen of the first Asparagus Festival, and married Fred Heimbaugh, who settled in Isleton after duty in the Pacific during World War II.

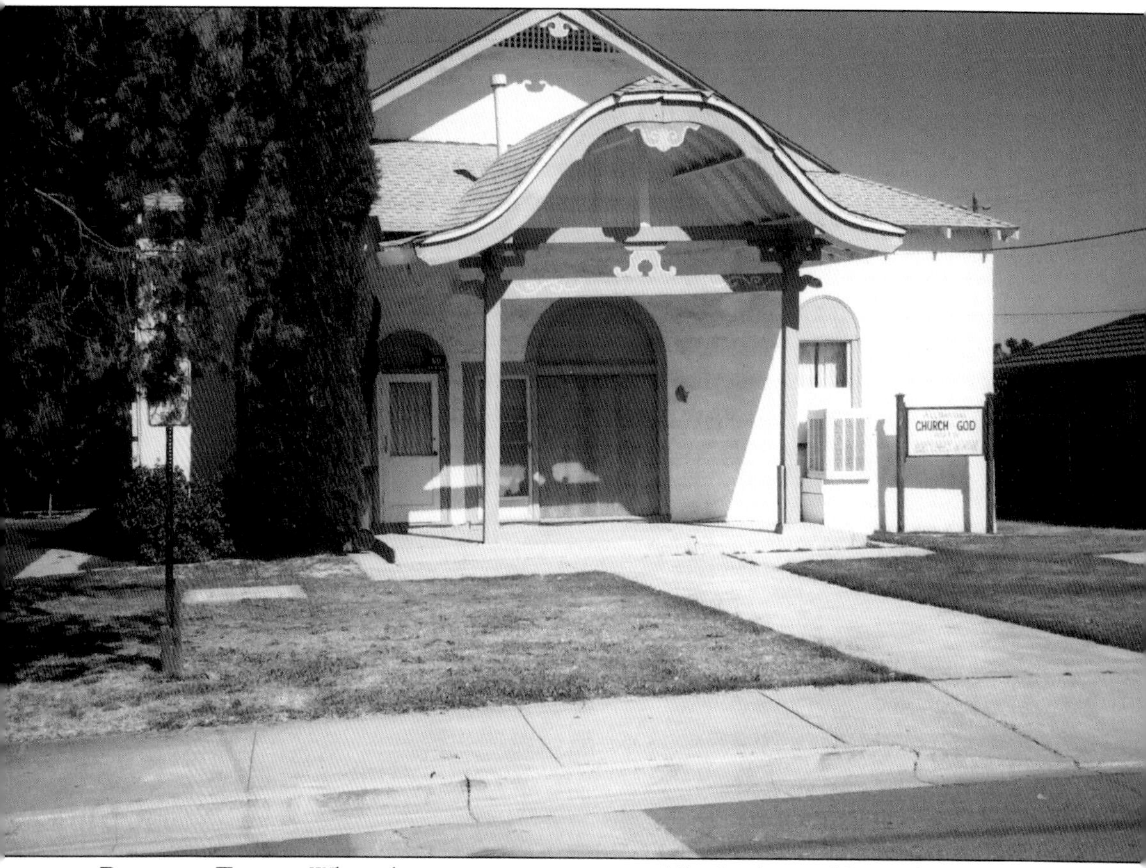

BUDDHIST TEMPLE. When the canneries were going full tilt, the world was demanding white asparagus, and the business on Main Street good, the Japanese community was strong and built their Buddhist Temple. A large Buddha was on the front concrete foundation. Today it is an "All Nations Church," but still has a Japanese façade.

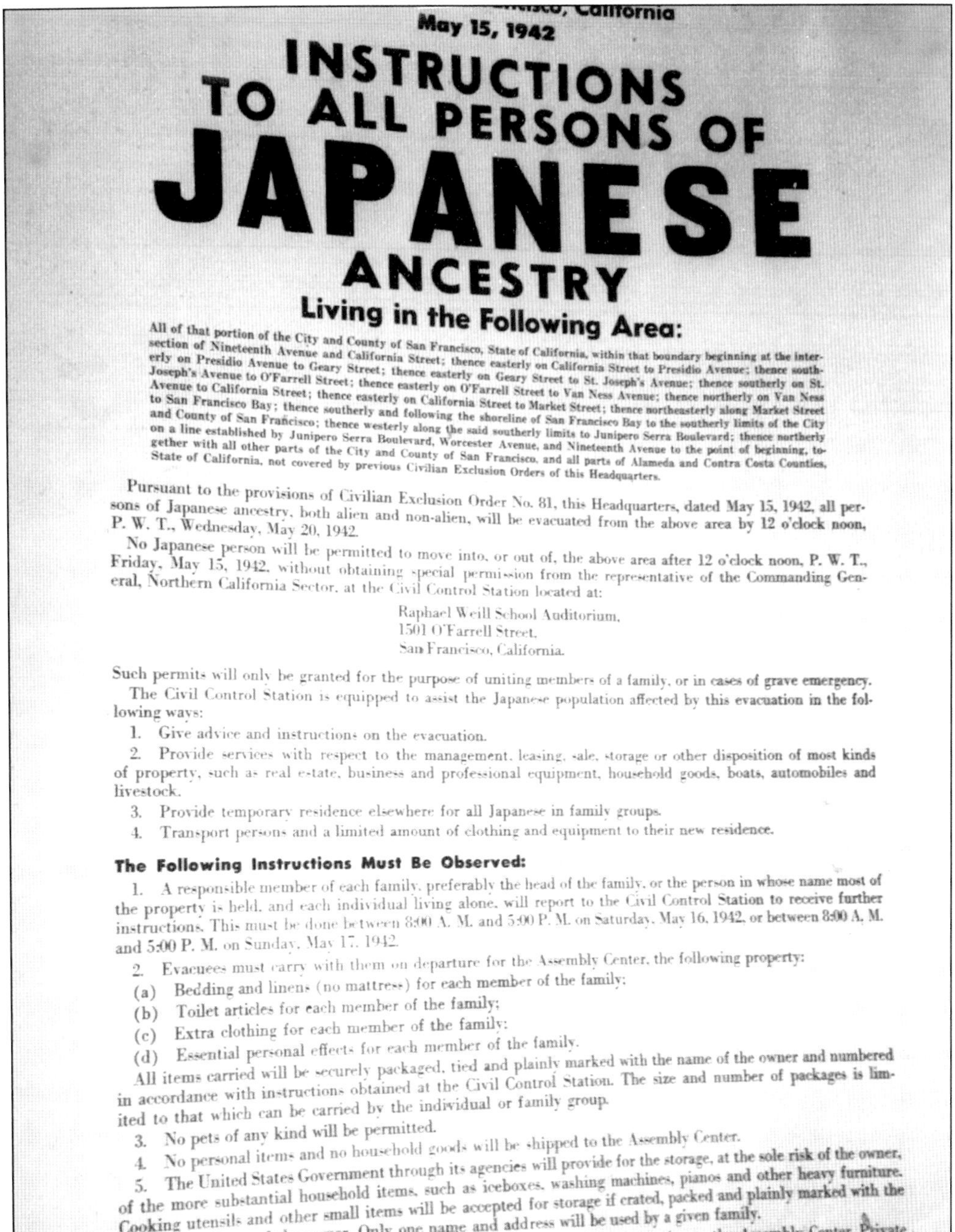

cisco, California

May 15, 1942

INSTRUCTIONS TO ALL PERSONS OF JAPANESE ANCESTRY

Living in the Following Area:

**All of that portion of the City and County of San Francisco, State of California, within that boundary beginning at the inter-
section of Nineteenth Avenue and California Street; thence easterly on California Street to Presidio Avenue; thence south-
erly on Presidio Avenue to Geary Street; thence easterly on Geary Street to St. Joseph's Avenue; thence southerly on St.
Joseph's Avenue to O'Farrell Street; thence easterly on O'Farrell Street to Van Ness Avenue; thence northerly on Van Ness
Avenue to California Street; thence easterly on California Street to Market Street; thence northeasterly along Market Street
to San Francisco Bay; thence southerly and following the shoreline of San Francisco Bay to the southerly limits of the City
and County of San Francisco; thence westerly along the said southerly limits to Junipero Serra Boulevard; thence northerly
on a line established by Junipero Serra Boulevard, Worcester Avenue, and Nineteenth Avenue to the point of beginning, to-
gether with all other parts of the City and County of San Francisco, and all parts of Alameda and Contra Costa Counties,
State of California, not covered by previous Civilian Exclusion Orders of this Headquarters.**

Pursuant to the provisions of Civilian Exclusion Order No. 81, this Headquarters, dated May 15, 1942, all persons of Japanese ancestry, both alien and non-alien, will be evacuated from the above area by 12 o'clock noon, P. W. T., Wednesday, May 20, 1942.

No Japanese person will be permitted to move into, or out of, the above area after 12 o'clock noon, P. W. T., Friday, May 15, 1942, without obtaining special permission from the representative of the Commanding General, Northern California Sector, at the Civil Control Station located at:

Raphael Weill School Auditorium,
1501 O'Farrell Street,
San Francisco, California.

Such permits will only be granted for the purpose of uniting members of a family, or in cases of grave emergency.

The Civil Control Station is equipped to assist the Japanese population affected by this evacuation in the following ways:

1. Give advice and instructions on the evacuation.
2. Provide services with respect to the management, leasing, sale, storage or other disposition of most kinds of property, such as real estate, business and professional equipment, household goods, boats, automobiles and livestock.
3. Provide temporary residence elsewhere for all Japanese in family groups.
4. Transport persons and a limited amount of clothing and equipment to their new residence.

The Following Instructions Must Be Observed:

1. A responsible member of each family, preferably the head of the family, or the person in whose name most of the property is held, and each individual living alone, will report to the Civil Control Station to receive further instructions. This must be done between 8:00 A. M. and 5:00 P. M. on Saturday, May 16, 1942, or between 8:00 A. M. and 5:00 P. M. on Sunday, May 17, 1942.

2. Evacuees must carry with them on departure for the Assembly Center, the following property:

(a) Bedding and linens (no mattress) for each member of the family;
(b) Toilet articles for each member of the family;
(c) Extra clothing for each member of the family;
(d) Essential personal effects for each member of the family.

All items carried will be securely packaged, tied and plainly marked with the name of the owner and numbered
in accordance with instructions obtained at the Civil Control Station. The size and number of packages is lim-
ited to that which can be carried by the individual or family group.

3. No pets of any kind will be permitted.
4. No personal items and no household goods will be shipped to the Assembly Center.
5. The United States Government through its agencies will provide for the storage, at the sole risk of the owner,
of the more substantial household items, such as iceboxes, washing machines, pianos and other heavy furniture.
Cooking utensils and other small items will be accepted for storage if crated, packed and plainly marked with the
and address of the owner. Only one name and address will be used by a given family.
transportation to the Assembly Center. Private

Japanese Relocation. This is one of the ways the government alerted the Japanese residents of Isleton that they were to be relocated. This poster was placed throughout California in 1942. It told persons of Japanese ancestry that they had five days before they would be evacuated, that they would be assisted by the Civil Control Station to dispose of their belongings, and that they would be transported to their new residences. Each person was only allowed blankets, soap, and clothing. No personal items or pets were allowed. Storage was provided at the sole risk to the owner. Relocation camps were inland in extremely isolated and barren areas. The camps were maintained with armed guards and barbed wire fences.

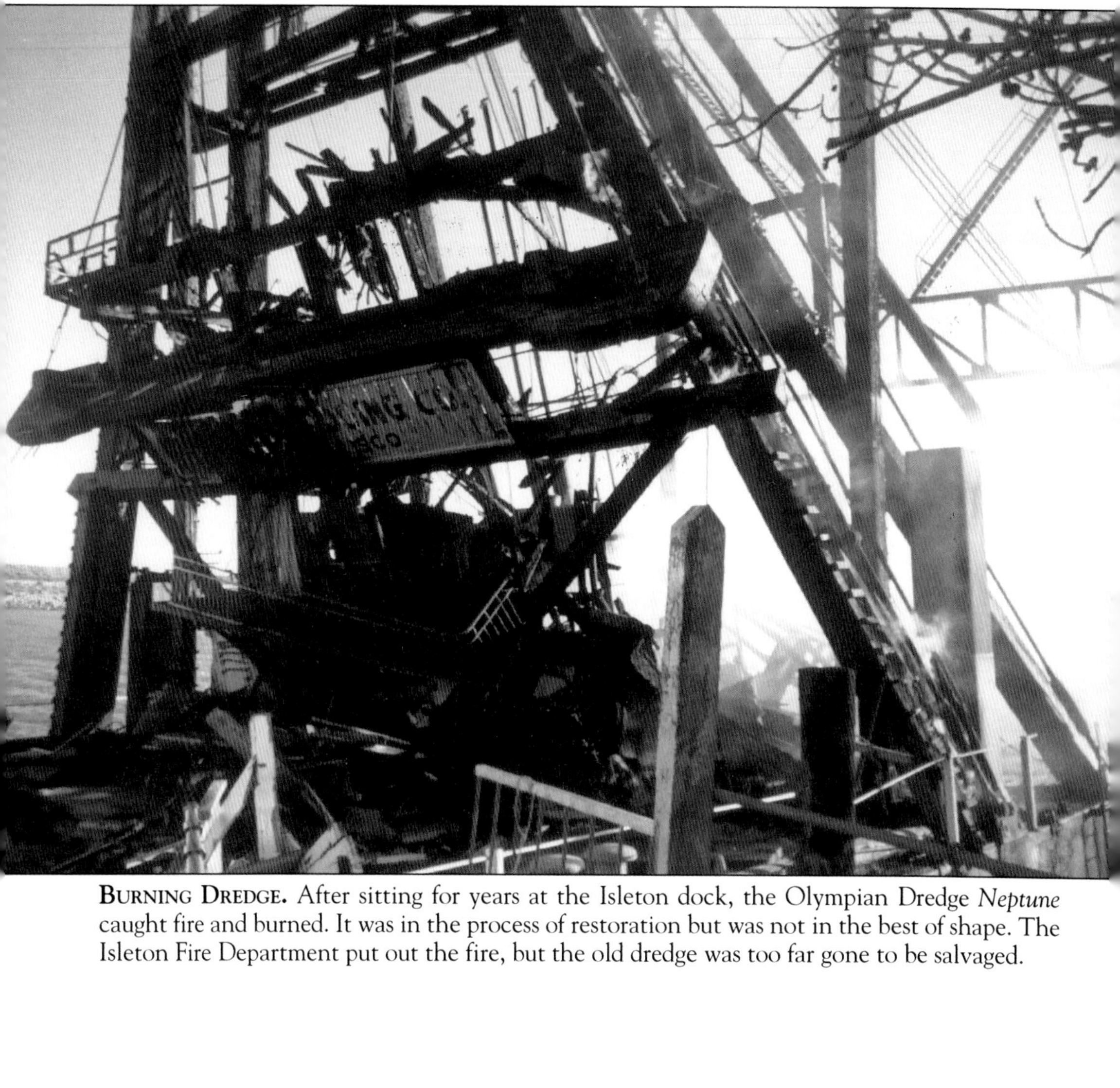

Burning Dredge. After sitting for years at the Isleton dock, the Olympian Dredge *Neptune* caught fire and burned. It was in the process of restoration but was not in the best of shape. The Isleton Fire Department put out the fire, but the old dredge was too far gone to be salvaged.

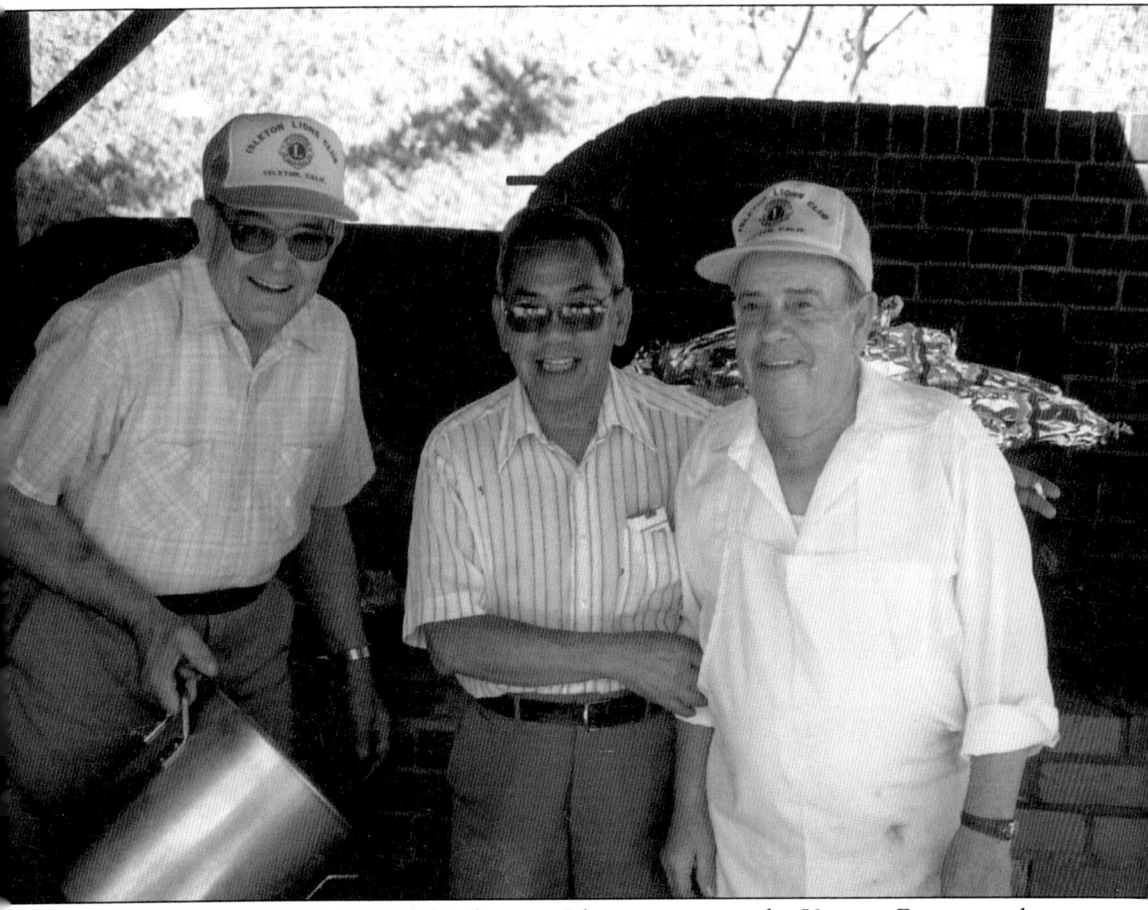

LIONS BARBEQUE. The Lions Club has been an Isleton institution for 50 years. Every year they held a barbeque at the city park. The old city park was located where city hall is today. Paul DeMesa gives his fellow Lions something to laugh about at this Lions barbeque.

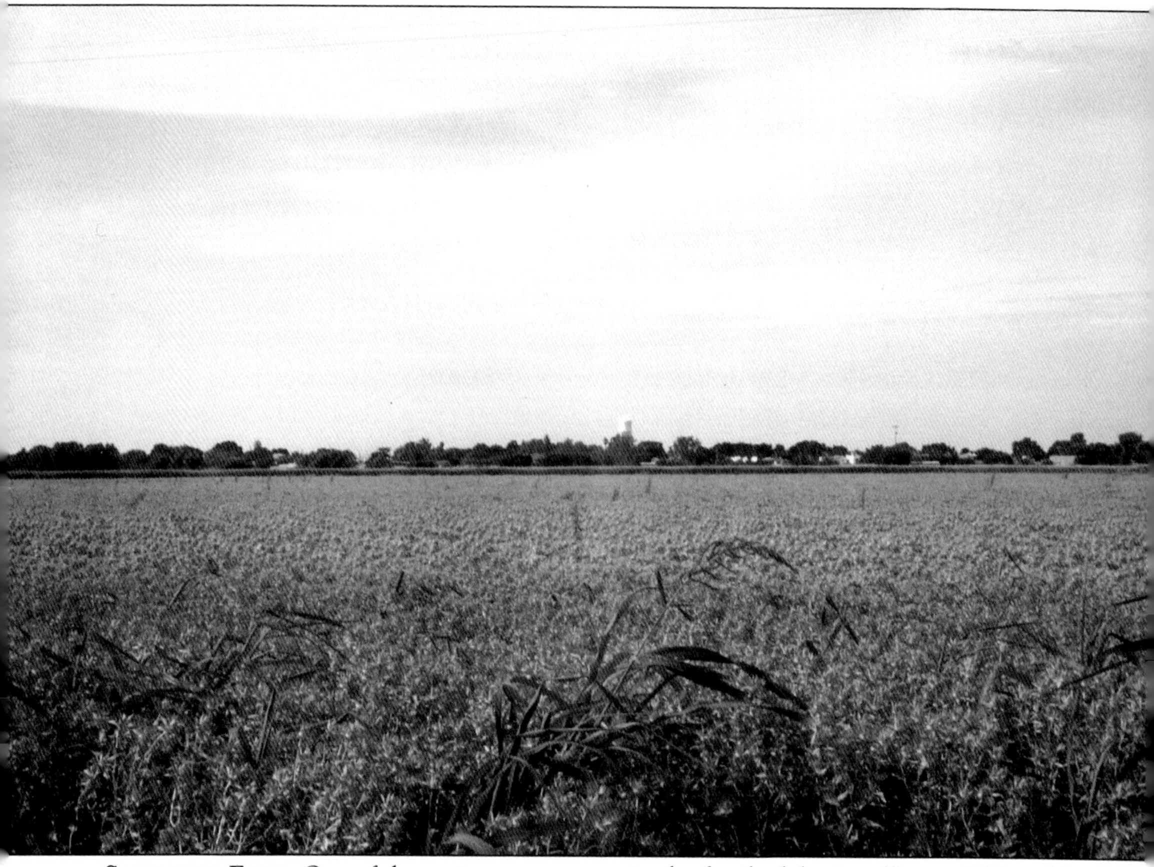

Safflower Field. One of the major crops grown in the fertile delta is safflower. This golden field, with the Isleton water tower in the background, is part of the Correia ranch. Most of the oil is sold on the international market.

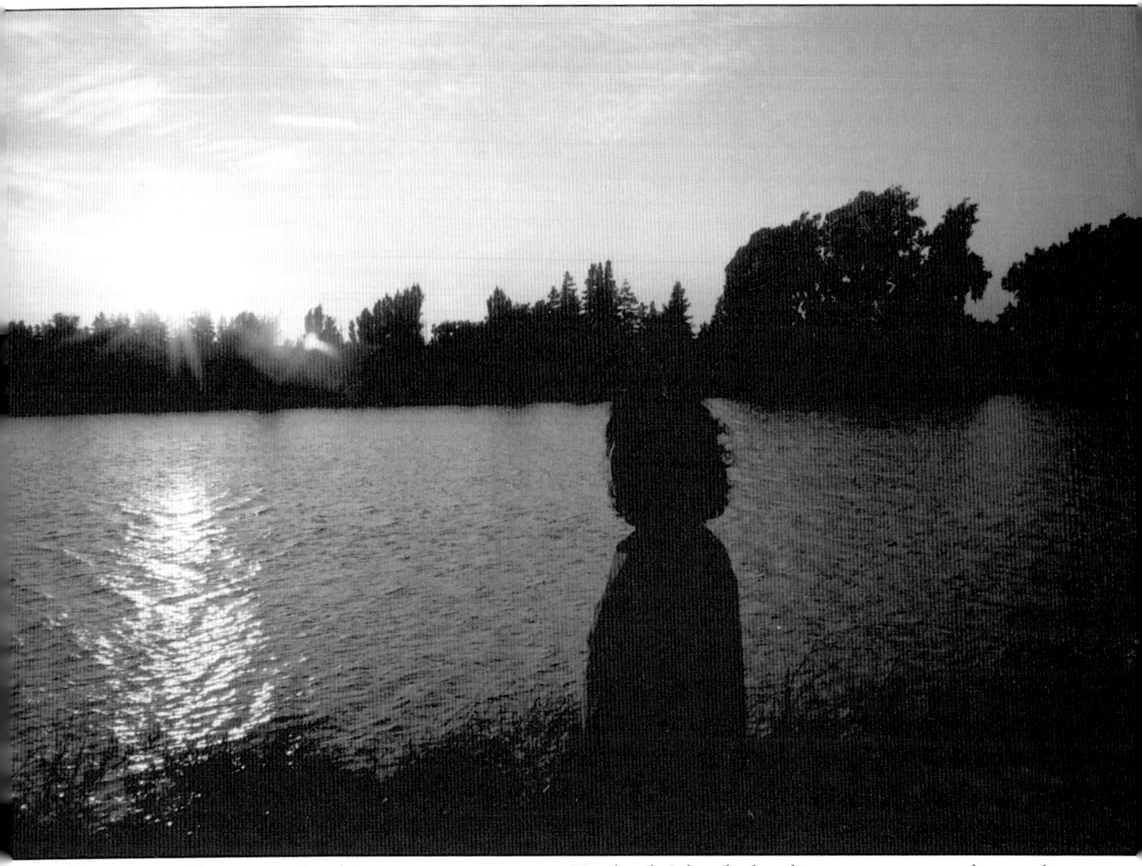

SUNSET ON HOGBACK. Looking west at sunset on Hogback Island, the distance, topography, and river make for excellent sunsets in the spring and fall.

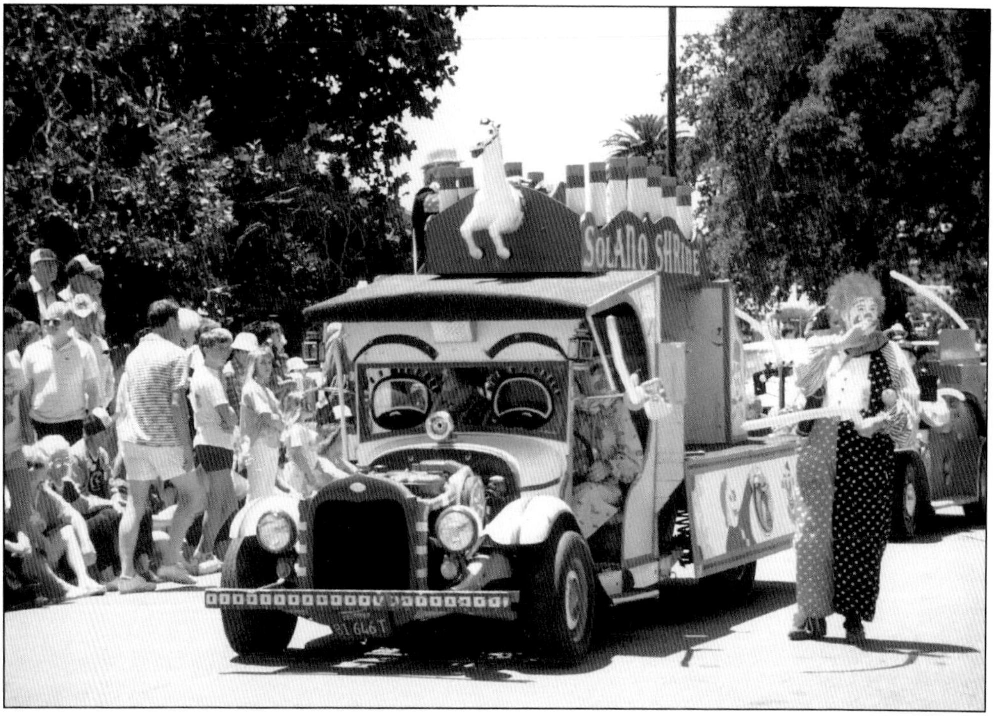

PARADE CLOWN. The Asian Festival Parade is a community event with laughter, a fun crowd, and a New Year's celebration that brings friends and happiness to a deserving community.

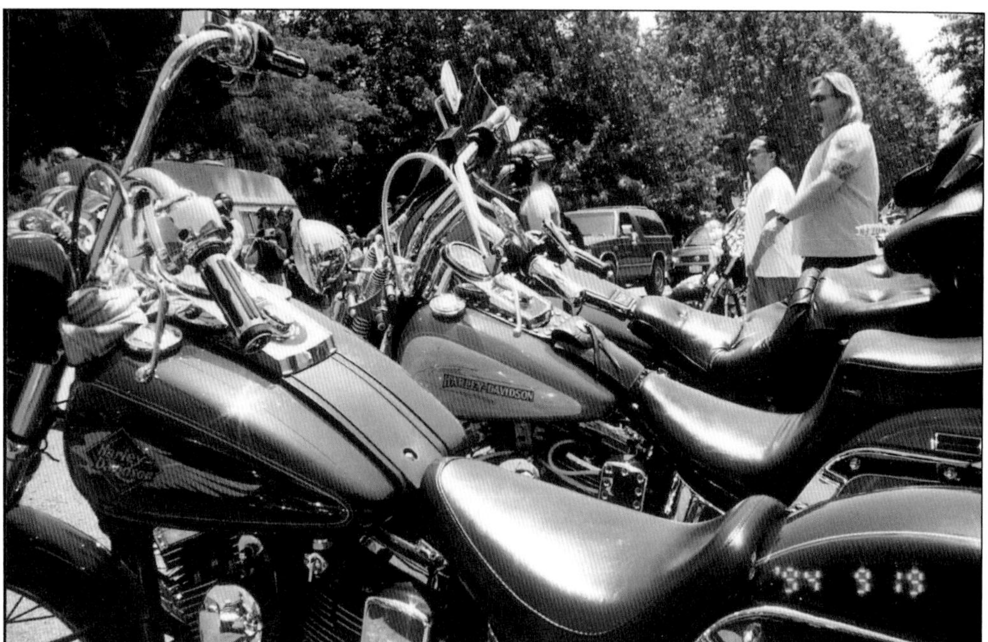

BIKERS AT CRAWDAD FESTIVAL. The stream of motorcycles coming to the Crawdad Festival is always impressive. Thousands of bikers add to the festive occasion with their leathers, beautiful machinery, and sense of community.

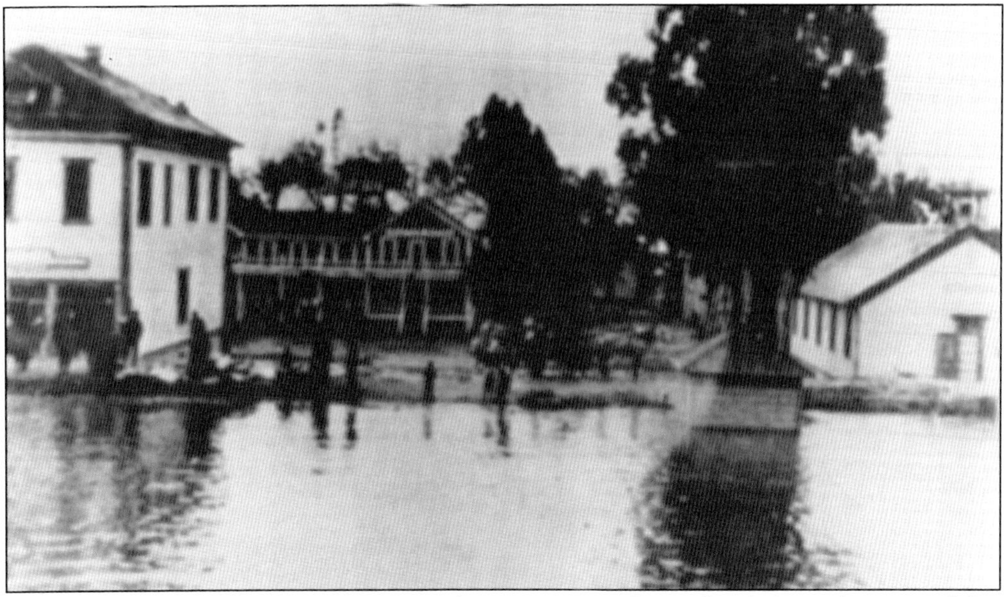

Flooded Gardiner Building. In 1907 the Sacramento River flooded. At the time of this photo the water was up to the top of the levee. Soon after, it spilled over and Second Street was under water. The Isleton Hotel, Gardiner house, the new Perkins home, and the Balsmeiers were all under water.

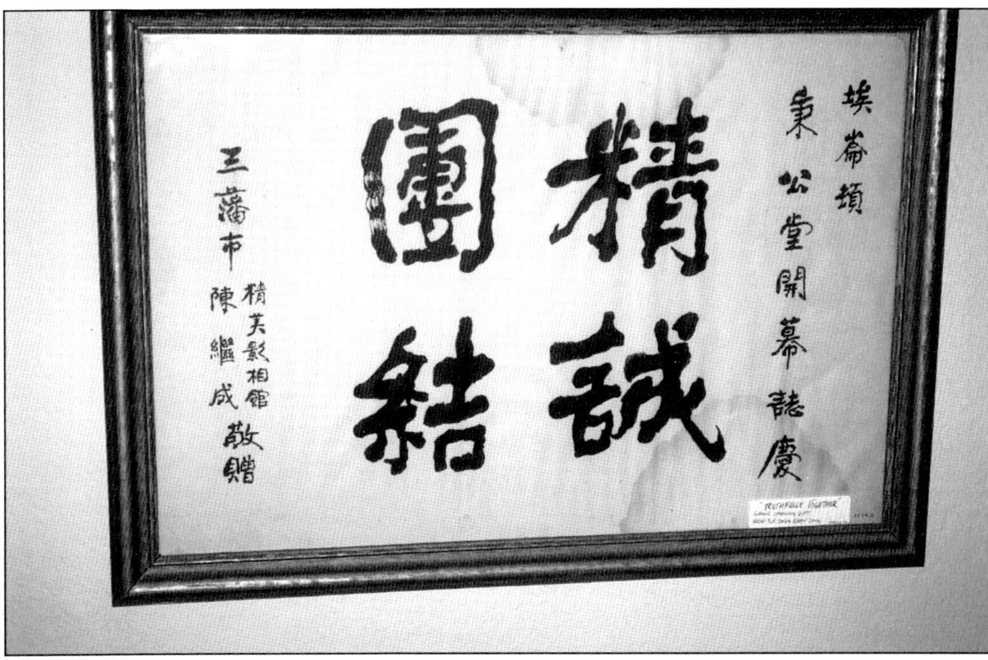

Gift from San Francisco Tong. This framed gift from the San Francisco Tong, Chun Qhay Sing, translates, "Truthfully together," a plea for unity with integrity.

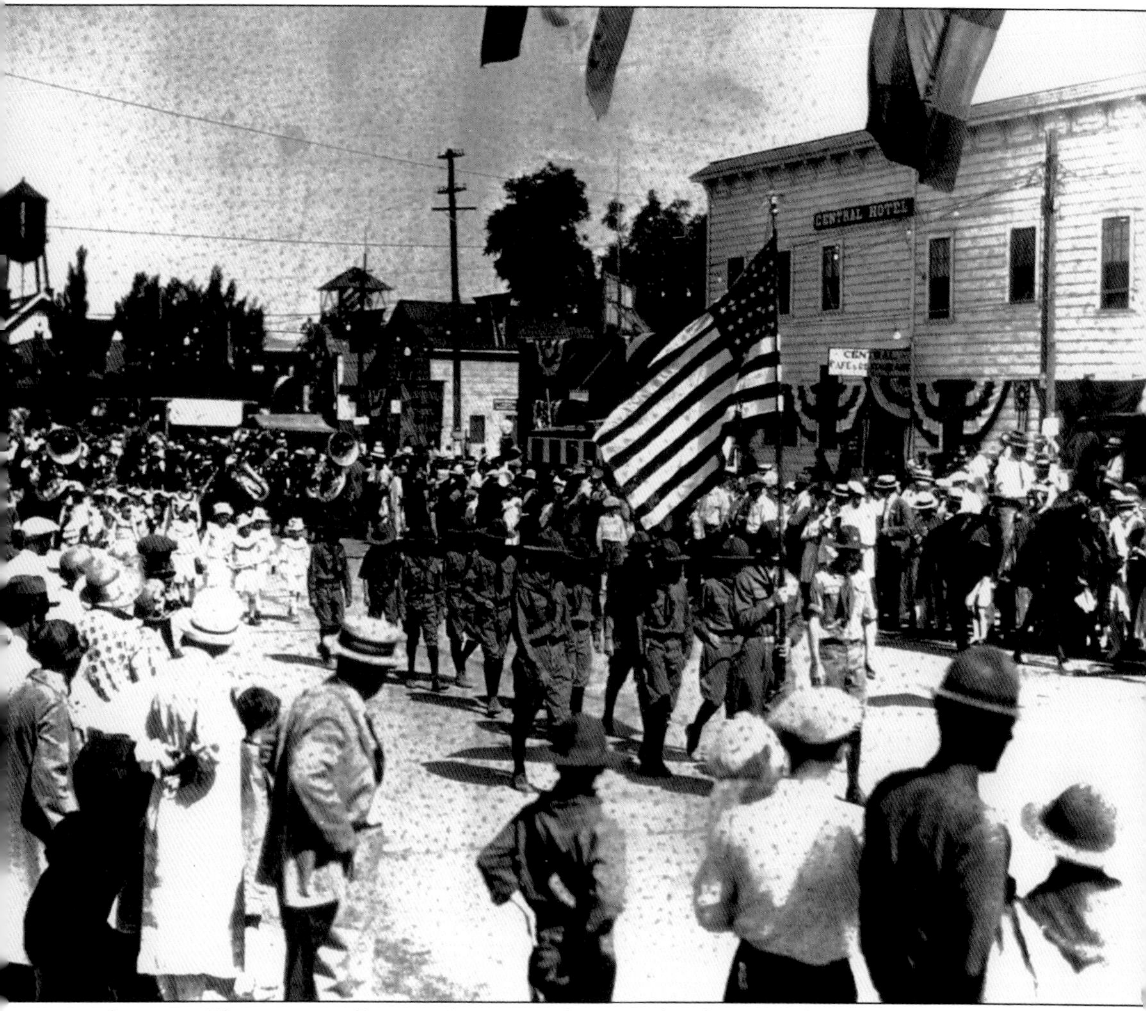

Central Hotel with Parade Soldiers. Support for the war effort took place on Second Street during World War I. John Gardiner was responsible for the Bond Drive. The Central Hotel was to be replaced by the Bank of Isleton. This photo was taken from the porch of the Gardiner Improvement Building.